Peter F. Gunther
Isaiah 52:7

The Fields at Home

THE FIELDS
AT HOME

Studies in Home Missions

Compiled and Edited by
P ETER F. G UNTHER

MOODY PRESS
CHICAGO

266, 2
G 958f

Printed in the United States of America

25144

Contents

The Chicago Skyline

The patriotic hymn, "America, the Beautiful," alludes to America's alabaster cities. But one impressed with the great buildings of an urban skyline often forgets the human need of the city dweller. (Courtesy of the **Chicago Tribune**.)

1

The Neglect
of Home Missions

PETER F. GUNTHER

IN THE PROGRAM OF THE CHRISTIAN CHURCH, foreign missions have always received much greater emphasis than home missions. The challenge to reach the millions without Christ in other parts of the world has been accepted in all evangelical missionary-minded churches. Usually, however, there is greater response to the challenge to reach the economically poor and illiterate in the so-called backward countries than to reach those in more modern and aggressive countries. But the evangelistic need is the same. The educated are as much lost and in need of Christ as the uneducated. The rich are as hopelessly lost as the poor. The literate need Christ as much as the illiterate. Somehow, the Christian church has not fully realized this, with the result that missions have become, in a sense, lopsided.

The needs overseas, among both the rich and the poor, cannot

PETER F. GUNTHER served with the Rural Bible Crusade in Indiana for three years following his academic training at Wheaton College and the Graduate School of Theology. Since 1950 he has been with Moody Literature Mission, which has a wide literature program in various home mission areas. As assistant director of this Moody Bible Institute department, Mr. Gunther has been able to visit extensively throughout the States to observe and evaluate the problems and needs in connection with the home mission field. For two years, he also taught the home missions classes at Moody Bible Institute.

be ignored. Exploding world population makes it all the more imperative that the church be spiritually alert to its responsibility.
Christians are obligated to evangelize the world, even though it
means long periods of separation from home, learning a new
language, and heavy cost to maintain the program.

At the same time, however, we cannot ignore the "heathen" at
home. The foreign mission program can only be as strong as the
home base. This home base includes the home church and the
effectiveness of its outreach in its own community and to all people
throughout the homeland. The injunction of Acts 1:8 is still in
force, that we be witnesses "in Jerusalem, and in all Judea, and in
Samaria, and unto the uttermost part of the earth" — in that order.
The local church cannot ignore any of these areas. The home
mission field is a necessary and vital link between the local church
and the foreign field.

A pastor once told me his church was committed entirely to
foreign missions. It is true the Lord has blessed his church in a
remarkable way. Its membership has more than doubled, and its
foreign missionary budget has grown even more. Yet not one item
appears on the church budget that could be considered home
missions, unless it might be a local radio broadcast which the
pastor conducts regularly and effectively. The people are good
givers to the program of their local church as well as to foreign
missions. But they have completely ignored the important gap —
home missions — and as far as the membership is concerned, the
responsibility of reaching the Negro, the migrant, rural youth,
mountain people, Mormon communities, or prison inmates, is not
theirs. "Our job is to support the local church and foreign missions"
is the voice from the pulpit. This church, by the way, has now
moved from the poor neighborhood to a prosperous section and has
failed in its obligation to witness to the needy people in a neglected
part of the city.

This absence of vision and responsibility for the needs around us
is prevalent in far too many churches in this land, with the result
that home missions have had to curb their activities for lack of
personnel, money and the necessary tools to do an effective job.
Is it any wonder that we have less freedom to witness today than a
decade ago? That opposing forces are extending their programs by

taking over our hospitals, for instance, which means that the gospel witness often becomes extremely limited or even impossible? That the once Protestant Negroes are being won over to the Catholic faith? That the Mormon church has become one of the fastest growing churches in America and is even considered an evangelical church by some Protestant leaders? That churches in metropolitan New York, Chicago and other large cities have had to close their doors along with many rural churches?

It is my firm conviction that unless the local church gives greater emphasis to home missions, there will be a gradual weakening in our foreign missionary outreach. Churches, Bible colleges, Bible institutes, missionary committees have a responsibility to train home missionary personnel, encourage them with their financial support, and give them the tools needed to do an effective job for the Lord in the homeland.

It may be true, at least in part, that home missions have been unpopular in some areas because of the many independent missionaries not responsible to anyone. We have been able to observe them carefully and some have not been too effective in their work. But could it be that the local church has been partly at fault by not giving them proper guidance and the tools needed to do the job? Is it fair to pass judgment on the entire home mission field because some have failed? What about those who have established a very effective work in spite of limited encouragement and help from the local church?

While there are still some independent missionaries, and in a few places they seem to be stepping on each other, this situation has improved greatly in the last few years. Most home missionaries are now identified with either a denominational or interdenominational organization. The National Home Missions Fellowship has, in recent years, done much to encourage the independent missionary to become identified with a reliable organization, to correlate work in a given area so as to avoid duplication, and to screen carefully missionary volunteers wanting to join the fellowship. Another factor that has probably led to the decline of the independent missionary is the need to supply a donor with a tax-exempt receipt for his support of the home missionary program. Qualified organizations must issue such receipts.

The Need For This Book

For a number of years Moody Press has felt a need for a book on home missions. It is true that some of the denominations have given comprehensive reports of their own home mission program. A few general surveys have been published, such as *Concerns of a Continent,* edited by James Hoffman. But some important areas have not been covered. In fact, it has been difficult to get reliable and up-to-date source material on some fields, such as the mountain work in Kentucky and the Ozarks. Then, too, the work of non-denominational or interdenominational organizations has never been described in book form.

It is recognized that, even in this book, some important aspects of the home mission field have not been covered and the thrilling stories of many organizations have not been told. Still an attempt has been made to give a comprehensive view of the home mission field so that the student, pastor, chairman of the missionary society or the lay person may become acquainted with the field, its needs and opportunities, and be encouraged to take his place in the program of home missions.

Some chapters have been written by persons connected with denominational home mission programs, while others are by missionaries identified with the so-called independent organizations. Each writer has had first-hand experience in the field he has written about and can speak authoritatively on his subject. Most of the writers have supplied a bibliography along with the material. In some cases this was not possible because of the lack of source material available.

Definition of Home Missions

Perhaps it is well to explain exactly what is meant by home missions. The term *missions* itself simply means a sending forth. Webster defines Christian mission as a "sending forth of men with authority to preach the Gospel and administer the sacraments," as well as "the authority or commission from God or the church to do this."

A simple definition of home missions could be "a sending forth of workers with the gospel message within the boundaries of the sending country." This does not mean that all home mission groups limit their activities to the geographical boundaries of the United States. Some include the territory of Puerto Rico. Others include Canada, Central America and the West Indies. In this book, all fifty states have been included, as well as Quebec, which in a sense is a foreign field in that the people are predominantly French-speaking.

In this book the term "home missions" is used in the sense of an organized effort to bring into a vital relationship with Jesus Christ persons who are not normally touched by the ministry of the local church. However, a chapter has been included on city and urban work, in which the starting of branch Sunday schools and churches is the theme. This work generally is initiated by a local church.

Organization of This Book

It is difficult to list, classify, and describe all types of home mission work. Complete statistics are hard to get. Diverse types of organization (independent, denominationally unrelated and denominationally related) or lack of it are found on most home mission fields. The sheer multiplicity of movements on the home field defies complete analysis. In this book it seems best to divide the field into four broad categories: minority groups, geographical areas, social and economic groups, and specialized service agencies.

Minority groups: Minority groups include those that may be of racial, national or religious character. Some retain the use of their own language, at least in the home. Others hold to various parts of their own culture. The American Indians, Negroes, Latin-American or Spanish-speaking peoples, Jews, Mormons, the Cajuns of Louisiana, all can be classified as belonging to a minority group of people living in our Western culture but, in a sense, isolated or living among themselves in specific areas. One could also mention the 125,000 Chinese, the 145,000 Japanese, the 70,000 Filipinos, and other groups of foreign descent, but these are not covered specifically in this book.

Geographical area: Some home mission groups attempt to reach people living in certain geographical areas. For practical purposes we can include the people living in the Appalachian and the Ozark Mountains, the rural population, the city and urban people, as well as the people of Quebec who, in a sense, could also be classified as a minority group, and Alaska and Hawaii. As intimated above, some denominational mission boards would include here also the people of Cuba, Mexico and other Central American countries.

Social and economic groups: The third group consists of those with social and economic problems, including those in such public institutions as jails, penitentiaries, reformatories, old people's homes, hospitals and orphanages. Work among these can also include ministry in rescue missions and in depressed areas of large cities. The work among migrants would certainly come under this category —a constantly shifting group of people very difficult to reach in any permanent way.

Specialized service agencies: The fourth group has been called specialized service agencies. Some of these are closely tied in with the church program, but still very much a part of home missions. It would be impossible to give a description of all such groups, but included here are brief descriptions of such representative ministries as Inter-Varsity Christian Fellowship, working among university students; the Young Life program, which seeks to minister to high school students; Pioneer Girls, Christian Service Brigade; and Child Evangelism, organizations such as the Moody Literature Mission, which helps supply literature to needy people; and the Open Air Campaigners.

One could mention such aspects as home visitation, which is sadly neglected in many local churches (and even on the home and foreign mission fields), and the ministry among seamen and servicemen. These are all part of the home mission program but so sadly neglected.

This book is sent forth with the prayer that the home mission field may be better understood, and that young people will be challenged to give themselves in larger numbers for this service.

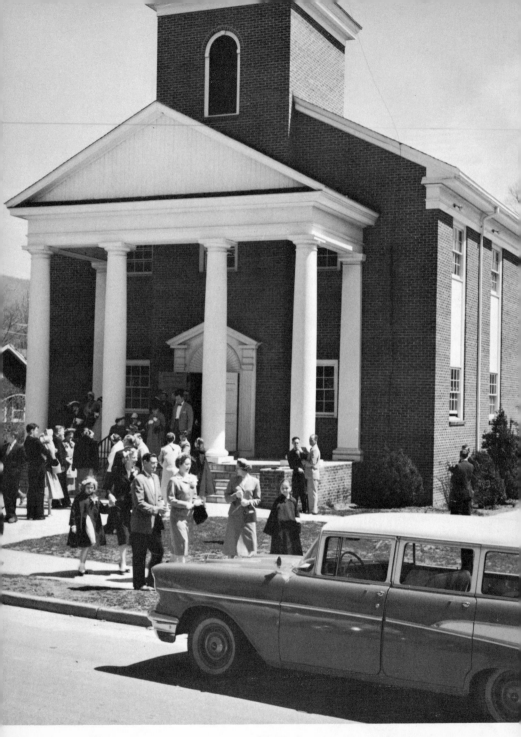

At a missionary conference in his local church, the missionary candidate often learns much about basic principles and practices of missions.

2

Basic Principles and Practices for Home Missions

Harold R. Cook

THE STUDY OF HOME MISSIONS is very broad in its scope. It includes city missions and rural missions. It includes Indians on reservations and students on university campuses. It goes into jails and penitentiaries and out to isolated homes in mountain areas. It ministers temporarily in migrant labor camps and starts permanent churches in new housing developments.

In all the varied activities that home missions carries on, there is an underlying unity. Even though many practices vary from place to place, and from ministry to ministry, there are some that have a universal application.

Objectives

If there is one thing more than any other that unifies the work of home missions, it is its objectives, its purposes. While each

HAROLD R. COOK, after taking his B.A. and M.A. degrees at the University of Southern California, spent two terms as a missionary in Venezuela, South America. Obliged by the ill health of his family to return to this country in 1936, he was then called to a ministry of teaching. At present chairman of the Department of Missions at Moody Bible Institute, he has been teaching missionary subjects there for more than twenty years. In this capacity he has given considerable attention to home missions as well as foreign. A large number of his former students are now serving in a variety of home mission fields. Mr. Cook has written numerous articles on missionary themes and two books, *An Introduction to the Study of Christian Missions* and *Missionary Life and Work*.

separate activity may constitute a different path toward the goal, the goal is one.

It is surprising how many Christian organizations do not have a clear statement of objectives. They almost seem to be afraid to define just what they expect to do, for fear it may limit their freedom of action, or make it difficult for them to do something else later. To justify its existence a mission must have some clearly defined objectives. In addition, these same objectives will help keep it from wandering off into numerous sidepaths that use up its resources without helping its cause.

1. *Evangelism first*

In the very nature of the case, evangelism is the prime objective for home missions, as well as for foreign missions. The great commission that Christ gave to His Church is that of evangelizing, giving the good news of His salvation to men and women and children in such a way that they will believe it and accept the life that He offers.

This seems quite obvious, and we seldom hear any objection to it. Yet we often lose sight of this objective in actual practice. We become absorbed in the operation of a school or hospital, the organization of a church, the provision of recreation, social services or physical aid, and we forget that for the Christian these things are worthless apart from the life that is in Christ Jesus.

This objective is common to all types of home missionary work. The rescue mission does indeed offer food and shelter and clothing to the down-and-outer. The offer carries with it no obligation to accept the gospel that the mission preaches. But apart from that gospel the material provision loses its significance. The mission then becomes just another flophouse, a free-lunch counter. What keeps it from being such is the belief of the mission that through Christ the man on skid row can, if he will, become a new creature.

In mission schools, orphanages, and the like, the same objective ought to dominate. In such places young people are being prepared for life. But a life that is not centered in the Giver of all life is fruitless. It is not enough to give class instruction in Christian ethics and Bible study. Unless the pupil himself makes Christ the center of his life these things become marginal. They are easily dropped off when he leaves the school or home.

The same objective is important even in the extension of the church into a new area. Sometimes the plea is made, "We ought to start a church in that place because people of our denomination are there and they would welcome its ministry." Such a plea might be legitimate if the church were only a social club. But since Christ intends it to be more than just a fellowship of believers, since He wants it to be a witnessing community, it must look further. What is the need of the community for the gospel of Christ? Will a new church really help in evangelizing the people? Or will it just add to the divisions among those who are already Christian? The objective, you see, will decide the practice.

2. Edification

While evangelism is the prime objective in home missions, it is not the only one. It is foundational, but a house needs more than a foundation. The author of the Epistle to the Hebrews speaks of the foundations already laid and urges his readers, "Let us go on." The Apostle Paul was not a hit-and-run evangelist, as some would make him out to be. He was concerned about the growth of those who believed his word, that they might come to Christian completeness, maturity of Christian experience. The same desire should be in the heart of every home missionary.

In some types of work it is more difficult than in others to build up people in their faith, once they have believed the gospel. For example, those who are converted in servicemen's centers often do not return to that place again. And it may not be easy to follow up those who make a profession of faith in a one-week Bible camp. Yet some way must be devised to provide continued nourishment and care for this new life.

The objective of home missions is not just to bring individuals to the experience of the new birth through faith in Christ. It is also to establish and nourish them to the point where they will be able to take over the full responsibilities of a mature Christian. This means principally two things: help in the continued study of the Word of God, so that it can sustain and guide the life; and continued interest and availability to counsel the new convert in applying the Word effectively.

3. *Church establishment and strengthening*

Evangelism and edification of individuals is good. But Christ has also established the church, and it has pleased Him to ordain that much of His work should be accomplished through the church. So a third objective of home missions has to do with the church. Where there is no church as yet, home mission workers seek to establish one. Where the church already exists, but in a sickly state, they try to bring new strength and inspiration. Even where conditions make it impossible to have a church as such, they try to relate the work as far as possible with the total program of the church.

Of course this is usually quite evident in the work of denominational missions, but it is not so evident in those of an independent character. Sometimes they seem to pursue a course entirely unconnected with the work of the churches. But if they really are fulfilling their mission, they don't dare to do so. Some, like the various student movements, not only try to avoid any competition with the churches, but encourage their young people to take a more active part in the work of the church. Others, like the rescue missions, see their ministry completed only when their converts leave the mission to pursue their Christian life in the more normal atmosphere of the local church. On the other hand, the church lends its support to the mission.

In any event, the work of home missions has as one of its main goals the participation of its converts in the life and work of the church.

The Place of Auxiliary Services

While only three main objectives for home missions have been mentioned, there are countless ways of trying to reach those objectives, and many more ways will be found in the days to come. The great problem is that some of these methods may themselves at times take the place of objectives. Even such a salutary exercise as the memorizing of Scripture by children may lose its value if it becomes simply a way to win a week at camp. It is even easier to let the provision of food, clothing, medical care, and the like crowd out any attention to the main objectives.

Not that these things should be neglected. Far from it. But their proper place is as auxiliaries to the main purpose. They are services that should be performed, demonstrations of the reality of the interest in the people being served. They are the necessary expression of Christian concern for others, not simply bait for the gospel. At the same time they are not substitutes for it. They can aid, but they cannot take the place of the main spiritual objectives.

Relationships

Fully as much as foreign missionary work, and perhaps even more so, home missionary service involves our relationship with other individuals and groups. We do not work in a corner. We work together with others, and our work brings us into contact with other groups and organizations as well as with various civil authorities.

1. Critical nature of this matter

It is easy to see how the relation with civil authorities can affect the work of a mission. One mission works with delinquent boys who are referred to it by the authorities. The very real accomplishments of the mission depend to a large degree on the continued confidence of those authorities. The same thing is true of the work in penal institutions and public hospitals.

What is not quite so apparent is the effect that the attitude of a community can have on the work of a mission. Yet we know that the present crisis in the South in the matter of school integration is presenting real problems to those who work with the colored people. Whatever the personal opinions, to flaunt the opinion of the community would probably spell the end of the work.

Yet even more critical are the relationships between the missionaries themselves. A mission that once seemed very flourishing has come to a shadow of its former self because the missionaries lost confidence in the leadership and withdrew from the work.

2. To the church in the field

Where it is of the same denomination. Every home mission faces the problem of its relationship to the already established churches. In the majority of communities there is a church of some sort. It may be small and weak, but the fact that it is there makes relationship to it important.

It may be a church of one's own denomination, even one established by the mission itself. In that case the issue is clear. There
are already ties of common interest. The one thing to do is to
co-operate.

Not that it is always easy to do. Both missionaries and churches
are often likely to want their own way. Yet they both need each
other. Fellowship and co-operation is not a matter of choice, but
essential for the work.

Where it is different but co-operative. There will probably
always be some people who think that they have a monopoly on
the truth. There is little use in talking to them about co-operating
with others. Co-operation always involves identity of belief or else
a measure of compromise. But truth cannot compromise with
error. So they must pursue their lone way.

On the other hand most of us are quite ready to acknowledge
that within the Christian faith there is room for many differences
of opinion in matters that are not essential. We may prefer it our
way, but we must admit that the other fellow is serving the same
Lord in all sincerity, and there is something to say for his point
of view.

Our primary concern is not that people shall follow after us, but
that they shall become followers of the Lord. The missionary task
that He gave us was not to win all men to our church or denomination, good as we think it to be, but to make them disciples of the
Lord Jesus Christ.

What does this mean in practice? To the strictly denominational
mission it means personal fellowship, consultation and co-operation
in matters of common interest. It means getting acquainted with
our neighbors, first of all. How many misconceptions can be removed by an hour of friendly conversation! Then on the basis of
that friendly relationship we can find out what things we can best
do together.

To the interdenominational or independent mission the matter
may be of even greater importance. It depends largely on the
character of its work. Sometimes its whole ministry is made possible through the co-operation of a number of churches, as in some
of the institutional chaplaincies. At other times, though it has an
independent organization, it deliberately seeks the co-operation of

the churches. The work of such an organization as Child Evangelism Fellowship would be greatly restricted if it did not enjoy the co-operation of numerous churches. In return, its work is beneficial to those same churches.

Where it is antagonistic. There will always be those who oppose our work. Some oppose it because they have a different faith. Others oppose it either because they don't understand it, or they think it is unwise, or for other more personal reasons. What should the relation to these people be?

Missionaries whose work takes them to a number of communities have often found it wise to get in touch first with the local church, if there is one and if it might conceivably be friendly. This is just courtesy, and it often leads to friendly co-operation.

But what if the leaders of the church are unfriendly? Then there is only this to say: We must be careful that unfriendliness doesn't find a good basis in our own actions and attitudes. If their opposition is based on misunderstanding, it can be removed. If they think our work is unwise, it is a challenge to us to demonstrate its usefulness. If the issue is more personal, let us be sure our own conduct as Christians is irreproachable.

3. *Relation to the denomination and the supporting churches*

Home missions, like foreign missions, are not self-supporting. They must have the support of the established churches or of interested individuals. In seeking this support they have at least one major disadvantage and one great advantage. The disadvantage is that home missions do not have the same romantic appeal that generally attaches to foreign missions. The very idea sounds drab and commonplace. On the other hand, that romantic appeal is often very superficial. Those who are really committed to the Christian cause find a special appeal in home missions. Dealing with people very much like themselves, home missions covers many situations they can understand. They can easily identify themselves with the home missionary and picture themselves in his situation, while the foreign missionary's life is quite remote.

Through many years of introducing both home and foreign missionary speakers to student groups, I have noticed that home missionaries generally get the largest active response to their messages, in spite of the fact that many are not exceptionally good speakers. So if home missions are not enjoying the support they should have, the likelihood is that the missions are not giving the same careful attention to church relations that foreign missions do.

There are some quite obvious reasons for this. Home missions seldom employ deputation secretaries. Their missionaries do not have furloughs, when they can minister in the supporting churches. And the periodical literature that they issue is sometimes irregular and often inferior in quality.

4. *Relation to other missions and missionaries*

The multiplicity of home mission organizations in the United States, especially of an independent sort, is very confusing. Some, like the American Sunday-School Union, are very widespread. Others, as the various rescue missions, are limited to one specific place. In a few cases a mission may be alone in its field. In many other cases, as among the Navajo Indians, there is a wide variety of missions engaged in the work. What should be the relation of these missions to one another?

This is not the place to go into the problem in detail. We must admit, though, that there is a great deal of overlapping and even of competition. There have been various attempts to bring some order out of the apparent chaos. The National Council of Churches, through its Division of Home Missions, is performing a useful service for some of the major denominations. A number of the smaller independent missions have formed an association known as the National Home Missions Fellowship. While not a strong organization, it has been helpful in bringing the missionaries together for fellowship and consultation. There is also a national association of rescue missions, and in some local areas there are fellowships such as that formed by missionaries among the Navajo Indians.

There is still vast room for improvement. The spontaneous springing up of so many independent works is not necessarily bad. It may rather be considered as an evidence of the vitality of faith in many churches today. The operation of the Spirit is not under the control of any human organization. But sometimes it seems that much more could be accomplished if those missions that have a common faith would diligently seek the ways and means of letting the work of each one complement that of the others.

5. *Relation to civil authorities and the community*

The critical nature of this relationship has already been mentioned briefly. Perhaps one more word should be added. In foreign missions we often speak about the importance of identification with the people we serve. The same thing should be true in the home field. In fact, it is much more possible here than it is abroad. Being one with the people means much more than simply living in the same type of house and eating the same kind of food. It means observing the same etiquette, taking part in the same civic functions, identifying our interests as much as possible with theirs. We must not defy the laws of the state, but neither should we defy the laws of society, except where one or the other comes in conflict with the higher law of God.

6. *Personal relationships*

The relationship of missionaries to one another within the same mission is a matter of extreme importance. Whenever people are called on to live and work *together* there will be problems. The important thing is to keep those problems from multiplying and to handle them wisely when they do arise. Otherwise the work will face recurring disruptions and there will be a heavy turnover of personnel.

This is a field in which good leadership shows its worth. Missionaries are very much like anyone else. They like to follow people whom they respect. They are glad to be associated with organizations in whose work they can take pride, even though their own part may be small. They long to have their work recognized and appreciated. They like to feel that what they are doing is really important and that they are being trusted.

A mission's most important assets are its missionaries. Therefore they should be chosen with the greatest care. But once chosen, they should be made to feel that they are an integral part of the team. They should not be treated as temporary employees, to be dismissed at will. Any complaint they make should get a prompt and fair hearing. But by all means discourage criticism of one another. It can ruin the work. Don't even listen to a criticism unless the person is willing to have his complaint investigated. The work of the

Lord cannot flourish in an atmosphere of suspicion. The loyalty and devotion of the workers of some missions, in spite of a few personal differences, is beyond price.

Of course no mission, no human organization, is perfect. They are all made up of fallible human beings who on occasion may show traits of pettiness, jealousy, irritability, and the like. In other words, they are just like we are. So the missionary should not expect perfection. What he should expect is that he will find such satisfaction in serving the Lord in fellowship with these others that he can overlook petty annoyances. He should have the confidence that the Lord has called him to that service, so that the minor trials he experiences are meant for his own spiritual profit.

Practices

Some practices in home mission work have already been mentioned. In fact, it is not always possible to separate the principles from the practical examples of their outworking.

1. Applying indigenous principles

The word *indigenous* is not the exclusive property of foreign missions. The idea applies fully as much at home as it does abroad. In other words, while there are some types of work, such as jail visitation, that will always depend on the coming in of workers from the outside, the objective of most home missionary work is to make it stand on its own feet as soon as possible. In organizing Sunday schools, the American Sunday School Union always looks to the community to provide teachers and leadership, with the help of the local missionary. Even such an organization as Inter-Varsity Christian Fellowship emphasizes the autonomy of the local chapter on each college campus.

In some cases, as with the work in new housing developments, the local group may soon be able to dispense with the help of the home mission. In other more sparsely settled communities, the church may always have need of help. It cannot carry the whole load, but its work is too important to be dropped. Yet we should always aim at the maximum participation of the local people in the work. One of the major weaknesses in work among the Indians is the lack of trained Indian leadership after so many years of labor.

2. *Giving all-important Bible instruction*

For many there is no need to emphasize this point. The Bible is the basis of their faith, their own source of spiritual inspiration. So they naturally want to teach it to others.

But others, though sincerely Christian, have not had the same experience of the power of the Word. So they tend to emphasize other activities in their work, sometimes to the exclusion of the Bible. What they fail to realize is that while a sort of secondary Christianity may be induced in some people with only a remote reference to the Scriptures, this is not the road to a really vital faith. "Faith cometh by hearing, and hearing by the word of God."

The rote memorization of Scripture verses that some missions use seems too mechanistic to others. Yet it is no more so than the memorization of vocabulary that we use in carrying on the affairs of life. Words are useless except as we employ them to express thoughts. But thoughts without words are equally vain. Scripture verses are like the vocabulary of God. They can be just meaningless symbols. But if we have them stored in our memory they provide the means by which God can speak to our hearts.

3. *Making good use of literature*

The Bible is our most important piece of literature. We can perform no more important ministry than that of getting it into the hands and hearts of the people. But there is a vast quantity of auxiliary literature that increases the effectiveness of home missionary work.

Books can continue to speak when the living messenger is not present. They never tire of saying the same things over and over until they are mastered. They are always available, always ready to give their message. They are never in a hurry, never impatient with the one who is slow to grasp the ideas they present. Neither are they inclined to speak "off the cuff"; their messages are always carefully prepared. Besides, in a handful of books there is not the wisdom of a single teacher but the teaching of several.

The important thing is to find out what literature will be of most use in our ministry, get familiar with it and push its distribution, selling, lending, or if necessary, giving it away. It will be money and effort well spent. The colportage ministry itself is a very valuable missionary endeavor. The rapid growth of some of the sects is due in large part to their use of literature. Why should those who teach the truth neglect such a powerful aid?

In some cases home missions find it wise to prepare their own literature. This is especially true of periodical publications and follow-up literature. But for general purposes there is an abundant supply of literature already available in English. The Colportage Library of the Moody Literature Mission contains scores of titles on a variety of subjects. There are not only sermons and Bible studies but Christian stories, and all for a price that anyone can afford.

4. *Teaching others to witness*

This is a matter on which the success of any missionary work will depend. The missionary is not an isolated worker carrying by himself the full burden of the work. He may serve as a sparkplug and a steering wheel, but he depends on the explosive power of the gospel in each life to push the work forward.

Rescue missions make good use of the testimonies of those who have been saved. Much of their success depends on it. Boys' clubs count on the witness of the boys themselves to bring in others. Bible memory missions figure that as the children learn their verses, repeating them to their parents at home, the parents themselves will be affected. And they all know that the most effective workers in any area are likely to be those who have come from such a background themselves.

5. *Taking advantage of other available aids*

Literature is not the only aid that is available to home missionary workers. Here are several others.

Radio. Many small local stations are scattered over the United States. The mission worker should get on one if possible, even if he has to buy time. For small stations the expense is not great and the people of the immediate neighborhood will be reached. But the program should be worthwhile. A consistently good program will often be given free time.

Correspondence courses. Many good Bible courses are available by correspondence. The people and the work in general will be benefited if these courses are encouraged.

Training schools and conferences. Home missions are one of the most important sources of students for the Bible training schools of the country. Some of them return to their own field to work for the Lord. Many others become foreign missionaries, and their going stimulates even greater interest in the gospel at home. Attendance at Bible conferences, too, benefits not only the ones who go, but the church to which they return.

Films, slides and other audio-visual aids. The amount of this material available is being multiplied year by year. Some of it can be rented for a fixed price, but a great deal can be borrowed free or on the basis of a freewill offering. There is also the possibility of constructing many audio-visuals. Those who wish to know how may get instruction in the subject in a summer course from a school like Moody Bible Institute.

BIBLIOGRAPHY

While a fair amount of literature dealing with individual home missions or types of home missionary work is available, studies of the basic principles and practices involved are exceedingly sparse. One book, though rather old, deals exclusively with home missions:

MORSE, HERMANN N. (ed.). *Home Missions Today and Tomorrow.* New York: Home Missions Council, 1934.

Another book deals with missions generally, but has a considerable section on work in North America:

LAMOTT, WILLIS. *Committed Unto Us.* New York: Friendship Press, 1947.

There are two books that deal especially with basic matters in relation to rescue mission work:

PAUL, WILLIAM E. *The Rescue Mission Manual.* Minneapolis: Osterhus Publishing House.

SEATH, WILLIAM. *A Study of Rescue Missions.* Chicago: Chicago League Print Shop, 1952.

One recent book written chiefly with foreign missions in view is nevertheless important for any type of missionary work:

KRAEMER, HENDRIK. *The Communication of the Christian Faith.* Philadelphia: Westminster Press, 1956.

The author, Harold R. Cook, instructing a class in missions at the Moody Bible Institute.

3

Qualifications and Preparation of the Home Missionary

Harold R. Cook

Qualifications

THE HOME MISSIONARY is a minister of Christ. His is the responsibility, by all means at his disposal, to represent Jesus Christ to men, women and children, to win them to the Saviour and help them grow in Him. As he goes forth he is conscious that he has a responsibility to God who has called him, to the people to whom he ministers, and also to the church that has set him apart and identified itself with him in the task.

So in speaking in general of the qualifications of the home missionary, we would say that he must be called of God, and that he must be such a one as the church will be willing to entrust with this important job.

But doubtless we ought to be much more specific. Not that we can ever perfectly define what a home missionary ought to be, but we can set up a number of standards that will help a young person evaluate his own qualifications for the work and that may even be of some use to those who will send him out. We shall group them under four heads: spiritual, intellectual, personality, and experience.

1. Spiritual

Obviously for Christian service the spiritual qualifications are

29

of supreme importance. Others are needed; in fact, they may have much greater importance than some are willing to assign them. But the spiritual qualifications are basic. Without them there cannot be a truly Christian ministry. We may call it Christian. We may even conduct it under the auspices of the Christian church. It may be very beneficial in bettering the social and economic situation of the people. But it is still not Christian unless the Spirit of Christ motivates it and unless its objectives are distinctively Christian. And this can only be when the missionary is spiritually qualified in a Christian sense.

Devotion to Christ and His gospel. Wholehearted devotion to Christ is imperative for the true home missionary. He must take up the task, not because he loves the work, but because he loves the Saviour. It is not so that he can find self-satisfaction, but so that he can satisfy the soul needs of others. With Paul he must be able to say, "The love of Christ constrains me." He must see the need of a world dead in sin and feel keenly that Christ "died for all, that they which live should not henceforth live unto themselves, but unto him which died for them, and rose again."

Consistent Christian living. The life of the missionary counts fully as much as the messages he may give. It may count even more. Few are going to believe what he says if they don't see it borne out to some extent in his own life. The hypocrisy of professing Christians is one of the favorite arguments brought against the acceptance of the gospel. Only a consistent Christian life can silence such an objection. The home missionary is called to represent Christ. To represent Him fairly he must know Christ intimately by personal experience.

Unselfish concern for others. When Paul wrote to the Philippians about sending Timothy to them, he said, "I have no man like-minded, who will naturally care for your state. For all seek their own, not the things which are Jesus Christ's." In Paul's estimation Timothy was an excellent missionary, but he was a rare individual. And if such concern about others was rare among those who surrounded Paul, it is no less rare today.

What a shame to have to say, "All seek their own." Yet even in missionary company there are those who are self-centered. They serve, not through interest in others, but to satisfy their own souls.

They are willing to suffer and sacrifice in order to hear the Lord's "Well done." Yet they lack the love that sent God's great Missionary into the world to die for men, "while we were yet sinners." To follow in His steps as missionaries, we must have some of that same concern for others.

Willingness to serve. To minister is to serve. And those whose whose concern for others leads them into a home missionary ministry will be glad to serve in whatever way they can. In seeking secular employment we usually bargain. We prefer congenial work, but most of all we are interested in the salary it will produce. In missionary work, while we cannot entirely disregard the material side, our orientation is different. We are primarily concerned with the contribution we can make. What talents has the Lord given us? Where can they most fully be used to His glory and to accomplish His purposes?

The call of God. Most of us think of the missionary call in relation to foreign service, not that at home. Yet such a distinction is purely arbitrary; it is not found in the Scriptures. In fact, the idea of a call in the New Testament refers primarily to salvation, not to service.

Yet we are not wrong in thinking that our entering into the Lord's service should be at His invitation. We can say that the ministry is a calling, not a profession. We do not choose it of our own desires and to satisfy our own ambitions. Just as Christ said to His disciples, "Ye have not chosen me, but I have chosen you, and ordained you, that ye should go and bring forth fruit," so today He continues to choose those who are to be His witnesses. Whatever else the calling of God may mean, it means that the course we are following is His choice for us.

The sense of a call — the sense that we are doing what God wants us to do — is extremely important in home missionary service. The minister of a church can sometimes cover up his lack of a call. He can develop his professional capabilities to the point where he can command a comfortable living and a certain amount of social satisfaction. The foreign missionary without a call would find it much more difficult to escape complete frustration. Yet he does enjoy a large measure of prestige in the eyes of the church at home, and there is a certain amount of glamour that attaches

to his life and work. But the emoluments of home missionary work
are always small, and there is little glamour to it. So the one who
engages in it must find his satisfaction in the consciousness that
he is in the place of God's choosing and that the Lord Himself
will be his reward.

The home mission field needs men of God-given vision. How easy
it is to become stultified in the routine of the work, to become so
burdened down with details that we cannot catch a vision of the
broad purposes and scope that it should have. But there will never
be workers with such vision, workers inspired by the tremendous
potentialities of home missions, unless they are men and women
conscious of the call of God to this ministry.

2. Intellectual

The demands of home missionary work on the intellectual abilities of the workers are exceedingly varied. There are some places
where people of very modest attainments, but deep devotion, can
have a very fruitful ministry. With superior abilities, though, they
could doubtless do a better job. The Lord's work should have the
best. We should not try to "get by" with less. And there are many
places where our best is none too good for the task to be done.

Knowledge of the Bible. The Bible contains the very heart of
our message. It would seem obvious, then, that every home missionary ought to have a good command of Scripture. Yet it is
apparently not obvious to some. Otherwise why would they write
asking about the possibilities of home missionary service when
they admit they have had very little instruction in the Word of
God. It is not a question of classes, diplomas and degrees. It is a
question of having well in hand the message that must be delivered.
However the missionary gets that knowledge, he must have it.

Ability to communicate. To know the message is fundamental.
To be able to communicate it to others is fully as important. In the
United States this does not often mean the mastery of a language
other than our own. In this the home missionary has an advantage over the one who goes abroad. Besides, even though there
are variations, he is already familiar with American culture. So he
doesn't have to learn the radically different customs of other people
and their different ways of thinking to make them understand the

gospel. His problem of adjustment in these matters is comparatively minor.

Yet the fact that English is our native tongue does not guarantee that we are able to use it well. Here is one of our most common weaknesses. It is not simply our inability to speak clearly and forcibly in public. It is the fact that even in private conversations we are unable to convey to others exactly what we want them to understand. Businessmen tell us that this one thing is a major reason why many otherwise capable young men have not been able to reach places of real leadership. Good ideas are powerless unless they can be communicated. The missionary's message is useless if he cannot get it across to others.

Capacity for growth. No missionary is fully qualified for his job when he first begins it. He should be qualified to make a start. But it is expected that he will develop greater ability as he goes along. This capacity for growth is something that is difficult to evaluate, yet it is extremely important. The best missionaries are those who never cease to grow. With Paul, they are always conscious that they have not yet attained, but they "follow on" right to the end.

Many a young man has complained that he was given a job that was beneath his abilities. It happens in missions as well as elsewhere. What he does not realize is that the very complaint shows his lack of stature. Only a very mediocre person has to have a job tailored to his abilities. One who is outstanding will tend to glorify even a minor task, with the likelihood that he will soon have more important work. Perhaps the choice was to increase the scope of the task entrusted to him. And if the job is too big for him, he will tackle it with the expectation of growing into it.

Special services: necessary talents and training. There are many special types of ministry in home missions. Doctors, nurses, teachers, and many others need special talents and training that we cannot deal with in detail here. Their qualifications in these special lines, however, do not exempt them from the basic qualifications required of other home missionaries. Their special abilities enable them to fill a particular need in the work, but they should still be missionaries — in spirit and in the character of their ministry.

3. Personality

How can we assess personality? How can we measure the impression that people make on others? Such an evaluation is not easy. Yet personality has a great deal to do with success in missionary work. The impression the missionary makes will determine to a large extent whether people will pay any attention to the gospel he proclaims. We cannot go into detail in this matter but will simply mention four items.

Ability to work with others. Some kinds of missionary work may permit the missionary to decide by himself what is to be done and expect others to follow his orders. But this type of work is rare. Many a missionary may indeed attempt such a thing, but sooner or later he runs into difficulties.

Most missionaries soon learn that they can do very little by themselves. The very heart of their work is dealing with people, and they can't do very much unless the people co-operate. This is even true of children's work, though children are much more ready to obey orders than are adults. To secure that necessary co-operation, the missionary must have learned how to work *with* other people.

This does not mean that he cannot be a leader. In fact, he should be a leader. But a leader and a dictator are two different things. The dictator rules by force because he is unable to persuade. The leader inspires confidence so that people are willing to go along with him. But there are times when he has to give in on some things so as to keep their support and co-operation. He has learned to work with people.

The "lone wolf" has very little place in missionary service. What is needed is one who can work with others, can inspire them by his example, can help them to accomplish what no one alone could ever do. And then he will also have companions in rejoicing, which adds to its sweetness.

Persistence. There are some very difficult and discouraging fields of service overseas. But it is questionable whether any are more frustrating to the missionary than some of the fields at home. Indifference is much more difficult to face than open opposition. And the churches that support the work are often less considerate of their home workers than of those who served abroad.

So the home missionary needs to be a person of great persistence. The man who accepts a job and then drops it as soon as the going gets rough will never do. The one who has to be encouraged constantly with visible evidences of success is not a good prospect. The "plugger" sometimes lacks the fire and imagination of some of the others, but he is the backbone of the work. If you have learned to tackle a job and carry it through to the end, regardless of difficulties and discouragements, you are a good missionary prospect.

Responsibility. As has already been said, a home missionary should be a leader. Most people look at leaders simply as those who occupy places of prominence. In that sense they would like to be leaders, too; they would enjoy being leaders if they didn't have to, as they express it, "stick their necks out."

But that is exactly what a leader has to do. He must be willing to take responsibility, he must be ready to make decisions. If he hesitates to make decisions, if he doesn't want to take responsibility, he just doesn't have what it takes to be a leader.

But responsibility involves more than a willingness to make decisions. It includes dependability. If we speak of a man as responsible, we usually mean not only that he is the one to blame if things go wrong, but that he usually shows good judgment and can be trusted to do his utmost to carry out any agreement he makes. In other words, he is trustworthy.

Enthusiasm. Every good missionary is an enthusiast. He is zealous for his faith and for the work the Lord has given him to do. Some are vigorous and effervescent. Others are less demonstrative but more intense in their zeal. The manner of showing it is not important; but the fact is important. The person who has no room for emotion in his faith has never experienced real faith. Neither will he ever be able to kindle faith in others.

4. *Experience*

In the "help wanted" columns of the newspaper we sometimes read, "No experience needed." Does that statement really mean what it says? Usually not. What it does mean is that no experience is needed in the special type of work for which help is wanted. If we were to ask for the job we would find that the employer is keenly interested in whether we have ever worked before and in what kind of work.

In some sense it is the same in home mission work. For some types of work no previous experience is required. But there are still certain kinds of experience that are needed.

Maturity of Christian life. The home missionary must not only be a Christian; he must be a mature Christian. Paul had a word to say about this in his first letter to Timothy. He warned that the one who was chosen to lead the church should not be "a novice." He should be one tested by experience. Christian training schools also have learned this lesson. They usually require that a student must have been a Christian for at least a year before he is accepted for training. This is not to question the sincerity of his conversion, but in order to lead others he himself must first be well established in the Christian life.

Practice in presenting the gospel. One of the most common questions asked of missionary candidates is this, "Have you ever led a soul to Christ?" This is not curious prying; it is an important question. If evangelism is the very heart of home missionary work, and the candidate has had no experience in it, how does he know that he can do it?

No matter how sincere our own faith, we need experience in communicating it to others. Basic, of course, is personal evangelism, which will be needed in any kind of home mission work. But many a missionary will also have to preach. So he needs some experience in this more formal way of presenting the gospel message.

Leadership experience. It never ceases to amaze me that some young people who aspire to missionary service have never taken advantage of the opportunities for leadership in their home church. They have never so much as occupied an office in the young people's society or planned the games for a church picnic. Some have never even taught a Sunday school class. Yet they expect by some magic to become missionaries!

Any experience in leading is valuable; it does not have to be an important job. In fact, the important jobs are usually given to those who have already demonstrated their ability. Every Christian should seize any opportunity for leadership experience that comes his way. It will help qualify him for a missionary ministry.

Specialized experience. Those who expect to be dealing with churches in their home mission work should certainly have church experience. How can one who has only sat in the pew possibly know how to direct what goes on behind the scenes? How can he help to organize a new church or counsel its leaders? He needs experience in this field, just as the doctor needs internship and the school teacher a period of supervised practice teaching.

Value of similar background. It is perhaps not strange that many men in rescue mission work are themselves the product of that work. By personal experience they know not only the need but also something of the way to approach the problems on skid row. Some of the most effective workers in the southern highlands, too, are those who have come from that background. Their personal experience is a great help.

Yet this is not always the case, and we should guard against thinking that because one has come from a certain area of home missionary work he should plan to go back to that same work. Some of the finest workers among the Jews, for example, have been Gentiles. At the same time some outstanding missionaries to other lands have been Jewish Christians.

Preparation

In dealing with the qualifications of the home missionary we have necessarily touched somewhat on the matter of preparation also. The two go together. Some qualifications may seem to be inherent in the person; but many are the result of cultivation, of preparation, whether planned or not.

Preparation, of course, can be both formal and informal. It has to do with what the prospective missionary does on his own and with what he is taught to do in the schools he attends. It concerns the general preparation that he needs as a minister of the Lord Jesus Christ, and also the specific skills and instruction that he ought to have for the type of ministry he is entering.

1. *That which depends on the candidate*

It is a mistake to suppose that missionaries get the preparation they need in Bible schools. That they get some important preparation there is certainly true. But much of their preparation—in fact, some of the most basic parts of their preparation—comes outside the school. To a large extent it depends on the initiative, the dedi-

cation, the diligent interest of the young person himself. Even
in school the amount that he profits by the instruction will depend
to a large extent on himself. Schools do not "give" an education;
they only help the willing student to get one. They provide the
opportunity, but it depends on the student what he will do with it.

Personal spiritual development. In the list of qualifications the
spiritual was first. Yet when all is said and done, there is comparatively little that a school can do to develop spirituality among
its students. We wish there were. We wish it were as easy to communicate as knowledge. But that is not the case.

The most that a school can do is emphasize the things of the
Spirit in its program and teaching. It can try to demonstrate them
in the lives of its faculty and staff. It can counsel and urge and
try to inspire. But that is all. Some students will still be left "cold."
The same meeting that inspires renewed dedication on the part of
one student seems a useless waste of time to another. The difference
is in the students themselves.

Spiritual development does not come through instruction. It
does not come through listening to a series of messages on the
Spirit-filled life. We all know much more about the theory of it
than we have ever put into practice. Sermons and lessons give something in the way of instruction. They provide more in the way of
incentive. But what really counts is the practice. Spiritual development comes through spiritual exercise, and the opportunity for
that exercise comes in day-to-day living.

Actually our spiritual development begins from the time we are
born again. It can be encouraged and helped by a wise pastor and
good Christian friends. It can be stimulated by Christian activity
within the church and outside of it. But most of all it depends on
a close walk with the Lord who gave us this new life. As He said
to His disciples, "I am the vine, ye are the branches . . . As the
branch cannot bear fruit of itself, except it abide in the vine; no
more can ye, except ye abide in me."

Participation in the work of the home church. To most people
this seems like a haphazard way of preparing for home missionary
service, since few churches have any planned program for instructing their young people in the work of the church. In fact, if the
young people were to ask for some kind of instruction or experience,

the church fathers might have a hard time knowing just what to suggest.

Nevertheless the church is an important training ground. For one thing, it soon shows whether a young person is a "self-starter" or whether he needs someone else to prime him. The one with interest and initiative will always find some service to perform. Home missionary work needs "self-starters." Then, too, it is work among those who know us best and are not so easily misled by outward appearances. This makes it difficult, but rewarding. And nearly all this work is on a voluntary basis, so it comes from the heart and there is little question of professionalism.

All this, of course, is beside the fact that much of the work done in the home church is the same sort of work that will be done in home missions. There will be differences, it is true, and with further instruction and experience it is to be hoped that the worker will do much better. But it gives the candidate a good beginning in his course of preparation.

Part-time service, or assistance of others. The apostles of our Lord were prepared for their ministry largely through being with Him, listening to His teachings, watching His works and doing the tasks that He gave them to do. This very personalized training, or apprenticeship, is unusual today in its full sense. But many part-time opportunities are available.

There are such opportunities as assisting the director of the boys' club or helping in the vacation Bible school. During summer vacations many organizations want help for their camp programs or vacation Bible schools, sometimes for the whole summer. In many cases they will give some instruction ahead of time, and a chance to work with and observe experienced leaders. Some will also pay something for the service. In home missions, where the field is nearby, a missionary might be persuaded to take on a helper just for the training and experience it will give.

Going the "second mile." There used to be an advertisement for a correspondence school that said, "It is what you do with your spare time that counts." In other words, the one who merely fulfills the requirements of his job will probably never advance very far. It is the extra effort that makes the difference between mediocrity and real success.

This is just as true in Christian work as it is in business. Those who do the best work are the "second milers," the ones who go beyond what is required of them. This is a lesson that can be told us, but we have to learn its truth for ourselves. After considerable time we can look back and see how some of the most valuable lessons we learned were not in the regular course of instruction. They were things we learned on our own initiative. And those are the things that usually make the difference in missionaries as well as others.

2. Schooling

How much schooling should one get? What kinds? And where is the best place to get it? These and similar questions are constantly asked by those who want to enter home missionary service. Frequently they take it for granted that this kind of work does not call for much schooling. They couldn't be more mistaken.

Depends on prospective service. The amount and kind of training needed depends to a large extent of course on the type of work to be entered. The broader the scope of work, the more extensive the training. But immediate objectives should not blind one to the possibilities for the future. It may be that the job in view right now does not call for a very lengthy preparation. But is the candidate sure that this will be his ministry through the rest of his life? Would he be prepared if the Lord should call him to a broader ministry?

In general we would say that the best idea is for him to get the most complete preparation that he can, consistent with his purpose. This means completing high school, by all means. It also means Bible school. In many cases it will mean college and perhaps some other specialized training. A missionary is the Lord's servant; he should be prepared to serve Him in the best way possible.

Bible institute and Bible college. The minimum amount of schooling for most purposes should be graduation from high school and from a good Bible institute. This will usually mean three years at least beyond high school, and it is little enough in our present day.

The difference between the Bible institute and the Bible college is this: The Bible institute provides one or more courses, now customarily three years in length, of specialized preparation in Bible and related subjects. Among the other subjects besides Bible and theology are gospel music, Christian education and missions. The Bible college combines the specialized training of the Bible institute with some of the liberal arts subjects of the usual college course. Its courses usually take four years to complete and lead to a degree. Each of these types of schools has its own advantages and disadvantages.

The school should be selected with care, keeping in mind the purpose of the training. The school should be accredited. The better ones of both types are accredited by the Accrediting Association of Bible Colleges. This doesn't mean that some non-accredited schools may not be giving good instruction. Neither does it mean that all accredited schools are on the same level. It simply means that those who are accredited have met certain minimum standards that the Association believes are important for a good educational program.

The extracurricular activities of a school are an important part of preparation. Does the school selected give regular assignments in Christian service to carry out? Will there be opportunity to participate in other groups that will fit in with the objective?

College and seminary. The missionary candidate should give serious attention to the question of going to college. Even if it is not actually required for the work he is to do, it will enrich his life and enlarge his ministry. But it should not be considered a substitute for the Bible institute or Bible college, unless he goes on to graduate work in the seminary. The liberal arts college is planned to give a broad cultural background, not to prepare specially for home missionary service. Only a few of the "Christian" colleges give anywhere near enough Bible and related subjects for home mission needs, and that only if the major is Bible or Christian education.

In many cases young people find it advisable to take the three-year course in an accredited Bible institute, and then by transferring some of these credits they can finish college in another two years or slightly more.

Seminary, of course, is a graduate school of religion for those who already have earned their first collegiate degree. Its primary purpose is the training of ministers, so its value to the home missionary may depend on the kind of work he is called to do. It can be very valuable, but it can also create in some students a high-mindedness that will turn them aside from their purpose to serve in home missions. Much depends on the student and the depth of his fervor to be used in this humble way.

Specialized training. For special types of service, the schools are too numerous to list. There are schools of medicine and schools of nursing. There are teachers' colleges. There are schools of social service, though not often on a Christian basis. Some schools offer special courses in rural problems. There are also brief courses such as the one Child Evangelism Fellowship offers for its workers. The advisability of taking some of these courses is more or less an individual matter and may call for counseling with missionary leaders.

3. *Special studies*

We have already said that Bible and communications (speaking, writing, teaching) are basic studies for the one who wants to be a home missionary. Beyond this there are many other useful studies. Some are valuable in one type of ministry, some in another. Actually the home missionary is in a situation somewhat similar to that of the foreign missionary. He knows better just what studies are most useful in his work after he has had a term of service. The pattern is not always the same, even for different individuals who work in the same field.

One of the most important needs is to understand the people among whom you work. Not all people are alike, even in the United States. In those things in which they are similar, perhaps study of psychology will be helpful. But there are many customs, ways of thinking, patterns of life among different peoples here in our homeland. Unless the worker understands these things, he may unwittingly offend the ones he wants to win. At least he will always be an outsider to them and they will keep him at arm's length.

Studies that will help in this matter are not available in most schools. Sometimes a class in rural life or the rural church may be offered. Often there will be a class in child psychology. Occasionally there are classes in urban problems and juvenile delinquency. But most often the missionary will have to make the study on his own, or he may be able to make it as a term project in a class where such projects are called for. The important thing is that in some way he try to gain an understanding of the people and their background. In some cases, as with the Indians, this may mean a study of their history, especially their relations with the white people.

Besides an understanding of the gospel and of the people to whom he ministers, the missionary would do well to learn something about personal counseling. Somehow we seem to take it for granted that anyone who has had experience is able to counsel another in the same matters. We don't realize that good counseling is more than just presenting facts or giving advice. It takes understanding and skill to lead the other person to make his own decision and to make it a right one. This is a ministry in which all home missionaries engage. They should learn to do it well.

Then there are practical studies of special methods that are useful in the work. For work with children and young people, the missionary needs to know about the Sunday school, the vacation Bible school, recreational leadership, and how to conduct an effective Bible camp. How to prepare and use the rapidly increasing variety of audio-visual aids is important to know both for children and adults. And if he has any musical ability at all, he will find that a little training will make it an invaluable aid in carrying on his ministry.

BIBLIOGRAPHY

Studies of qualifications and preparation for home missionary work are very rare. One pamphlet on the subject has been published recently:

SCHREIBER, JAMES C. *Qualifications and Standards for Home Missionaries.* Chicago: National Home Missions Fellowship, 1959.

There are many more studies that have to do with qualifications and preparation for *foreign* service. In some cases these are broad enough to be helpful for *home* missions, since the basic spiritual preparation is the same. Representative of this type are:

COOK, HAROLD R. *An Introduction to the Study of Christian Missions.* Chicago: Moody Press, 1954.

PULLENG, A. *Go Ye Therefore . . .* London: The Paternoster Press, c. 1958.

Why should this Navajo child smile? His spiritual and material poverty leave little room for optimism. (Courtesy of Navajo Missions, Inc.)

4

The Indian American

D. CLARENCE BURD

In the introduction, home missions were defined as reaching those not normally reached through the normal channels of the local church. In this chapter we are not considering work among the Indians where the local church may have an extension program including these people. Instead, we are primarily concerned with missions whose entire program is geared to that of bringing the gospel of Christ to the Indian.

Dr. Burd has given considerable emphasis to the history of the American Indian. In a sense, this is necessary to appreciate fully their spiritual needs. It is also necessary to appreciate fully the complexities involved in trying to reach these people with the gospel.

The greatest concentration of home missionary work among the Indians has been on the Navajo reservation — probably because here is the largest single group of Indians. Missionary activity among the Indians elsewhere is very limited.

A look at the map will show how scattered the Indians really are. In many areas their life and activities have become intermingled with the white man, and missionary work among them is considered the responsibility of the local church. There are some exceptions, however; for instance, among the various denominational groups as the Southern

Born in 1887, D. CLARENCE BURD received his business education at Rider College, Trenton, New Jersey. He also studied at Biblical Seminary and graduated from the Department of Religious Education in 1912 and Department of Theology in 1927. Postgraduate work was taken at Princeton Theological Seminary.

Dr. Burd held pastorates in Presbyterian churches in Farmington and Las Vegas, New Mexico. He taught Bible at Navajo Methodist Mission School, Farmington, and Cook Christian Training School, Phoenix, Arizona, from which he retired in 1955. Since writing this chapter, Dr. Burd has gone to be with the Lord.

Baptists, American Baptists and the Mennonites working specifically with the Indians in Oklahoma, or the Christian and Missionary Alliance in South Dakota.

Rerefence should also be made to the work among the Indians in Alaska and Canada. Actually, a separate chapter in this book is devoted to Alaska, and missionary work in this state includes an outreach among the Indians.

As for Canada, probably the largest faith mission concentrating on reaching the Indians in the far north is the Northern Canada Evangelical Mission with headquarters in Meadow Lake, Sask. The Indians here are scattered all the way from the West Coast to the East Coast, and to reach them requires a great deal of travel from one reserve to another — usually by airplane. The work is progressing, however, but the need for more well-trained Indians to work among their own people is acute.

At our request, Mission Aides, Inc.,* recently made a Navajo survey. While it was impossible to get a complete picture of missionary work on the reservation, some interesting information was found.

There are about 185 Protestant groups with 470 staff members who reach approximately 12,700 Navajos once a month, and four times that many at least once a year. Roughly, half of these have stations located within the confines of the reservation. In addition, at least fifty Catholic and Mormon stations are found on the reservation. Actually, there are only a few Mormon stations, but they have sent out missionaries two by two using Indian trading posts as their base of operation. There seems to be evidence of communistic activity among the Navajos as well.

The Navajo language is still being used extensively by the Indians themselves. There are, however, relatively few missionaries who know the language. Of 350 non-Navajo staff members, only 33 speak the language, 62 can read Navajo, 23 speak well enough to teach in the Navajo, and three can preach if given ample time for preparation.

It is difficult to determine the number of organized Navajo churches. There are probably twenty-five to fifty groups of Navajos who consider themselves to be churches. At least a third of these should be classified as mission outstations. As far as is known, only four may be considered to be self-supporting. In two of these instances, the pastors receive some outside support although it does not come from a mission board. In the other cases the pastors are self-supporting through outside employment.

Mission Aides has compiled a list of forty-four Navajos who might qualify as pastors if they were given the opportunity to serve in that

* 100 East Montecito Ave., Sierra Madre, Calif.

capacity. The majority of these, however, serve as interpreters. Some are in charge of mission stations, and probably five or six have been ordained. Only a few are graduates of Bible training schools or have had some seminary training.

Perhaps among Indian missions today, the greatest need is for trained Indian teachers, pastors and workers who can minister to their own people. They know the customs and language. The Indian is often suspicious of the white man — not so with his own people.

The following schools have been established for the purpose of training Christian Indian leadership:

Navajo Gospel Crusade, Cortez, Colorado.
Navajo Mission and Bible School, Window Rock, Arizona
Southwestern School of Missions, Flagstaff, Arizona
Cook Christian Training School, Phoenix, Arizona
Navajo Gospel Mission, Oraibi, Arizona
Mt. Echo Bible Institute, Great Valley, New York (on the Seneca reservation but open to all tribes)
Indian Bible School, La Ronge, Saskatchewan, Canada (sponsored by the Northern Canada Evangelical Mission especially for the Cree Indians)
Mohahum Bible School, Cass Lake, Minnesota
Brainerd Indian School, Hot Springs, South Dakota

All schools are relatively small, but plans call for expansion and greater emphasis in the training of Indian Christians who, in the long run, can reach their own people more effectively than the white man can possibly do.

The Editors

I F THERE IS A PEOPLE in the whole world to whom the United States owes a great debt, it is the Indian American. We call these people Indians, or we speak of them as red men, but both terms are incorrect. Columbus called these people "Indians," thinking he had reached India. "Red men" is also a misnomer, for the Indians are really all shades of brown rather than red in color.

The Indian was the first to discover two continents. He antedated the coming of the white man by centuries. "He made the trails which are now some of our highways. He found the useful plants, trees and animals. His ways of hunting, cooking and house building were taught to the first white men and often saved their lives."[1]

[1] Ruth M. Underhill, *Red Man's America* (Chicago: University of Chicago Press, 1953), p. 1.

As early as the last glacial period there were people in America, late archaeological finds indicate. It is rather generally thought that the first people in America came from Asia, perhaps by way of the Bering Sea. How many came and from just what area they migrated may never be known. It would appear, however, that there must have been many migrations because of the many locations in which remains are found and because of the different cultures which developed.

When the white man arrived, he was confronted with inhabitants who had been here for a long time. Drake's *Indians of North America,* published in 1880, gives a list of some 460 tribes who were the ancestors of the numerous tribes of today. Archaeologists go much further back and give fascinating tales of the cultures of the Chimus, Incas, Aztecs, Mayas, all to the south of us.

Estimates of the Indian population of the American continent today vary from 25 to 50 million. If we should agree on a figure of 40 million, we would say that approximately 1 per cent, or 400,000, live within the United States. Contrast that with the something less than one million residents here when the early settlers arrived.

The Indians Considered Regionally

Northeast Area

Virginia, 1607; New York, 1613; Plymouth, 1620; Massachusetts Bay, 1629 were sorrowful dates for the Indians. By 1640 there were 20,000 settlers living mostly in the Northeast. The story of the first Thanksgiving proves that there were friendly relations between the early settlers and the Indians. The Indians taught many valuable lessons to the settlers, but peace did not long endure, for the settlers continued moving inland.

Rebecca Reuben, a student at the Cook Christian Training School, Phoenix, wrote a paper in 1957 entitled "History of the American Indian." This is but one example of similar experiences by other tribes; therefore her account is given in full:

"The United States made a promise in 1778 that guaranteed the Delawares full rights to land bound by earlier treaties. If another tribe would like to join with the Delawares, the United States and they would agree to join and form a state of the Union.

If this should take place, the Delawares would be entitled to send one representative to Congress. The Delawares accepted, but later were forced to leave their territory despite the treaty.

"The government tried later to offer the Indians money, but the Indians explained that money was of no use to them. Why not give it to trespassing whites and let them move out of Indian territory? The government representatives refused, holding that it would be too much trouble for settlers who had violated the treaty to move off. The Indians persisted, so the commissioners reported that the Indians refused to make peace. The army then attacked and seized the land. The Indians sued for peace and were promised that payment would be made. The promise that no more land would be taken from them was repeated. Later they had to give up more land. Five treaties specified annuities forever or permanently, but finally these gave out. The Delawares were moved to different land. They still received promises of the government's faithful protection. They stayed there for twenty years before they were required to cede more land. This continued for treaty after treaty until we see the Delawares pushed clear back to Oklahoma. They were now under the jurisdiction of a state, when once they had been promised they could become a state."

Today in Oklahoma they may number 1,250 with less than 20 per cent full-blooded Indians.

2. *The Iroquois*

To the west of the Algonquian tribes of the Northeast and in the middle Atlantic states dwelt several Iroquois tribes. These were village people united in a confederation of tribes. Often they were scourge of the Algonquians to the east of them. Originally, their league consisted of five tribes: Seneca, Cayuga, Onondaga, Oneida and Mohawk. This league of nations dealt with matters of war and peace and intertribal difficulties. Each member was pledged not to fight the other. There had to be unanimous consent for any common action. Through warfare they captured other tribes who often became members of the league. This league continued until the Revolutionary War, when the various members of it separated. Some of the tribesmen moved to Wisconsin and some to Oklahoma. There are still six small reservations of these people in New York today.

Their home area before the settlers came was mostly central and southern New York, which abounded in fish, birds and wild turkey. The soil gave good yields of squash, beans and corn. Wild plants, berries and nuts were also found in abundance.

3. Southeast Area

In southeastern United States the Cherokees and Creeks were the most important tribes. Less populous tribes were the Chickasaws, the Seminoles and the Choctaws. These were later listed by government records as the "Five Civilized Tribes."

These tribes did not have a common tongue, but came from at least two language stocks. Their area was well supplied with foodstuffs gathered and prepared largely by the women, while the men spent much time in warlike activities. Shamanism[2] was a common practice among all of these. Dances were common to celebrate the ripening of various foods, with particular emphasis on the arrival of the first green corn.

DeSoto first contacted these tribes in 1540. His kidnapping and looting were long remembered by the Indians. Contacts with the Spanish, French and English, each of whom sought to gain allies against the other, proved to be no more peaceful.

One of the outstanding men was the Cherokee Sequoya (1770-1843), who worked out an alphabet and system for writing his language. His system consisted of eighty-six letters or characters representing that many sounds in the Cherokee language. As soon as one learned the alphabet he could read. It was said that a clever boy could be taught to read in a single day.

Today remnants of these tribes are to be found in Oklahoma. The Seminoles, largely under Osceola, were too smart for the soldiers and many of them remained in the Everglades of Florida. Some of the Cherokees also escaped from the soldiers in the round-up and fled to the mountain fastnesses. Approximately 3,500 members of the tribe are to be found today on a reservation in western North Carolina.

One of the saddest chapters in our treatment of the red man is embodied in the "Trail of Tears" march, as the removal to Oklahoma is frequently called. Of the estimated 16,000 moved across the Mississippi from their beloved lands, one-fourth perished on that

---

[2] Religion in which the unseen world of gods, demons and ancestral spirits is conceived to be responsive only to the medicine man.

1,200-mile trek. The Cherokees were disarmed and herded into stockades by some 7,000 soldiers under General Winfield Scott. This included the aged, the infants, those in sick beds or from the fields or the loom. They were marched over weary trails to the stockades, and then were prodded along with oaths, blows and bayonets over wet and sometimes frozen ground. Colonizers then moved into the territory from which the Cherokees had been removed.

Space will not allow any detailed account of the tribes immediately west of the Iroquois. A comment from the historian James T. Adams indicates how they were displaced:

"A steady stream of settlers had poured ever westward from the east and the pioneers had preceded them in a restless advance. The Indians were in treaty possession of much of this old Northwest. Treaty after treaty had been made with the 'savages' only to be broken, reserving lands to them with an ever-retreating line against the inflow of the whites. In the dozen years preceding 1809, the savages sold 48 million acres, not seldom when made drunk for the proposition and without any apparent satisfaction of the whites' insatiable demand for the land."[3]

"The next thirty years saw treaty after treaty in which tribes ceded their huge hunting territories for the benefit of settlers who expected to farm or cut timber on almost every square foot of it. By 1840 all the tribes in this area had moved across the Mississippi, usually in several stages, each of which both they and Congress thought would be the last."[4]

4. Plains Area

West of the Mississippi and stretching from the river to the Rockies through the central and northern half of the United States, the Plains Indians make their home. Here is the colorfully dressed Indian, the one commonly visualized by the average American when he hears the word *Indian*. The eastern part of this large area was suited for growing native foods, while the western sections were buffalo country. Tribes from the north and east both came to this country after being driven from their former lands. Of the many tribes in the area, the Dakota (Sioux) are best known today. This

---

[3] *March of Democracy* (New York: Charles Scribner's Sons, 1933), II, 76.
[4] Underhill, *op. cit.*, p. 137.

Siouan group had in it different bands from the common linguistic
stock.

One of today's Sioux leaders raised the question why his people
had not made good like other minority people of today. He pointed
out the differences in culture and outlook between the American
way of life and the Indian style of living. He said: "The American
way is 'future oriented' while the Indian thinks only of the present.
The non-Indian life is one of self-conquest over nature, as against
the Indian way of self-harmony in nature. A second difference is
in relation to time. Clocks, watches, calendars, day of the week
are not as important to the Indian as they are to the non-Indian.
In the third place, saving as a means to achieve economic development has not been a part of the economic life of the Indian. He
lived largely by hunting, fishing and food gathering. Again, hard
work to earn a living was not in the Indian system, especially for
the man."[5]

Warfare was the major occupation of the men. As the white
men pushed ever westward, the Santa Fe Trail and the Oregon
Trail proved to be happy hunting grounds for booty from the white
man.

Conflicts were sure to arise. The Indian was not aware of actions
taken by the government. There was much misunderstanding on
the part of both Indian and white. A government representative
met with the northern tribes and promised them annuities of
$50,000 a year for the next fifteen years. In return, roads and
military establishments were to be built for the protection of those
on the trails. Boundaries were established for the various tribes.
The southern tribes were also contacted and similar arrangements
made with them. The Indians did not understand these agree-
ments and went on the warpath.

"The Sioux were promised that all whites would leave the Black
Hills and those hunting grounds would be theirs forever. One
year it looked as though the Black Hills would never be wanted for
settlement. The next year gold was discovered there and the story
changed. So year after year the holdings promised to the distant
red man were revised downward."[6]

[5] Ben Reifel, address to the Northern Montana Work Conference, Nov. 27, 1956, entitled "Cultural Factors in Social Adjustment," issued by the Department of Interior,
Bureau of Indian Affairs, Washington, D.C.
[6] Underhill, op.cit., p. 160.

The Severalty Act of 1887 allotted acreage to the individual Indian with a deed to his holdings. The sale of acreage cut up a reservation into farms. When there was land left over it was thrown open to the homesteader (white man). This plan has proved detrimental to the Indian, with results still apparent today.

The Great Basin Area has an equally dismal picture of the white man's conquest of the lands inhabited by the Flathead, Klamath, Nez Percé, Shoshone, Ute, Paiute, Yakima and other tribes. To the west of these were the Pacific Northwest tribes, whose settlements reached up into Alaska. South of them the California tribes numbered some 200,000 when the Spanish arrived in 1769.

5. Southwest Area

The Treaty of Guadalupe Hidalgo, signed February 2, 1848, along with the Gadsden Purchase of 1853, rounded out the boundaries of the United States and gave the nation jurisdiction over the vast territory of California, Nevada, Utah, Arizona and a portion of New Mexico. The United States thus became responsible for the many tribes of Indians who roamed the plains and deserts of this great region or lived in long established villages along its streams and fertile valleys. Except for a thin line of settlements, established by Spain and Mexico along the Rio Grande River and in California, and the newly planted Mormon colony in Utah, the Indians were virtually the only inhabitants in this huge area.

The Pueblos. Today there are nineteen villages of Pueblos along the Rio Grande River and its tributaries. These do not have a uniform language and come from at least four different language stocks. The archaeologist tells us that some of these may have had the cliff dwellers as their ancestors. Their known history has shown them to be a peaceful people given to agriculture.

It has been said that the Pueblo Indian had the first apartment houses ever built in the United States. The Taos Pueblo had five-storied apartments. Some of these houses are built around a court, each story receding in a terraced effect. Others are built in long rows terraced back from the streets. Adobe brick has been a common building material.

In 1540 Coronado explored through southern Arizona into New

Mexico, looking for the Seven Cities of Cibola. The story of gold
had circulated in old Mexico, but the gold was never found by
Coronado or his successors. The Pueblos were raided again and
again by the Apaches, Navajos and other tribes after the Spaniards
came. Our government thus inherited a most unhappy situation
in 1848.

Pueblo life today in the nineteen villages is not greatly changed.
Spanish influences are still seen, particularly in religion. Roman
Catholicism is mixed with the old beliefs and customs. Prayers to
the gods are mixed with prayers to the saints in strange manners.
"The Indian built himself a new religion, genuinely synthesizing
pre-conquest components with Roman Catholic components."[7] And
the former is seemingly the more important.

The Navajos. The government's early efforts to control the
Navajos included a fort built at present-day Fort Defiance, Arizona.
There were no rail or telephone connections with Washington and
communication was so slow that it took three months for a request
from the field for advice or action to get to the capital. Serious mis-
understandings between the government authorities and the Indians continued until the Civil War. Then the soldiers were largely
removed and the Navajos were permitted to continue their raiding
of Pueblos and white settlements on a large scale.

News of these conditions resulted in a government decision to
clean out the raiders. The Navajos offered peace by treaty, but
neither side trusted the other. Finally a plan was evolved whereby
Navajos were to be moved to a place where they could be supported until they became respectable citizens. Someone suggested
that it was "cheaper to feed them than to fight them."

At this point Kit Carson entered the picture with nine companies
of 400 volunteers. The job given him was to round up and subdue
some 10,000 Navajos. He used the scorched-earth policy. Be it said
to his credit that no more than fifty Navajos were killed.

Finally the Navajos took refuge in Canyon de Chelly. Kit pursued them, and literally starved them into submission. They fled
to Fort Defiance in droves and in April, 1864, 2,400 surrendered
Navajos made up the first caravan to Fort Sumner in eastern New
Mexico. This migration, dubbed by the Navajos "the Long Walk,"

[7] John Collier, *The Indians of the Americas* (New York: W. W. Norton & Co., 1947),
p. 142.

was some 300 miles. The sick and infants rode, but all others walked some fifteen miles a day, fording any necessary streams. More than 7,000 reached Fort Sumner.

During the years all efforts to educate and make farmers of the Navajos failed. They were discouraged and disgruntled and did not respond to any efforts put forth on their behalf. Because of their pleas to go home, a treaty was offered and accepted by them. Not until in the 1950's did the United States government fulfill all the terms of the treaty.

The Navajos were allowed to return to their old lands, with some 8,000 going back. They were given sheep — and sheep have been their economy largely to the present time. Today the number of Navajos has grown to about 85,000 and is growing at about 2 per cent a year. As the population has increased the boundaries of their reservation have been extended eighteen times, until today it is by far the largest Indian reservation. Yet it is not adequate to support the tribe on a sheep economy.

Beautiful and intricate in design are the rugs which the women weave from the wool of the sheep and goats. The men learned the art of silversmithing from the Mexicans, and they do exquisite work with the most primitive tools.

During World War II, 3,400 Navajos entered the armed forces and about 15,000 left the reservation for work in mines, on railroads, in factories and fields. The Navajo soldier proved himself. He not only was a good soldier, but with his difficult language performed a unique service in the communications department, having a language too difficult for the enemy to decipher. He came home the buddy of many a white boy and wearing many decorations. The tales he told and the knowledge he brought have caused a real desire for education, so that almost all Navajo children are in school today. The adult population, however, is still 75 per cent illiterate.

The discovery of uranium, along with gas and a vast and largely untapped pool of oil beneath their wastelands, has brought wealth to the tribe as a whole. The use of this wealth is now in the hands of the tribal council of seventy-four members, with the help and advice of the Indian Bureau. Work has already begun on the Navajo Dam on the San Juan River, which will provide irrigation for more than 100,000 acres of land for farming and fruit growing. Five million dollars have been set aside for a scholarship fund, and $7,000,000 will be used to build a new sawmill to handle their valuable stand of yellow pine. Thus Navajo wealth is to be used in constructive ways.

"And what more shall I say, for time would fail me to tell of" Apaches, Pimas, Papagos, Maricopas, Yavapais, Walapais, Supais, Hopis and others in the Southwest area. Oklahoma is omitted, since there are no Indian reservations as such in the state. Five per cent of its population are Indian who live on allotted lands.

The one saving feature of the advent of the white man is described by Charles Journeycake of the Delawares, who has remarked: "We have been broken up and moved six times. We have been despoiled of our property. The white man came into our country from Missouri and drove our cattle and horses away; and if our people followed them, they were killed. We try to forget these things, but we do not forget that the white man brought us the blessed gospel of Christ, the Christian hope. This more than pays for all we have suffered."[8] This is our opportunity and our challenge to repay at least a part of our immense debt to the Indian American by bringing him the gospel.

Missionary Endeavors

Indian people are religious. Religion permeates all their daily life. Here one is reminded of Paul's visit to Athens when he saw a religious people, but a people who needed Jesus Christ. This is exactly true of the Indian people of today. Much has been written concerning their religious virtues, but these virtues are not sufficient without the knowledge of the Lord Jesus as Saviour and Lord of life. We must not forget the statement of Christ: "No man cometh to the Father but by me." For this reason mission work has been and still is being carried on among the American Indians.

1. *Northeast*

John Eliot may be described as an early pioneer missionary to the Indians of America. Born and educated in England, he arrived at Boston in 1631 at the age of twenty-seven. After language study, his first meeting with the Indians was held October 28, 1646. His first message was an explanation of the Ten Commandments.

[8] E. Russell Carter, *The Gift is Rich* (New York: Friendship Press, 1954), p. 77.

From this time on Eliot gave himself unreservedly to the gospel for the Indians. After winning the Indians to Christ, he organized them into Christian villages, with 1,150 "praying Indians" set up in fourteen villages. Warfare and disease proved destructive to these villages and they disappeared in the course of a hundred years.

In addition to his preaching, traveling and organizing, Eliot did a tremendous amount of translation. This included the whole Bible into the Massachusetts (Algonquian) language, the first Bible printed in America, *Baxter's Call*, a grammar, a psalter, a primer, and a catechism.

Another outstanding name is that of David Brainerd (1718-1747) who labored among the Mohicans in New York and New Jersey. Seventy-seven converts were recorded in one year. His diary inspired William Carey to go to India. His devotion and early death turned the thoughts of Jonathan Edwards toward the Indians, among whom he was laboring when called to the presidency of Princeton University in 1758.

Samuel Occum, a Mohican, became the first Indian missionary to his people. George Whitefield took him to England, where he raised some $60,000. This was invested in the founding of Dartmouth College, originally planned for Indian youth.[9]

Basin Area. The March 1, 1833, issue of the *New York Christian Advocate and Journal* carried the famous letter from William Walker which told of the arrival of four Indians in St. Louis. These came from beyond the Rockies in search of the "white man's book of heaven." Four Indians had come on this errand from the Nez Percé and Flathead tribes in the fall of 1831. Two of these died while in St. Louis and the third died on the way home, leaving only Rabbit-skin-leggins to reach his people.

Excerpts of this letter indicate their reception in St. Louis: "I came with an eye partly open for my people who sit in darkness. I go back with both eyes closed. How can I go back blind to my blind people? I made my way to you with strong arms through many enemies and strange lands that I might carry back much to them. I go back with both arms broken and empty. My people sent me to get the white man's book of heaven. You took me to where

---

[9] Thomas C. Moffett, *The American Indian on the New Trail* (New York: Missionary Education Movement, 1914), p. 75.

you allow your women to dance as we do not ours; and the book was not there. You took me to where they worship the Great Spirit and pictures of the good land beyond, but the book was not among them to tell me the way. . . . When I tell my poor blind people, after one more snow, in the big council, that I did not bring the book, no word will be spoken by our old men or by our young braves. . . . My people will die in darkness, and they will go on a long path to other hunting grounds. No white man will go with them, and no white man's book to make the way plain. . . ."[10]

Jason Lee and a nephew, Daniel Lee, responded to the stirring plea for missionaries published in the *Christian Advocate*. Shipping their possessions around Cape Horn, they made an overland journey across the Rockies to Oregon. They established their mission in the Willamette Valley, sixty miles from Fort Vancouver. The Methodist Foreign Missionary Society had sent them.

Soon Marcus Whitman followed to the Nez Percés. He was joined by H. H. Spalding. With their two brides they made a honeymoon crossing of the Rockies, the first white women to make such a journey.

After eleven years of faithful labor among the Cayuse Indians, Marcus Whitman perished with eleven others at his station. Some fifty others at the station were taken prisoners in a revolt.

In the meantime H. H. Spalding was building a mission at Lapwai among the Nez Percés. He is described as having been "preacher, teacher, doctor, farmer, horticulturist, mechanic, printer, lumberman, weaver, miller, carpenter, musician, translator and author."[11]

Spalding was at Waiilatpu at the time of the Whitman massacre. His escape and return to his home at Lapwai is one of the thrilling flights of missionary life. Mrs. Spalding was taken from her home and protected by friendly Nez Percés, but the home was looted and partly destroyed.

The Whitman massacre marked the end of the American Board Mission to Oregon. Spalding retired from the field for a period, spending his time mostly in preaching to the white settlers. Then the Presbyterian Church asked him to take up work again among

---

[10] *Ibid..* p. 89.
[11] Clifford M. Drury, *Henry Harmon Spalding* (Caldwell, Idaho: Caxton Printers, 1936), p. 312.

the Nez Percés, which delighted his heart. Revival fires swept over the Nez Percés. Within a year more than 600 of these tribesmen were baptized and received into the church on confession of their faith.

Sue MacBeth was sent by the Presbyterians to Lapwai in 1873 as a teacher. Not too successful at that, she devoted her time to the training of young Nez Percés for the ministry among their people. She was remarkably successful in this, and her pupils filled the pulpits of established Nez Percé churches. She was joined by her sister Kate, and together they operated a small Bible school, the influence of which is still felt today though the school has been closed for years.

Some claim the Nez Percés are the most Christianized tribe in the United States. They are certainly one of the most advanced in the arts of civilized life.

Southeast

Moravian missionaries were the first to go to the Cherokees. Samuel Worcester is another of the outstanding missionaries sent by the American Board of Commissioners for Foreign Missions (Congregational, Presbyterian and Dutch Reformed). He settled at the Cherokee capital, Echota, Georgia, in 1827. In addition to preaching, he aided in the establishment of the first Indian newspaper, the *Cherokee Phoenix.*

Worcester accompanied the Cherokees on the "Trail of Tears" to Oklahoma and ministered to the sick and dying en route. Much of his time in Oklahoma was spent in translation work at his mission. His "mission press printed many books and pamphlets for the missionaries laboring among the Creek, Seminole, Choctaw and Chickasaw nations. His own translations included large portions of the Bible, tracts, hymn books, school books and a Cherokee almanac."[12]

Southwest Area

Charles H. Cook heard of the need of the gospel among the Pima Indians, and responded to God's call in 1870. He made his intentions known to the Methodist Church, but it "had no money to spare for sending the gospel to the Indian."[13] Dr. Cook con-

---
[12] *Encyclopedia Americana.* XXIX, 511.
[13] *Among the Pimas* (out of print), p. 23.

tinues: "The thought came to me that the same Lord who had protected me during the war could also protect me in Arizona; and as to my temporal support, the same God who provided for George Mueller's orphans must be able to provide for me as long as I was willing to work."[14]

Since there was no railroad running to the West Coast at that time, Dr. Cook had to make his way by mule train after his arrival at Kit Carson, Kansas, the railroad terminus of that day. He moved from army post to army post, preaching wherever opportunity afforded.

Dr. Cook did not arrive at Sacaton, Arizona, until December 23, nearly four months after he left Chicago. A month later, in January, 1871, he opened the first Pima Indian school with thirty-five pupils. This he taught for seven years, the government paying his salary.

Dr. Cook saw the need for a trained native leadership and conceived the idea of a training school. The Cook Bible School was opened in 1911 at Tucson, with Dr. Logie as superintendent. In 1914 this school was moved to Phoenix. In 1940 the school became interdenominational and the name was changed to the Cook Christian Training School. Practically all the leadership in the Indian churches in southern Arizona has been trained at Cook School.

The school plant has grown until it can now adequately care for sixty-five students in a three-year course. There are usually from ten to twenty different tribes represented in the student body.

This pioneer missionary to the Southwest left a record rarely if ever matched in Indian missionary annals. Today one may visit eighteen Presbyterian churches and chapels among the Indian people, all the outgrowth of his work. The membership is in the thousands, counting the adherents.

Chaplain A. H. Donaldson began work among the Navajos as early as 1851 at Fort Defiance, where he was stationed. It was not until the beginning of this century, however, that the gospel really came to these neglected people.

Mrs. Mary E. Eldridge and Miss M. E. Raymond, who went to the Navajos in 1891 under the Methodist Church, might be called the pioneers. Mrs. Eldridge acted as missionary and nurse, conduct-

---

[14] *Ibid.*

ing her work largely on horseback as she traveled around on the
reservation from the station which had been opened near Shiprock,
New Mexico.

The Navajo Methodist Mission School, which was the first mission school for the Navajos, developed from her work and was
opened in 1896 as a day school. This day school proved to be un-
satisfactory and a boarding school was established two years later.
The school was later moved up the San Juan River to larger quarters. A flood destroyed it in 1911, so that now it is at its third location. It has a fully accredited grade and high school.

A large number of the graduates of the school have gone on to
higher education. One of the graduates is the first Navajo medical
doctor and another is executive secretary of the tribal council.
Others are missionaries, teachers and government employees in
various forms of tribal work.

The second mission school to be opened for the Navajos was the
Ganado Mission School, started by the Presbyterians in 1901. Ganado has grown to be the largest Indian mission in the United States.
In addition to the school, there is the Sage Memorial Hospital, with
sixty beds and twelve bassinets. This school is a fully accredited
junior and senior high school. The Ganado church with its evangelistic outreach is serving a large area with several outstations.

The Christian Reformed Church was the third Protestant group
to open a mission school. They began in 1903 at Rehoboth, New
Mexico. The Rehoboth Mission also has a hospital and ministers to
several outlying stations. The Christian Reformed Church lists
twenty-four churches and preaching stations in New Mexico. The
Presbyterians list fifteen mission stations in Arizona. This state division of work was a comity agreement entered into by the two
churches early in the century.

The Episcopal Church has a mission station at Fort Defiance,
one at Farmington, New Mexico, and a mission center at Bluff,
Utah.

The American Baptists have been operating a junior college for
American Indian students at Bacone, Oklahoma, for nearly eighty
years. Bacone College offers basic liberal arts subjects and a general academic program leading to a continuing college education
or to a terminal certificate based upon vocational courses.

At Flagstaff, Arizona, an Indian Bible institute, the Southwestern School of Missions, trains American Indian leadership from at least seven different tribes.

Farther north, the Brainerd Indian School at Hot Springs, South Dakota, offers junior and senior high school courses to American Indians. There is also a four-year Bible course to train Indians for Christian service.

In addition to these there are a number of smaller missions. Connected with these are some units which might be called Bible training, often connected with academic work.

This is the opportune time for the evangelization of the Navajo. The vast natural resources recently discovered on the reservation, the emphasis on education, the loss of confidence in the old ways, all call for a gospel presentation such as there has never been in Navajo history. If the various missions will co-operate in spreading the precious Word to these long-neglected people, great things may be accomplished for our Lord.

Conclusion

The American Indians today are beset by many problems. They left the reservations in droves during World War II to work in mines, factories and to serve in the armed forces. They earned what to them was big money. This usually was not wisely spent, and when employment did not continue after the war, they were back where they started. The relocation plan of the government established some in cities in good positions. Yet by and large the adjustments of city life have proved too difficult, so that many have returned to the reservations.

Education has increased among the tribes, particularly the Navajos. Yet without the stabilizing influence of Christianity this results merely in breaking down the old mores and substituting the white man's evils. Excessive alcoholism, the use of peyoti, and immorality are more apparent than under the old culture. Only Christ can provide the controls needed to establish new cultural norms based on sound principles. This is where home mission work and training schools for native leadership can play a vital role.

BIBLIOGRAPHY

ADAMS, JAMES TRUSLOW. *March of Democracy.* Vols. I and II. New York: Charles Scribner's Sons, 1933.

Board of Navajo Missions. *Sourcebook on the Navajo.* New York: United Presbyterian Church of U.S.A.

CARTER, E. RUSSELL. *The Gift Is Rich.* New York: Friendship Press, 1954.

COLLIER, JOHN. *The Indians of the Americas.* New York: W. W. Norton & Co., 1947.

CONGDON, G. K. *Navajo Indian Missions.* Mentmore, N. M.: Mission Press.

COOK, CHARLES H. *Among the Pimas.* Albany, N. Y.: Ladies Union Mission School Association, 1893.

CORY, DAVID M. *Within Two Worlds.* New York: Friendship Press, 1955.

DALE, EDWARD EVERETT. *The Indians of the Southwest.* Norman, Okla.: University of Oklahoma Press, 1949.

DANIELS, WALTER M. *Indian Americans.* New York: H. W. Wilson Co., 1957.

DRAKE, SAMUEL G. *Indians of North America.* New York: John B. Alden, 1880.

DRUCKER, PHILIP. *The Indians of the Northwest Coast.* New York: McGraw-Hill Book Co., 1955.

DRURY, CLIFFORD M. *Henry Harmon Spalding.* Caldwell, Idaho: Caxton Printers, 1936.

DYKHUIZEN, DOROTHY. *Go Quickly and Tell.* Grand Rapids: Wm. B. Eerdmans Publishing Co., 1946.

EDBRY, CARLOS B. *America's Concentration Camps.* New York: David McKay Co., Inc., 1956.

FEY, HAROLD E. *Indian Rights and American Justice.* Chicago: Christian Century Foundation, 1955.

Franciscan Fathers. *An Ethnological Dictionary of the Navajo Language.* St. Michaels, Ariz.: St. Michaels Press, 1929.

GODDARD, PLINY EARLE. *Indians of the Southwest.* New York: American Museum of Natural History, 1927.

Ha'asiidii (diglot publication). Cortez, Colo.

HASSELL, SANDY. *Know the Navajo.* Denver, Colo.

Indians of South Dakota. Bulletin No. 67A, South Dakota Department of Instruction, 1956.

KLUCKHOHN, CLYDE, and LEIGHTON, DOROTHEA. *The Navajo* Cambridge, Mass.: Harvard University Press, 1946.

Lindquist, G. E. E. *The Indian in American Life.* New York: Friendship Press, 1944.

McGroarty, John Stevens. *Mission Memories.* Los Angeles: Neuner Corp., 1929.

Moffett, Thomas C. *The American Indian on the New Trail.* New York: Missionary Education Movement, 1914.

Newcomb, Franc Johnson. *Navajo Omens and Taboos.* Albuquerque, N. M.: author.

Nixon, O. W. *Whitman's Ride Through Savage Lands.* Chicago: Winona Publishing Co., 1905.

Reichard, Gladys. *Navajo Religion.* 2 Vol. set. New York: Patheon Books, 1950.

Sanchez, George I. *The People.* U. S. Indian Service, 1948.

Sherman Pamphlets, No. 3. Washington, D. C.: Department of Interior.

Spinden, Herbert J. *Ancient Civilizations of Mexico and Central America.* New York: American Museum of Natural History, 1928.

Smith, Mrs. White Mountain. *Indian Tribes of the Southwest.* Stanford, Calif.: Stanford University Press, 1935.

Underhill, Ruth. *Here Come the Navajo.* Lawrence, Kan.: United States Indian Service.

————. *Red Man's America.* Chicago: University of Chicago Press, 1953.

Wissler, Clark. *Indians of the United States.* New York: Doubleday & Co., 1954.

Wright, Muriel H. *A Guide to the Tribes of Oklahoma.* Norman, Okla.: University of Oklahoma Press, 1951.

You Asked About the Navajo. Lawrence, Kan.: Department of Interior. Distributed free.

Young, Robert. *The Navajo Yearbook.*

A minister calling to develop a Bible study group in a home.
(Courtesy of the Chicago City Missionary Society.)

5

The American Negro

B. M. NOTTAGE

In 1954 the United States Supreme Court ruled that our Constitution forbids any state or school district to separate school children according to their race. This monumental decision has focused particular attention on the American Negro. Although they are a minority group in this country, they have become an explosive problem in many parts of the nation.

In the past the Negro has been the object of much scorn. He has been needed but unwanted. He has received unjust treatment physically, mentally and economically. And the Christian church has, to a large degree, ignored his spiritual need. The gospel "is the power of God unto salvation to everyone that believeth." This gospel is meant for the Negro as well as anyone else, and it alone is able to meet many of his problems.

Slaves From Africa

Where did the American Negro come from? Why are we faced with the problem of integration and segregation? To discover this we need to go back to the beginning of the slave trade in America.

Born in the Bahamas in 1889, B. M. NOTTAGE received all his formal education in the government schools of the islands. In 1909 Mr. Nottage went to New York City, where with others he began his ministry, especially to people of his own race. In 1932 he moved to Detroit and from this center he has served across the entire United States, Canada, the Bahamas, Bermuda and Jamaica. He has been instrumental in establishing churches and providing support for Sunday schools, summer camps, rescue missions and other places of gospel activity.

It is believed that Columbus had a Negro in his party when he landed in Haiti in 1492. Large numbers of Africans were brought into the West Indies during the 1500's. In 1619 a Dutch ship landed in Virginia with twenty Africans who were purchased by Virginia colonists. For the next two hundred years Negroes were brought to America largely as slaves. By 1790 one out of every five Americans was a Negro. In 1801 the total slave population stood at 1,007,037.

Most of the slaves were found in the South. Often they were treated with cruelty. In New England, the Negroes were sometimes used as domestic servants and treated as part of the family. They had little educational opportunity. In the South, the master sometimes would teach a slave to read, write and do accounting so as to keep his master's books.

Slavery Abolished

There was considerable opposition to slavery, especially by the Christian church. The Quakers in 1688 decided to abolish slave trade among their own members. Later they made efforts to abolish slave trade altogether and to give the Negro his freedom. Other denominations (such as the Puritans, Congregationalists and Presbyterians) began definite missionary work among the Negro the last half of the eighteenth century. The Baptists admitted Negro membership in Virginia in 1758.

The influence of the gospel had its effect. In 1807 Congress passed a law to prohibit the continuance of African slave trade, and slavery was abolished in 1863.

The Negro Today

At the present time about one out of every ten Americans is a Negro. According to the 1960 census, the total Negro population was 18,871,831. This represented a gain of about 25.4 per cent since the 1950 census, when the population was 15,042,286.

More than 10 million Negroes still live in the South. The rest live largely in the northern centers east of the Mississippi. California is almost the only western state with a sizable Negro population.

A few statistics of the Negro distribution by states might be of interest: Texas, 1,187,125; Georgia, 1,122,596; North Carolina,

1,116,021; Louisiana, 1,039,207; Alabama, 980,271; Mississippi, 915,743; Florida, 880,186; South Carolina, 829,876; Virginia, 816,258; Arkansas, 388,787. California has 883,861.[1]

Northern states with large Negro populations include: New York with 1,417,511; Illinois, 1,037,470; Pennsylvania, 852,750; Ohio, 786,097; Michigan, 717,581; Maryland, 518,410; New Jersey, 514,875; Washington, D.C., 411,737.[1]

It is estimated that about 13,800,000 Negroes live in urban areas and only 5,000,000 in rural. Cities with the largest populations include New York, with more than 1,000,000; Chicago, with about 700,000; Detroit, 475,000; Philadelphia, 465,000; Baltimore, 280,000; Los Angeles, 260,000; St. Louis, 225,000; Cleveland, 220,000. These figures are changing constantly because of the large movements from the South seeking to escape the discrimination so common in that part of the country. As the people move to the cities, many become skilled or semi-skilled laborers.

Social and Economic Conditions

There is no doubt that the African background, the conditions of slavery and discrimination since slavery have had their natural effects on the Negro. But in spite of all the handicaps of race and color, marked progress has been made. The movements to the North have been with the hope of economic improvements. Cities, such as Chicago, have done much to provide modern housing projects for the Negroes. Even in the South, the finest consolidated schools have been provided for the Negro and, in general, the one-room school with the big pot-belly stove and inadequate teaching facilities is gone. As late as 1950 about 4 per cent of the Negroes between fourteen and twenty-four years of age were illiterate. Today there are well over a hundred public and private institutions offering college training for Negroes. More than 15,000 are graduated from college a year.

While the struggle for national and political recognition, for economic progress, education, good homes and church buildings continues, there are still problems that must be faced.

Intermarriage, for instance, is not approved by either group — white or Negro. Thousands of white Negroes leave their own

[1] *Information Please Almanac, Atlas and Yearbook* (New York: Simon and Schuster, 1963).

people each year because of the disadvantages of the Negro. On
the other hand, others who may be white continue to call themselves Negroes and are trying to do their part in giving the Negro
his rightful place in society.

The United States government has passed laws that would
prevent industry from discriminating against the Negro. But that
does not change the heart attitude and, no doubt, in many instances the Negro will still be the last to be hired and the first to
be fired.

Juvenile delinquency and crime among Negroes are greater
percentagewise than among other citizens. The Negro divorce
rate is higher. Illegitimacy and crowded living conditions tend
to hinder proper home life. Sin, of course, is the root of all this,
and no effort should be made to excuse the Negro; but it is true
that the economic and social disadvantages placed upon him by
American society encourage and increase these problems.

The Negro and Religion

There was a time when Negroes were the most religious people
in this nation. The Christian church has failed, however, and unless we awaken to their spiritual need, they will soon become
the most godless element in the nation. The faith of their fathers,
as expressed in the many well-known spirituals, is being given
up by ever-increasing numbers of Negro people.

Negro denominational organizations were started because the
people desired to enjoy greater liberty and responsibility than
was possible in the existing churches. According to the United
States census in 1963, there were 256 religious bodies in the
country. Fifty-nine denominations had Negro churches and thirty-
three were entirely Negro. There was a total of 38,303 Negro
churches. At that time 7,000,000 did not belong to any church.
The total Negro population in 1963 was over 12,000,000.

According to the *1952 Negro Yearbook*,[2] there were thirty-three
Negro church groups. The following five had membership of more
than 100,000: the African Methodist Episcopal Church, the African
Methodist Episcopal Zion Church, the Colored Methodist Episcopal
Church, the National Baptist Convention, U.S.A., Inc., and the

---

[2] J. P. Guzman, *Negro Yearbook* (New York: William H. Wise Co., 1952).

Church of God in Christ. The largest of these, the National Baptist Convention, U.S.A., had a membership of 5,500,000 in 1962.

Of the twenty-six predominantly white church groups having Negro communicants, the following are the better known: Congregational-Christian Church, Evangelical and Reformed Church, Lutheran Synodical Conference, Methodist Church, Presbyterian Church in the U.S., United Presbyterian Church in the U.S.A., Protestant Episcopal Church, Roman Catholic Church and Salvation Army.

Denominational Aims

The Negro Yearbook further states: "Three main purposes for which all Negro denominations work to bring Negroes together are: (1) They worship God in their own way, a God who is the Father of Negroes also. (2) They encourage and inspire Negroes to live the good life, which includes improvement in morals, social life, education, health, housing, politics, business and recreation as well as worship. (In this task, the dynamic idea of 'getting to heaven' has undoubtedly been the greatest motivating force for better living on earth.) (3) The Negro church preaches practical Christian brotherhood, and strives to have the Negro included in that brotherhood. Regardless of theoretical differences, all Negro churches easily unite to urge American acceptance of the Negro as a Christian brother through economic, political, civic and social justice. Thus, the Negro church has laid the spiritual foundation for many fraternal, business, civic and political movements. Strange as it may seem, the Negro church is founded more largely on a sociological than on a theological basis."

In a thesis on the American Negro by C. L. Roesler, we find the following: "Not only has the Negro church of today strongly embraced the social gospel, but it has, to a large degree, endorsed modernism and its accompanying ecumenical councils. Many of its better trained leaders were instructed in institutions in which the doctrine of the plenary inspiration of the Scriptures is not held. A large number of pastors who have not had the benefits of a higher education condone and encourage extreme emotionalism. In various places across the United States there are, however, those churches in which the fundamental doctrines of the Christian

church are taught and the gospel of the Lord Jesus is preached
in clarity and power."[3]

Hindrances to Religious Progress

The thesis further states: "There are many forces that hinder
the progress of evangelical Christianity among Negroes in the
United States. Among the foremost are Communism, Romanism,
modernism, emotionalism and racial discrimination."

It is a remarkable situation but, none the less true, that fellowship among all these groups and many others is more possible than
among evangelical Christians. Thus we have the tragic need for
a spiritual awakening among the nearly 20 million non-whites
in the United States of America. When this takes place, the program of Christ our Lord will feel the glorious impact not only
here at home, but in the far-flung mission fields of the world.
God alone knows how much this unchristian attitude has hindered
the gospel among colored peoples everywhere.

Catholic Negroes

Negroes are largely Protestant. It is only in comparatively recent
years that the Catholic Church has become alerted to the great
opportunity afforded by the Negro in the United States. It has
now gone all-out in its effort to remedy that situation.

When my white friends who are exercised about reaching the
Negro ask how it can be done, I usually suggest that they go into
some colored area and watch how the Catholics carry on. The
Catholics not only provide a place for them to worship, but also
give them the best in education, provide modern up-to-date
hospitals and, in many cases, have taken the lead in providing
integrated schools.

In years gone by it was a rare thing to meet a Negro Catholic.
Recent statistics indicate that there are now more than half a
million Negro Catholics in the United States. *Our Sunday Visitor,*
a Catholic publication, reports as follows: "There are 595,155
Catholic Negroes . . . in the United States. Catholic Negroes increased by about 20,000 over the totals given a year ago. Some
90,756 Negro pupils attend Catholic schools, an increase of 9 per

---

[3] Calvin Lewis Roesler, *The American Negro* (Columbia, S. C.: Columbia Bible
College), pp. 7, 8, 38.

cent over the previous year. Seven hundred and nineteen priests, 2,000 sisters and several hundred lay persons are engaged exclusively in the work among the colored."[4]

How may Negroes be reached for God here in the United States? Just like we reach people anywhere. Love them as people whom God loves and for whom Christ died. There is no other proper way to reach anybody anywhere.

"All Welcome"

Generally speaking, the "all welcome" sign on the doors of most evangelical churches does not include the Negro or some other minority group. Most Bible conferences, Bible schools and colleges, Bible camps, rescue missions and other Christian gatherings are not geared for the Negro. Usually he isn't welcome and is not allowed to enjoy such fellowship. He isn't exposed to that type of teaching which makes for godly character among white Christians. But if the Christian church doesn't take the lead in treating the Negro as an equal and giving him spiritual help and Bible training, who will? This is a responsibility that cannot be ignored.

When Billy Graham visited the British West Indies, he reported publicly that he found more Bible-believing Christians percentagewise in those countries than anywhere in the world. Yet about 90 per cent of these people are Negroes.

What is the reason for this? Preachers and missionaries from Britain, Canada and the United States worked among these people even before the abolition of slavery in the British empire in 1834. Negroes and others in Bermuda, Bahamas, Jamaica and British Guiana heard the good news of the gospel and responded to it. Had the same thing been done in the United States, doubtless there would now be thousands of large fundamental, Christ-loving, Bible-believing churches among Negroes here, with sufficient workers and means to support God's program at home and anywhere in the far-flung harvest fields of the world.

It is interesting to note that many of the colored people who were reached by Plymouth Brethren and other missionaries in the Caribbean area are now in the United States. Quite a number of them, including the writer, are engaged in seeking to meet the

---

[4] *Our Sunday Visitor*, March 1, 1959, p. 2.

great spiritual need that is evident everywhere. Some thirty to forty church groups have been established around the country through such activity. "God moves in a mysterious way His wonders to perform."

God Uses a Woman

As a girl in school she began to hate Negroes. Later she heard and believed the gospel, and joined the fellowship of a fundamental church. She still, however, had no use for colored people. This church sent out one of their finest members as a missionary to Africa, and this woman became a member of the missionary prayer band. Although she was active in praying for the Africans and the missionaries, she still hated colored people at home. She would not give a tract to a Negro or speak to one.

One day, during prayer, the Lord convicted her of this sin of inconsistency. She confessed the sin to others as well as to the Lord. Soon she began holding home Bible classes for colored women. Some of them were led to a saving knowledge of Christ. They brought their husbands along, who also confessed salvation. For the most part, these people had been members of churches for years. Some were church officers, but they had never really known the gospel. The church which was established through the effort of this woman still goes on, sound in faith, separated from the world and proclaiming God's message of grace and salvation in that part of the country. Not only that, but four or five other such church groups have been established as the outcome of God's blessing upon the woman's efforts.

God used this woman in spite of opposition from her white friends and misunderstanding by some of the colored people. She proved that nothing is impossible with God, and that the "gospel of Christ" is indeed "the power of God unto salvation to everyone that believeth," whether Jew or Gentile, red, yellow, black or white.

God Uses a Man

God used a man by the name of John Brooke, now pastor of a Baptist church in the Detroit area. At the time we met he was superintendent of the Detroit City Rescue Mission. This young man noted the desperate spiritual need of the Negro skid row element. He called a number of Christian men together for prayer and counsel about this situation. The Open Door Rescue Mission was the result. This was the first of its kind in the United States. Through his activity, similar missions have been started in Chicago, Toledo and Baltimore.

In Detroit a number of sound churches and a Bible school have been established where the Negro is welcome to go and be instructed in the truths of the Bible. Such people are not only saved from hell, but they become a blessing to the community in every area of life. They are delivered from emotionalism, modernism, Romanism and every other "ism" because they are instructed in the Word of God.

Other Evangelical Work

The Bible school movement for Negroes is growing. Among them are: the Manna Bible School, Philadelphia, Pa.; Baptist Bible Seminary, Cleveland, Ohio; Community School of the Bible, Detroit, Mich.; Hope Bible School, Chicago, Ill.; Zion College, Chattanooga, Tenn.; Southern Bible Training School, Dallas, Texas; and Carver Bible Institute, Atlanta, Georgia. Some of these institutions have an interracial teaching staff.

There are various summer Bible camps around the country for Negroes. The leading one is located in Spring City, Tennessee, with over 800 in camp during a single summer season. The Pioneer Gospel Camp in Jackson, Mississippi, is also doing a good work. Another growing camp is Smith's Creek Bible Camp in Michigan. This and Grace Bible Camp in St. Helena, South Carolina, are operated by Negroes exclusively. A few Bible conferences have also been established.

It must be noted that a number of schools in the North have become available for the training of Negroes. A large number of Negroes are enrolled in the evening school of Moody Bible Institute. Many students from Moody Bible Institute and Wheaton College go into the Negro districts of Chicago, and help in young people's meetings, Sunday schools and churches. Columbia Bible College has also engaged in an energetic effort among the Negroes in and around Columbia, South Carolina.

Teacher training classes are being conducted in various homes in the Chicago area to strengthen the Sunday school teaching staff of the Negro churches. Many have enrolled in Bible correspondence courses, which are proving an effective means of training.

God is using the gospel radio and television programs to bless many. This can be done without the embarrassment of discrimination. Some programs in the South are geared especially to the Negro.

Yet all this is inadequate to meet the crying need among the millions of Negroes in this country, especially in cities like Washington, D. C., where the Negroes outnumber the whites.

The Mennonites

The work of the Mennonites among the Negroes should be mentioned. This denomination is facing the situation squarely. They are engaged in preaching the gospel and establishing missions, camps and churches in various parts of the country. The following statement indicates the official attitude of the Mennonite Church:

"The Bible teaches that it is the purpose of the Good Shepherd to bring all His sheep as one flock into His fold . . . . This one flock is the Church, His one body . . . . a new society of men recreated in the image of God. This new society transcends all human differences. . . . This transcendence is not a mere matter of theory, but it is a reality among men in whom Christ dwells."[5]

What Shall We Do?

While this increase of interest and effort on the part of churches and individuals around the country is commendable, it is clear that there is much room for improvement. The born-again colored people belong to Christ's Church. They are members of His body, of His flesh and of His bones, and members one of another. It is our obligation to love to serve one another.

In a book entitled *Epistle to White Christians*, Fred D. Wentzel writes: "To my white brethren in the churches in America: grace be to you and peace from God the Father and from our Lord Jesus Christ, who gave Himself for our sins that He might deliver us

---

[5] *Christian Race Relations* (Goshen: Mennonite Community Association, 1955), p. 8.

from this present evil world . . . . I write to you concerning the Negro whom God hath made to differ from us in color only, but whom we have rejected as a lesser creature . . . . I write not to judge but to urge repentance and deeds born of repentance . . . . He that loveth his colored brother abideth in the light and there is no occasion for stumbling in him . . . . I write to you about God the Father and about Christ His Son in whom there is neither bond nor free, neither superior nor inferior, white nor black, but all are one."[6]

Surely divine love is the grand solution of this problem. There are great efforts being made to reach the increasing number of literate people abroad. Why not slant some of this toward the non-whites here at home?

Then there is also the urgent need for the training of Negro leaders. They must be instructed in the Word of God so that they in turn can minister to their own people. Qualified Negro youth workers must be encouraged. Christian marriage counselors are needed among the adults. Workers among the delinquents are needed. It is true the whites can assist in this, but the greatest need is to train the Negro to do the job himself and to help him get the tools to do an adequate job.

A Testimony

I have had the burden of this great need at heart for nearly fifty years. I have endeavored to use every possible means to get the gospel out among everybody in general, and my own people in particular, from New England in the east to Kansas in the west, and from Minnesota in the north to Florida and Texas in the south.

I thank the Lord for sending white missionaries to the Bahamas where I was saved sixty years ago. I thank God, too, for the great blessing of belonging to the Negro section of the human family. God made me thus for His glory. God is a God of variety, whether of stars, angels or people. Soon our Lord will come to raise the dead and change the living and give us a non-stop flight through space into His blessed presence.

Believing as I do, our home and church in Detroit have always

---

[6] Fred D. Wentzel, *Epistle to White Christians* (Philadelphia: The Christian Education Press), pp. 7, 95.

been open to God's people, regardless of color, nationality or denomination. Praise God for our many white and colored friends in Christ.

BIBLIOGRAPHY

Christian Race Relations. Goshen: Mennonite Community Association, 1955.

GUZMAN, JESSIE P. (ed.). *The Negro Yearbook.* New York: Wm. H. Wise Co., 1952.

HAYNES, L. L. *The Negro Community.* Boston: Christopher Publishing House.

Our Sunday Visitor. Huntington, Ind.: National Catholic Weekly, March 1, 1959.

ROESLER, CALVIN L. *The American Negro.* Columbia, S.C.: Columbia Bible College.

U.S. News and World Report, March 18, 1959.

WENTZEL, FRED D. *Epistle to White Christians.* Philadelphia: The Christian Education Press.

A vacation Bible school class for Spanish-speaking children in Chicago. (Courtesy of Chicago City Missionary Society.)

6

Our Spanish-Speaking Neighbors

John K. Vincent

I f we ask a person of Spanish descent from where he comes, he might well reverse the question. Few people in the United States consider the fact that the Spanish people have been on the North American continent since the days of the early explorers in the beginning of the sixteenth century. Spaniards had settled in southeastern and southwestern United States long before the first Europeans arrived on the scene. In the Southwest some states are still officially bilingual and the English or Spanish language is equally acceptable for legal papers and in the courts. A large number of the businessmen and civic leaders are of Spanish descent, and though they speak English without difficulty or accent, they cling to the Spanish language and customs as a matter of choice.

Mexican-Americans

The largest number of Spanish-speaking persons are Mexican. More than a million Mexicans have migrated to the United States

John K. Vincent received his academic training at Brothers College in Madison, New Jersey, and Drew Theological Seminary. Since 1946 he has been working full time with Spanish-speaking people.

For eight years he served in Puerto Rico with the Methodist Church, founding the Vieques Island Mission. During this time 2,700 professed faith in Christ, each of whom was followed up with intensive Bible instruction. Before he left in 1954, 520 had become members of the local church.

In 1955 Mr. Vincent served with the Methodists in East Harlem among Spanish people. Later he came to Chicago under the Chicago City Missionary Society as director of their Spanish work. He has now returned to Puerto Rico to work among the Spanish-speaking people there.

in the last century, and are making a significant contribution to the United States economy in both agriculture and industry. They supply much of the labor force of the Southwest. They are also minority groups numbering up to 50,000 or more in many major cities. Chicago has the largest of these Mexican minority groups, with some 100,000 resident in the city. Most of these are bilingual and well integrated into cosmopolitan living.

It is unfortunate that much adverse criticism has been made of the Mexican group by the unfair presentation of them in the "western" movies and by the spectacular publicity given to the illegal entry into the United States of the so-called "wetbacks." Since 1954, when strict enforcement of the immigration rules was begun, there has been no significant number of illegal entries.

After 1954 the yearly number of legal entries into the United States from Mexico increased. In other words, it became generally known among those migrating that now it was necessary to go to the trouble to get the proper papers before adventuring into the United States. From 1820 to 1958, a total of 139 years, immigrants from Mexico to the United States numbered 1,180,131 (Immigration and Naturalization Service, 1961). This report gives a total of 299,811 Mexicans entering the United States between 1951 and 1960. In 1961 the figure was 41,476.

The People from Cuba

Another minority group found among Spanish-speaking people in the United States are the Cubans. They have settled chiefly in the cities on the southeast coast, particularly Miami, Tampa and Key West. There are also significant numbers in New York City.

The close proximity of Cuba to Florida, plus the similar climatic conditions in both places, has made migration from Cuba to Florida a very logical move for families wishing to change their way of life or seeking economic betterment.

In recent months, of course, thousands of Cubans have fled to the United States for refuge from the intolerable conditions under Communist domination. The United States has welcomed the Cuban people and the Department of Health, Education and Welfare has established a Cuban refugee center to provide registration, material support, medical, educational and resettlement facilities for the refugees. Statistics for 1962 show there were 360,000 Cubans in the United States.

A report from Mrs. Burt Cornelius, of the United Presbyterian Church in the U.S.A., states: "Church World Service has joined with the National Catholic Welfare Conference, the United Hebrew Immigrant Aid Society and the International Rescue Committee to help provide jobs and homes for Cuban refugees.

"The refugees have come from every walk of life and from all levels of society. Many are well educated. There are doctors, lawyers, teachers, businessmen, farmers, students and children. Parents have sent their children out of Cuba hoping to join them later. All children under eighteen years of age are processed through the Children's Service Bureau in Miami and placed in foster homes. Whenever possible, families are kept together.

"Along with the physical and material requirements also come the spiritual needs of those who have sacrificed everything to preserve their Christian and democratic principles. Most of the refugees are of the Roman Catholic faith, but many fall into the Protestant group, and Church World Service may, in the end, have to be responsible for the people who are of mixed religion or none. It is a program which has had to be treated with alacrity as well as with great compassion, as we remember this is the first time in many years that refugees have turned to the United States as their first country of asylum."

A personal testimony tells what the church is doing for the refugees:

> I was Catholic when I went for the first time to the United Presbyterian Spanish center. I don't have words to express my gratitude to God for the help you are offering to all the Cuban refugees who are running away from Communism. Your center means to me physical maintenance for my family, but more than that it means spiritual help for our souls, because through it I have known the gospel, which is joy, happiness and gladness. I used to cry very much, but now I am happy because I trust in my God.

With the Communist menace now close to our shores, our communities face a new challenge to prove to the Cubans and to the world that we value our freedoms and respect human dignity in

our democratic way of life. Their impressions of the way of life
in the United States will be based on the way we welcome them
and provide homes and job opportunities.

The Puerto Rican People

Since the end of World War II, the immigration of Puerto Ricans
has been significant and has claimed much attention. These are
American citizens moving from Puerto Rico to the mainland at a
rate close to 50,000 a year. In recent years, however, many thousands have returned to Puerto Rico and the migration seems to
have leveled off.

Migration varies with the economic picture in the United States.
Low-cost plane transportation makes it possible to come and go
with facility when jobs are available and to take advantage of seasonal labor opportunities harvesting crops. The improvement in
living conditions in Puerto Rico has contributed to the lessening
of the movement into the United States.

The great majority of the Puerto Ricans have settled in New York
City. The Puerto Rican population there has been estimated at
750,000.

The second largest grouping of Puerto Rican people is found in
and around Chicago. The St. Lawrence Seaway project has attracted
diversified industry to Chicago and has resulted in a job-opportunity
situation that is expected to last a decade.

Language presents the greatest single difficulty for the Puerto
Rican, although English classes are a regular part of the island's
public school curriculum. One-tenth of the Puerto Rican group are
non-whites and have their newcomer problems compounded by
color prejudice, while many in the white majority suffer the stigma
of the extension of this attitude. Other problems of customs and
adjustment to the industrial metropolitan environment parallel those
of the working-class groups of past and present who move in search
of better economic opportunity.

Indications are that the Puerto Rican people show a remarkable
adaptability and are integrating into their communities far faster
than did the other minority groups who came to this country in the
past. Outside New York City there are no noticeable social ghettos
or geographic areas belonging to the Puerto Rican people. The ten-

dency toward dispersion is facilitated and encouraged by the Commonwealth of Puerto Rico, the island government, which maintains labor employment and orientation offices in major United States cities as well as an island-wide orientation program for prospective migrants.

Persistence of Spanish Culture

It should be noted that there are many factors which will tend to cause the Spanish culture in the United States to persist for a long time. One of these is the ready access to their homeland, be it Mexico, Puerto Rico, or the Latin American countries, and the tendency to go back and forth for short or prolonged visits. This in turn brings relatives to reside in the United States and seek opportunities here beyond what they can expect in their homeland.

The popularity of Spanish music, Spanish foods, Spanish architecture tends to help these people retain their natural pride of their Spanish cultural background. Less and less are they inclined to discard the Spanish language which is being refreshed and perpetuated through television, radio and the printed page. Of course, the Spanish language itself is completely adequate and modern. All scientific and technical terms can be used with facility in the Spanish idiom. These facts, plus the natural beauty of the language, guarantee continued popularity for Spanish language and culture.

General Population Characteristics

The population chracteristics of the Spanish-speaking people in the United States might be summarized as follows:

1. Conservatively estimated, the total Spanish-American population on the mainland is more than six million.

2. Although the majority come from a rural background in their native country, they are rapidly becoming urbanized.

3. A million Spanish Americans are to be found in the migrant stream, but their permanence there is unlikely.

4. These people are rapidly rising in the economic scale. Evidence of this is seen where large numbers of them are now living in the more attractive residential parts of a city. However, the vast majority are still in the slum areas.

5. There has been a rapid increase in the number of young people

graduating from high school, and in more recent years, colleges and universities.

6. As in the case of all ethnic groups in this country, they are gradually, as opportunity affords, making a place for themselves as leaders in their community.

Missionary Outlook

As early as 1537 Spaniards came into New Mexico. It became a territory of Spain in 1595, at which time the Roman Catholics began their formal work. They had entire religious control until 1850.

In 1680 the Indians revolted and drove out the Spaniards, but the Spaniards regained possession in 1698. In 1846 General Kearny entered New Mexico and took possession of the territory, and in 1848 it was ceded to the United States.

The Missionary Society of the Methodist Episcopal Church sent out its first missionary, Rev. E. G. Nicholson, in 1850, for the purpose of preaching to the English-speaking settlers. In 1853 Benigno Cardenas, a converted Mexican Catholic priest, was sent to preach to the Spanish-speaking peoples. Dr. Thomas Harwood came to Tiptonville, New Mexico, in 1869, and started his work. The Harwood School for Girls in Albuquerque still bears his name.[1]

A number of other denominations also started work among the Spanish-American people of the Southwest. Many human interest stories can be told of the early days. A Mexican from the territory of New Mexico moved to southern Colorado. A Frenchman learned that the Mexican, Juan des Jesus Gomez, wanted a Protestant Spanish Bible and traded him one for $10.00 in gold, a fat ox, and the use of a yoke of oxen and a wagon for several months.

Juan read the Bible and was converted. A few years later a Presbyterian missionary went through the San Luis Valley in southern Colorado and wrote to his mission board: "I have found thirteen or fourteen persons here who show every evidence of conversion." They built a church and went to work! Five preachers came from that church — and that was the beginning of Protestant Spanish-speaking work in southern Colorado.

From this we can gather there is a Protestant tradition among the Spanish-American people and, though often not fully informed, the

[1] *History of New Mexico, Spanish and English Missions of the Methodist Episcopal Church,* Vol. 1.

Spanish Roman Catholics have an idea what Protestantism stands for and in many cases the Roman Catholics have a respect for the Protestants and their leaders.

This is especially true in Puerto Rico. Here, since the acquisition of the territory in 1898, the Protestant denominations have been working vigorously with an excellent program, fully supported by an especially strong lay movement. All the ministers are recruited from native Puerto Rican congregations.

In the case of Puerto Rico, it is especially interesting to note that the Protestant movement, with its numerous chapels, Sunday schools and vigorous rural church program, was able to do a job in Christian education the Roman Catholic Church failed to do. The Roman church, usually located on the plaza in the larger towns, rested on its reputation and its old-world philosophy, while the Protestant churches taught the Bible in memory verse, sermon, and song. Today almost every family has some professed Protestants in its number.

It is hard to find a professed Protestant in Puerto Rico who does not know the principles of his faith and who is not a militant Christian, ready to defend his theological position wth fervor. For this reason many Catholics are apologetic about their position.

This situation among the Catholics is being somewhat rectified by a vigorous religious education program in the many Roman Catholic private schools and by special "Holy Mission" campaigns in rural communities. These campaigns play up the many rituals accompanying the adoration of the Virgin Mary and the first communion pageantry. As in much of old-world Catholicism, the women play the prominent part in church attendance, and though the men are often seen in the processions on saints' days, they are seldom seen in church. In contrast, the Protestant church is noted for its strong support by the men in Latin America.

Until very recently the Catholic Church in Puerto Rico had no native clergy. In the Protestant churches, most clergy, including the denominational superintendents, come from the local church congregations with the exception of a few specialized missionaries. So much is this true that one can safely say there is no place for the Anglo-American missionary as pastor of a Latin-American Protestant congregation in Puerto Rico. In both the urban and rural work

it would be difficult for an Anglo-American missionary to enter the
field, for the Latin-American Protestants (popularly termed "Evangelicals" among the Latin-Americans themselves) no longer consider themselves a mission field. In educational, medical, and community work, and in special types of evangelism there is, however,
much to be done. Here and there some women have been used in
parish work in Christian education and in work with women and
children to good advantage.

Churches at Work

To be able to give accurate statistics about the number of Protestant churches among the Spanish-speaking people in the United
States is impossible. The following denominations are now engaged
in Spanish work: American Baptist Home Mission Society, Southern
Baptist Convention, Conservative Baptist Home Mission Society,
Christian and Missionary Alliance, Mennonite, Church of God, Congregational, Disciples of Christ, Evangelical United Brethren, Lutherans, Methodist, United Presbyterian Church U.S.A., Presbyterian
Church U.S., and Protestant Episcopal. In addition there are many
societies and city missions doing outstanding work. Among the latter are the New York City Mission Society and the Chicago City
Missionary Society, both independent organizations.

The churches and community projects of the New York City Mission Society have often served as models in showing denominations
how to undertake successful Spanish work. The Chicago City Missionary Society has helped denominations and independent churches organize Spanish congregations in the areas of Chicago where
a neighborhood study shows there is need. The personnel of the society assist locally in the ministry, as well as supply social work, material need, and orientation to newcomers. As the congregation
grows stronger the society's personnel moves on to other areas.

Group ministries, organized as Protestant city parishes, working
in the difficult areas of the cities, have come across many Spanish-
speaking newcomers. The East Harlem Protestant Parish and the
Cleveland Protestant Parish have successfully established Spanish-
language churches and extensive parish activities for these people.

Strong Pentecostal Influence

The Pentecostal churches, both organized as denominational and as independent churches, play a most important role among the Spanish-speaking people in the United States. They have taught their rhythmic hymns and Bible-verse choruses with such efficiency that it is not uncommon to find other churches singing them. Many Spanish-speaking people can quote Bible verses and tell Bible stories because they have heard them sung so many times. It is hoped that a more stable and better-trained leadership may correct some of the weaknesses of this group and there may be a significant future for these churches among the Spanish-speaking people.

Chicago Churches

Statistics of Spanish-speaking churches are somewhat vague in that they do not give an idea of the size of the congregations or the extent of their geographical area of influence. In Chicago there are about forty Spanish-speaking Protestant congregations including the small store-front churches. Of these, about 50 per cent are Pentecostal or independent. The other 50 per cent have somewhat loosely organized into a Fellowship of Protestant Churches that conduct many successful mass meetings and union activities. With a Chicago Spanish-speaking population of 275,000, it would seem that these people are better churched than in many other areas. However, the geographic dispersion in Chicago accounts for the larger number of churches percentagewise.

New York Churches

New York has more than one million Spanish-speaking people and about 250 Protestant congregations. Almost all of them are conducted by indigenous leaders, and the vast majority of the churches are self-supporting. About thirty of these are very small, however, and it is hard to determine their relationship to other Protestant groups. About sixty-eight of the total are denominational. Most of the rest are either Pentecostal or independent.

In regard to the Pentecostal and independent churches, the *Midcentury Pioneers and Protestants*[2] has this to say: "First, the churches of these two groups are largely a real indigenous expression of Protestant convictions. They receive no aid from denominational agencies, nor have they flowered from some central group's missionary vision. They have a strong evangelical spirit, a conservative

[2] *Midcentury Pioneers and Protestants* (New York: Department of Church Planning and Research of the Protestant Council of the City of New York, 1954).

theology, and are willing to work with other Protestant churches toward a limited number of specific short-term goals."

The number of Spanish-speaking churches found in New York City is growing. This growth is somewhat due to the division of congregations because of differences or because of the extreme mobility of the newcomer people within the city. The tremendous missionary opportunity present among the Spanish-speaking people of our cities is also a factor in this growth.

The 1960 edition of *A Report on Protestant Spanish Community in New York City*[3] indicates repeatedly that the great need today is for trained leadership among the Spanish-speaking people. Puerto Rico is not producing enough ministers to fill the pulpits there.

All things considered, it is not venturesome to say that the greatest present-day missionary opportunity among the Latin people is not in some far-off Latin American country at all, but rather in the great cities of the United States.

The Missionary's Approach

The dangerous pitfall confronting the Spanish-speaking newcomers in the United States is that, as they begin to adopt the new culture, they are apt to adopt the worldly non-Christian culture of the city. Many come with Roman Catholic backgrounds where religious education and Sunday school training, as we know it, are non-existent. They have had no real spiritual roots. Morals were taught by the social mores and customs and not by the church. Many do not have a Christian morality before becoming members of a Protestant congregation. Instead, they possess a peculiar morality coming from the ethical dictates of the culture. It is best to keep this in mind rather than class them as immoral. They are ethically neutral and can be considered potential materialists or potential Christians. It is certain that they will adopt one of the new ways of life much more rapidly than we are prepared to believe. It is sad to observe that the American churches, with all their wealth and spiritual preparation, have not taken advantage of this opportunity to evangelize these people who have come to our very doorsteps.

The Spanish people are friendly and eager to hear our message.

[3] *A Report on Protestant Spanish Community in New York City* (New York: Department of Church Planning and Research of the Protestant Council of the City of New York, 1960).

There have been cases where on one evening Roman Catholic groups have visited Spanish homes and persuaded the families to put a prepared sign on the front door saying, "WE ARE CATHOLICS, PROTESTANTS ARE NOT WELCOME HERE!" The very next evening Protestant groups, not intimidated by a sign, have been welcomed by the same family, who asked for literature, Bible reading and prayer. It is my opinion that it will be hard for the Roman Catholics to isolate these warm, friendly, open-hearted people by such methods. However, other more persistent indoctrination can take them away from the Protestant gospel message forever.

It is unfortunate that some Christian workers give so much attention to the religious tags that people carry. If a Spanish-speaking person says, "I am a Catholic," this statement should be elaborated before he is categorized or pigeonholed as unreachable. Further investigation may prove that this person has never had any religious education. Most Spanish-speaking persons consider baptism in a Roman Catholic church when an infant enough to make them "Catholic." Thus when the Spanish person says he is Catholic, he may be making a profession of faith, or he may be merely answering politely with a word empty of the meaning we associate with it. Many Protestants will call themselves Catholics and then staunchly declare: *"Católicos Apostólicos y no Romanos,"* that is, Apostolic Catholic — not Roman Catholic!

Establishing Spanish-Speaking Congregations

There are many approaches to the goal of establishing Spanish-speaking congregations. Much time has been spent in committees and conferences to determine which approach is correct. Some think that Spanish-speaking groups in ethnic isolation should be the only type of effort. These people point to the flourishing success of the many Spanish-language churches that have become strong institutions with hundreds of members, all with little or no help from the organized denominational churches or national mission boards. For the most part, however, the organized denominational churches and national mission boards support the position that it is best to organize the Spanish people as part of the established English-speaking churches and missions. Notice is made of the fact that, with few exceptions, the Spanish-speaking congregations within

English-speaking churches seldom grow larger than a hundred members. These congregations average around fifty in number.

There is really a difference in goals in these approaches. In the isolated Spanish-speaking church much emphasis is made on retaining the old culture and language. In some of these churches the children who go to public schools are actually taught to speak Spanish on Sundays in their churches. Thus the family finds a center of stability in the instability of a new and often hostile environment. Methods of family discipline and daily living receive the authoritative approval of the church. The children are more apt to stay in line with that which the old culture expects of them. Often in these churches the Christian way of life is taught as being essentially tied up with the Spanish way of doing things.

Where congregations of Spanish-speaking people are formed within an English-speaking congregation, little effort is made to preserve the old culture or language. The children are accepted in the English-speaking Sunday school and the parents are persuaded to attend the English church services where there is a good choir, organ, and an attractive sanctuary. If the Christian education of the Spanish newcomers is complete enough, there is no particular drawback to this approach. However, the method itself limits the size of the Spanish group. The Spanish congregations, under this plan, are small because their members have been absorbed into the English-speaking congregation. In this approach we must take care not to rob a family of its cultural inheritance without giving it an even greater stability — making its members citizens of Christ's kingdom. The real goal is that of conversion and Christian growth and no amount of church clubs can replace this need.

The Spanish congregation within the English church affords many opportunities for two-way orientation. In one church in Chicago where two large congregations meet every Sunday (one Spanish and one English) the English-speaking congregation sponsors special cultural events and activities that give occasion to point out the good features of the Spanish group. They do this because the Spanish people have little other opportunity to show or express pride in their own cultural roots.

Often the children and young people, in the interest of social approval here in the United States, have rejected their own language and culture and are embarrassed by their parents' clinging to the old ways. If by chance the new culture does not accept these children because they are "different," then the child or youth finds himself in a no man's land of social isolation and is easy victim for any organized gang of vice that would exploit him.

It has been the experience of this particular church in Chicago that the youth find a new and comforting assurance in the celebration of special Spanish traditional programs and are thus directed to a wholesome synthesis in their social adjustment. They begin to recognize the good in their own cultural background. The English-speaking congregation also becomes more appreciative of the Spanish way of doing things. Such programs also help to retain those of the Spanish group who attend church but who have not as yet been converted.

In regard to the separate Latin-American church, a California-born church social worker of Mexican parents makes these pertinent observations:

There is a growing trend toward Latin-American churches being independent and self-supporting. The paternalistic philosophy of the early missionary enterprises has made its contributions in the maintaining and sustaining of evangelical work with the Spanish-speaking peoples but has established a dependency attitude which has hampered the growth of independence, now evolving. However, the new Latin-American church (primarily Mexican) is a young church, young in years (in contrast to existing denominational churches) and young in the medium age of membership. The administration and leadership of the church, as well as the support, fall on the young adults and adults between the ages of twenty-five and fifty. Official boards and governing bodies are composed of bilingual members primarily, as well as members who can give financial and leadership support to the church program.

Churches where the older pillar-of-the-church leaders remain tend to die. They cannot retain the younger, vigorous, brighter and better-prepared membership. These in turn will move into English-speaking churches or move to other denominational churches, looking for a church which meets their spiritual, social and intellectual needs. Standards for ministers must be raised in view of the demands of the younger congrega-

tions. Spanish-speaking members remain in churches sometimes
primarily on the basis of cultural cleavage and not spiritual
communion. These are doomed to die, in my opinion, because a
church must have more than a cultural cleavage sanctuary.

Our Latin-American churches are bilingual, the level of
education is higher and continues to be elevated with a great
number of people engaged in the skilled trades, business and
professional occupations. Members are home owners, not migrant
or farm workers barely able to eke out an existence. We are
a bi-cultural group, retaining much of our heritage, adopting
much of the patterns of the land in which we were born. Why
do we, being bi-cultural, still cling to segregation? Not segregation, but to the security of a cultural family which is unique to
us. Realistically we are not, cannot be, Anglo-Saxon simply
because we know the language. Furthermore, the stings of
prejudice have not been totally erased. One remains where one
feels he belongs and this is the philosophy of our membership.
A worship experience is an intimate experience; it is not the
casual experience of just being a co-worker in the event someone should ask us. Why do they feel so different about worshiping? They go to school with Anglos, they work with them, etc.

I believe that general boards are not encouraging missionary
status for our Spanish-speaking churches. This means they must
struggle for survival, either maintaining themselves or combining
with other Latin-American churches, or integrate. We have all
of these patterns. (Faustina Solís, an outstanding social worker
well-known in Latin-American and Anglo-American. churches
of the Los Angeles area.)

In reality it is folly to speak of *the* correct approach. To insist
on one approach is like insisting on using a certain gun in battle
when there are many types needed for assured victory. In a crusade
to evangelize the Spanish-speaking people, intelligent Christians
will use every expedient method possible. If there seems to be sufficient need for a temporary totally Spanish-speaking church, then
there should be such an effort. This is particularly true where there
are large isolated communities of Spanish-speaking people. On the
other hand, there are hundreds within that same community who
shun the old culture and language and yearn to be taken into the
new. These people make a ready adjustment to church life within
the English-speaking church, and the adjustment will be easier if

they can come in via a Spanish-speaking group worshiping, with membership privileges, as part of the English-speaking church.

Any church or denomination, society or group considering Spanish work must know the seriousness of the question before them. These are a proud and honorable people. When confronted with the question of integration it is not merely a question of people of a different culture occupying a seat in the sanctuary, or sending their children to the Sunday school. There is the question of language which separates Spanish Americans from others in all walks of life. In some cases a dark skin pigmentation provides an excuse for unfair treatment from others. All these questions must be met squarely, honestly, and capably if there is to be a significant evangelical movement by the church among these people.

As churches, our first job is not that of "Americanization" (which still tends to persist in people's minds), but to bring the Spanish-speaking people the message which has been entrusted to us by Christ. Such being the case, it is easily understandable why leadership in the Council of Spanish American Work and elsewhere is more inclined to evangelism in its purest and most effective form than any other program of service. In fact, it is interesting to note that a great deal of concern has been generated over the tendency on the part of some to promote the idea of integration at the expense of making Pentecost a reality in the lives of our Spanish-American neighbors.

Home Visitation

Churches play an important role in evangelizing the Latin-American people, but many Latin-American newcomers do not come to the church and are not reached by the church. This is especially true in the cities. Our failure to evangelize is our failure to contact these people at all. It is precisely at this point where we see that home visitation evangelism by the home missionary, pastor, and layman is a practical, direct, and most important approach to the evangelization of Spanish-speaking families.

In crowded cities, it is not uncommon to find hundreds of families gathered fearfully behind closed apartment doors. The world outside the humble apartment is indeed a hostile one to any foreign language newcomers. For weeks and months the only persons knocking at their door may have been the truant officer, the rent collector, the practical joker, the drunkard, or a salesman who would show them something they wanted and needed but could ill afford. What of him who comes in the name of the Lord?

Many times, when they are sure that a Protestant pastor or worker is calling on them, there is a pouring out of hearts. At such a time one marvels at the confidence the missionaries have gained among these people. It can be taken for granted that in the old country sacrificing missionaries, men and women of great integrity, have paved the way.

Too often casework of great proportion is uncovered during these visits and the Christian worker will have many things pulling at his heart before visiting many homes. Soon it will be evident that material salvation is not possible for all these newcomers. But the Christian worker can preach a Saviour, adequate for all human needs and wants, a Friend who will walk with His own even through the valley of the shadow of death. What a Friend we have in Jesus! Oh, that we would share Him with these Spanish-speaking strangers who are so lonely in this land — the country's migrant and the city's newcomer! We must make this hymn their declaration of faith as they face the adversity of their new environment. Oh, the strength it can radiate to the hearts of those who brave the road of the migrant!

> O God, our help in ages past,
> Our hope for years to come,
> Our shelter from the stormy blast,
> And our eternal home!

Our ancestors walked this same road and most brought with them a solid faith. Not so with these new people who bring their Spanish language and culture to our land. They do not come, as our forefathers, seeking religious freedom. They come, as did the early Spanish conquistadores, seeking gold — economic fortune, a job. It is for us to see that they receive the greatest gift of all — the gift of salvation from the crucified and risen Lord. This is our privilege — this is our task.

Jewish young people reading the Scriptures in Hebrew.

7

The American Jew

VICTOR BUKSBAZEN

THE PLACE OF THE JEW in the divine and human scheme of things is unmatched and unparalleled by any other people. God in His sovereign wisdom and grace has made himself known to all mankind through Abraham and his seed.

The Jews were the human authors and custodians of the Bible. Israel was also the matrix from whence came forth Christ, the Saviour of all mankind. Persecuted, massacred, exiled, shut up in ghettos, driven from country to country, the Jew has survived and shows an amazing vitality and vigor. Israel is the burning bush which cannot be consumed, the only people whose history, past, present and future, was written in advance by the prophets of God.

Their importance cannot be measured by their numbers. Their contribution to religion, science, to philosophy and the arts, to commerce and industry, to medicine and indeed to all human endeavors, is beyond computation. Their restless quest for justice and truth has profoundly influenced and often given birth to many of the great movements of history. They are the spiritual forebears of the Christian faith.

Jewish ideals have profoundly affected our Western civilization, first in Europe and later in America. It is quite possible that Chris-

VICTOR BUKSBAZEN was born early in the century in a traditional Jewish home in Warsaw, Poland. As a young man he was converted and studied at the Theological Seminary of the University of Warsaw, where he became an instructor in Old Testament subjects. He then became a missionary among the Jews in Poland, and later continued a similar ministry in England. In 1941 Mr. Buksbazen came to the United States and is now the general secretary of the Friends of Israel Missionary and Relief Society, Inc.

topher Columbus was himself of Jewish descent. It is certain that
a number of his crew members were *Marranos* — Jews who in the
Middle Ages were forcibly converted to "Christianity" in Catholic
Spain. The first white man ever to set foot in the New World was
in all probability a Jew.[1]

When in the seventeenth century the *Mayflower* brought the
Pilgrim Fathers to the New World, its most precious cargo was the
Jewish Bible and a set of moral, spiritual and social values based on
the Hebrew heritage. Some of the Pilgrim Fathers were so impressed with this Jewish heritage that they seriously proposed
adopting Hebrew as their common language.

The American Jew

The history of the American Jew and the history of America are
closely interwoven. Each powerfully molded and shaped the other.
Among General Washington's associates were a number of Jews.
Hyman Solomon, who helped George Washington finance the Revolution (and incidentally was never repaid) was called "the financier
of freedom." Moses Frank, a Jewish lawyer from Philadelphia, was
among those whom General Washington entrusted with important
missions and responsibilities. Judge Moses Levi, also of Philadelphia, crossed the Delaware with General Washington's army.[2]

As anti-Semitism and persecution of the Jews in Europe increased,
Jewish immigration to America, the golden land of freedom and
opportunity, also increased. In 1880 there were about 300,000 Jews
in the United States, roughly .06 per cent of a total population of
50 million. Today their number is about 5,000,000, or three per
cent of the total population. Here in America under favorable conditions the economic status of the Jew improved and a profound
change took place in his intellectual and spiritual position.

The American Jew born and reared in freedom is in many re-
spects different from his European ancestors. His European grand-
father may have been a pious, orthodox Jew. His immigrant father
likely joined a conservative or reformed synagogue. His son, born
in America, if he goes to the synagogue at all, does it mainly on the
Day of Atonement. Although he may still feel proud of his Jewish
heritage, his attachment to Judaism is often very slender.

---

[1] Cecil Roth, *Jewish Contributions to Civilization* (New York: Union of American
Hebrew Congregations), pp. 72-76.
[2] Lee M. Freedland, *Pilgrims in a New Land.*

The restoration of the State of Israel has increased his sense of national pride and dignity. Yet, spiritually, the Jew is adrift. Traditional Judaism, with its stringent ritualism and antiquated mode of worship, does not appeal to him. Conservative or Reformed Judaism with its emphasis on ethical living does not seem to be able to nourish his deep-seated spiritual hunger for God. In the large cities, bigger and better synagogues are being erected. Yet these imposing edifices are becoming less and less a place of worship and devotional life, but more and more communal centers, where cultural, social and philanthropic activities are conducted. Many a great synagogue is the finest catering establishment in the city, but the poorest place where a soul may find nourishment.

One splendid and wealthy synagogue in metropolitan New York has a membership of some 1,600 families and a four-year waiting list of Jewish families who would like to join this magnificent temple. Yet on a Sabbath morning it is hard to get together ten persons to make up a *minian,* or a quorum, needed for public worship. This situation is only one of the symptoms of spiritual decline and presents a challenge to every earnest Christian.

The Jew Through Christian Eyes

The Christian who takes his faith and his calling in Christ seriously must face the Jew with a profound sense of gratitude and sacred obligation. The Bible-taught Christian knows that everything which has eternal value was transmitted to him through the medium of the Jewish people. By the grace of God he has become, so to speak, a naturalized citizen of Israel's spiritual commonwealth (Eph. 2:12-14).

The Jews' failure, in spite of their great heritage, to recognize in Jesus "the Lamb of God, which taketh away the sin of the world," is something which mystifies the Christian. The believer feels challenged by the Jews as nothing and nobody in this world could challenge him. In the case of the Jew, the commission of the risen Saviour to His disciples to go and preach the gospel to all nations, beginning in Jerusalem, takes on an added significance and urgency. The Jew is the touchstone which probes and proves the quality of our Christian faith, the spiritual tone of our lives.

From the very beginning, the Jew has always been in the center of the Christian effort to win him for his Lord. This dates back to the ministry of our Lord Jesus Himself, to the apostles and to the early Christian church. The Acts of the Apostles, the New Testament epistles and the literature of the early church are a testimony to this great effort to win at least a remnant of the Jews for their Messiah, Jesus.

The Church of Christ was born on the Jewish Feast of Pentecost in the city of Jerusalem, when three thousand Jews, who heard the gospel proclaimed by Peter, the apostle to the Jews, believed and were baptized. It was this Jerusalem church which sent out the first missionaries into the Gentile world (Acts 11:18-26).

The fourth-century church historian Eusebius records that the first fifteen bishops of Jerusalem, beginning with James, the brother of our Lord, were all Jews.[3]

For a true scriptural grasp of the proper relationship between Israel and the Gentile believer in Christ, it is absolutely necessary to read, study and inwardly digest Romans 9-11 and Ephesians 2.

It was only later when the church became predominantly Gentile and its spiritual center shifted westward into the Greek world and to Rome, that she lost her sympathy and her concern for the salvation of Israel. An arrogant church, forgetting her origin and the warning of the Apostle Paul (Rom. 11:18-25), became more and more contemptuous and hostile to the Jews. Instead of seeking to win them for Christ by love, she treated the Jews as social outcasts. Her theology, her ecclesiastical laws, and the social system which she helped to shape reflected the spiritual decay of the church.

In our literature the Crusaders who went forth to win back the tomb of our Lord and to liberate Jerusalem from the infidel Moslems appear as valiant knights, romantic and heroic. To the Jew the Crusaders bring back a vision of rivers flowing with the tears and the blood of his ancestors.

What effort the medieval church did make to win the Jew for Christ was generally crude and often cruel. As a result the Jew, instead of becoming attracted to Christ, became more hardened against the gospel of grace and against Christ. In fact, the very term *Christian* in the mind of the medieval Jew became a synonym for anti-Semitism. Even the modern Jew still suffers from this trau-

3 Eusebius Pamphili, *The Ecclesiastical History*, translated from the original by Christian Frederick Cruse (Grand Rapids: Baker Book House, 1955), p. 479.

matic shock once inflicted upon his forebears by the cruel Inquisition in Spain and in other "Christian" countries.[4]

Neither did the Reformation bring about an immediate change in the Christian-Jewish relationship. "Nearly every great Christian reformer has had at least one Jewish scholarly friend and associate."[5] The reformers, although greatly influenced and taught by Jewish scholars, were too preoccupied with their gigantic task of liberating the Christians from the shackles of Rome to give much thought to the Jew. Indeed some of them still nurtured long-ingrained and deep-seated prejudices against the Jew.

Nevertheless, the Reformation made a change in Christian-Jewish relations not only possible, but inevitable. In rediscovering the Bible the Christian was bound to rediscover the Jew and a new sense of responsibility and gratitude toward him. From then on one hears more frequently about individual Christians witnessing to the Jews.

In the eighteenth century organized missionary efforts began in Germany, in Switzerland, and in other Protestant countries. But the foundation for the most fruitful and lasting world-wide effort to evangelize the Jews started in London, England, when in 1809 the London Society for the Promotion of Christianity among the Jews was organized by a converted Jew, the son of a rabbi.[6] It was a missionary work sponsored by the Church of England, which continues its ministry to the present day. This work is responsible for the conversion of a considerable number of prominent Jewish men and women.

In 1843 another important organization representing the Free churches of Great Britain came into existence, the British Society for the Propagation of the Gospel among the Jews. This society also is still very active in Europe, in Israel, and in Africa. Later a number of new Jewish missionary organizations were formed in Great Britain and in Europe. Under the impetus of these European societies similar organizations were born in the United States and Canada.

---

[4] N. Carter, *The Shame of Christendom*.
[5] Louis I. Newman, Ph.D., *Jewish Influence on Christian Reform Movements*, Columbia University Oriental Series, XXIII, 4.
[6] W. T. Gidney, *History of the London Society for Promoting Christianity Amongst the Jews* (London: S.P.C.K., 1909).

Missionary Methods

An outstanding veteran missionary to the Jews recently stated, "The golden age of Jewish evangelism may be just around the corner."

The American Jew, generally well-educated, is frequently religiously illiterate. He has become a stranger to the Bible, even to the Old Testament. As a result, he is spiritually emaciated. Judaism, whether traditional or liberal, is not capable of meeting the needs of his soul. At the same time, consciously or otherwise, he is continuously exposed to Christian thought, whether it is by radio or television, through literature, or through the direct testimony of his Christian friends.

While the message of salvation in Christ remains the same forever, yet our methods of presenting the gospel must be adapted to the spiritual conditions of the American Jew. These methods should be flexible and subject to revision in the light of experience.

The old-fashioned dingy mission hall with a few Scripture texts on the wall does not command the respect of the modern Jew. The best place to meet with him may be a private home. If a mission center is used at all, it should be attractive and supplied with good literature written by Christian men with a true understanding of the Jewish mind and background.

No single method of reaching the Jew with the gospel is sufficient in itself. It should be reinforced by other valid methods. The greatest of these is the solid meat of the Word of God — teaching the Bible. Next is the living testimony of a consecrated life. Radio broadcasts, summer camps, open-air meetings, special classes for women or children, all can be used to great advantage. Mail evangelism, if the right literature is used, is valuable. Medical clinics, once very acceptable, today under greatly changed social and economic conditions are of questionable value, at least in America.

Christian workers among the Jews use a variety of missionary methods, according to their individual ingenuity or as local conditions may dictate.

Bible classes will always be the most important means of winning people for Christ and for grounding them in the faith. Whenever possible the study of the Bible, whether individually or in groups, should be started as soon as possible. Secure a competent teacher who can bring the Word to life.

Personal witness is also one of the most important means of reaching Jews for Christ, whether it be a visit at the home of a Jewish friend or wherever else there may be opportunity.

Reading rooms and display windows attractively arranged and stocked with good Christian literature often attract the attention of potential inquirers. It is important to have regular hours and a competent person to answer the questions of visitors. This approach has been found useful in Boston, New York and Philadelphia.

The community center is another avenue of approach (found successful in Chicago and Toronto). It gives the missionary many opportunities to work with young people and to reach their parents.

The luncheon forum where Christian and Jewish businessmen meet together has been very effective in some places.

Radio broadcasting directed to Jewish people can be used very effectively. Many Jewish people who would never enter a church or any other Christian place of worship may listen to the gospel in the privacy of their homes or while driving.

Distribution of literature, especially of New Testaments, is a good way of reaching Jewish people with the message of the gospel. However, it cannot be sufficiently emphasized that every tract must be well prepared, intelligently presented, and convincing.

The Hebrew Christian congregation (found in Philadelphia, Baltimore, Miami, Tampa, Detroit, Chicago, San Francisco) often attracts Jewish people, especially those of mixed marriages.

Work among students and Jewish people by men with academic training or in the professions is often very effective.

Work among children is of particular value since it brings the gospel message to young lives and sometimes also to their parents. However, we strongly recommend that in case of minors the consent of their parents should be secured previously.

The parish approach is an effort to reach the Jews who live within the neighborhood of a given church with the message of the gospel. This approach seeks to include the Jewish people in the regular visitation by the pastor and the elders of the church. Theoretically this is the ideal method. However, in practice the pastor and the officers of the church often lack interest or time to extend their effort to the Jews. Sometimes they do not know how to go about it, or find the church is not prepared spiritually, emotionally or socially to welcome Jewish people into their midst. A vast educational program is needed to prepare pastors and churches for this effort. Nevertheless some churches, both denominational and independent, have practiced the parish approach with some success.

Contacts with Jewish people are generally made:

1. Through the introduction by a mutual friend.
2. Through mailing of literature and magazines to Jewish homes.
3. Through personal contacts in daily life.

For the purpose of mailing literature, lists of Jewish names may be obtained through telephone and other directories. However, this method is not always reliable, as some Jewish-sounding names may not be those of Jewish persons, while common English names are often used by Jewish people. Mr. Hoffman may turn out to be a Gentile and Mr. Robinson or Mr. Smith, a Jew.

Follow-up of contacts should be done by carefully planned and timely visits, phone calls, invitations to meetings, or specially arranged events. Those who make a confession of faith should be brought into the fellowship of a church where they will receive spiritual nourishment and be encouraged in growth and service. To abandon a new believer is sometimes just as tragic as the abandonment of a newly born babe. Both may perish from lack of food, lack of loving care, and from exposure to the elements.

The importance of prayer for those to whom we witness can hardly be sufficiently emphasized.

The Qualifications of a Jewish Missionary

While every Christian is called to be a witness to all men for his Lord and Saviour, not every Christian is qualified to be a full-time missionary among the Jews. Just having an urge to be a missionary to the Jews is not enough.

The Christian worker among the Jews ought to be a consecrated person with a real love for Israel and with a passion for souls. He should be well prepared for his missionary calling.

The apostles were men trained in the greatest school of all times;

the Lord Jesus Himself was their teacher. In addition to his massive background of Jewish learning, Paul was fourteen years in the wilderness before the Lord prepared him to be the greatest missionary of all times. The Jewish mission should not be considered a dumping ground where any kind of misfit can be placed.

The Jews are a highly intellectual people and have great respect for learning. The modern missionary among the Jews should be a person of spiritual and intellectual stature, able to command the respect of the Jew. In addition to Bible schools and colleges, there is also an urgent need for an institute of postgraduate specialized studies where prospective or practicing Jewish missionaries may obtain additional training in their chosen field of Christian service. We would also strongly advocate a period of internship for missionary candidates under the supervision of veteran missionaries to the Jews.

The oft-discussed question of who makes a better missionary to the Jew, a Hebrew Christian or a Gentile Christian, is basically irrelevant. The Lord uses both for the salvation of Jewish souls. Both have certain natural advantages and disadvantages. Both need to be called of the Lord, filled with His Spirit, humble yet keen, loving yet wise, men of prayer who know how to depend on God and not on the arm of the flesh. They must be men who are not easily discouraged; men who, at the first sign of opposition, will not give up. To quote a veteran missionary: "There are many who consider evangelistic work among the Jews a stony waste, but when we walk in it in the fear of the Lord and at His command, it is a garden full of fair and fragrant flowers."[7]

When a Jew confesses Christ as his personal Saviour, this should not be considered the end of the missionary's task, but rather the beginning. The young Jewish believer should not be left alone, exposed to the onslaught of the enemy within. He should be nourished and nurtured in the Christian faith and in Christian living so that he may grow into the full stature of Christ.

The Jewish believer needs the fellowship of mature believers who will encourage him in his spiritual growth and testimony. Many Jewish believers feel at home among Gentile believers; others do not. Many Jewish Christians feel more at home among fellow

[7] *Kingdom Tidings,* January, 1959.

Jewish believers of like background and of a like burden for Israel. In any case, the Jewish babe in Christ, just like any newborn baby, must be placed in a community of love if the baby is to survive and thrive.

Educating the Church

A vital aspect of missionary work among the Jews is the education of the church to understand her responsibility to the Jew. While there are many Christians who have a true love for Israel, the vast majority are indifferent and sometimes even hostile to Jewish evangelism. "The Jew has had his chance," is one of those hackneyed platitudes handed down from past generations. Every Christian, but especially the pastor, has a great responsibility to train other believers to pray, to love and to help in the evangelization of the Jews.

Jewish missions can be divided into two main groups — denominational and interdenominational. Some Jewish missions seek to reach the Jews of their own city or community. Other organizations have a national or international scope, endeavoring to reach the Jews in America and also abroad.

Here is a list of some Jewish missionary organizations in the United States and Canada. The list is not complete.

INTERDENOMINATIONAL MISSIONS

American Association for Jewish Evangelism, Inc., Winona Lake, Ind., with work in Dayton, Ohio; Richmond, Va.; Seattle, Wash.; Montreal and Winnipeg, Canada.

American Board of Missions to the Jews, Inc., New York, N. Y., working in New York, New Jersey, Pennsylvania, District of Columbia, Ohio, Florida, Texas, Colorado, California, Oregon and Canada.

America-European Bethel Mission, Los Angeles, Calif.

American Messianic Fellowship, Chicago, Ill., working in Chicago, Milwaukee, Indianapolis, Miami and Tampa.

Buffalo Hebrew Christian Mission, Inc., Buffalo, N. Y.

Cleveland Hebrew Mission, Cleveland, Ohio.

Evangelization Society of Philadelphia, Pa.

Friends of Israel Missionary and Relief Society, Inc., Philadelphia,

Pa., working in Brooklyn, Oakland and San Francisco, Washington, D. C.

Hebrew Christian Fellowship, Inc., Philadelphia, Pa.

Hebrew Christian Society, Cleveland, Ohio

Hebrew Evangelization Society, Los Angeles, Calif.

International Board of Jewish Missions, Inc., Atlanta, Ga., working also in New York City.

Israel Covenant News, Minneapolis, Minn.

Israel's Remnant, Hebrew Christian Congregation, Detroit, Mich., working in Detroit and Boston.

Jewish Evangelical Witness, Inc., Whittier, Calif.

Messengers of the New Covenant, Inc., Newark, N. J.

Messianic Witness to Israel, Nampa, Idaho.

Midwest Messianic Center, St. Louis, Mo.

New York Gospel Mission to the Jews, Inc., New York, N. Y.

New York Messianic Witness, Inc., New York, N. Y.

Ohio Messianic Testimony, Cincinnati, Ohio, working in Akron and Canton.

South Side Witness to Israel, Chicago, Ill.

Toronto Jewish Mission, Toronto, Ont., Canada.

DENOMINATIONAL MISSIONS

American Baptist Convention: Los Angeles and Philadelphia.

Assemblies of God: Chicago.

Christian and Missionary Alliance: New York, Philadelphia and Toronto.

Lutheran Church: Minneapolis, Chicago, New York, Baltimore, Philadelphia, Pittsburgh and Los Angeles.

Mennonite Church: Philadelphia, Lancaster, Pa., New York and Tampa.

Reformed Church in America: Passaic, N. J.

United Presbyterian Church in the U.S.A.: Philadelphia, Baltimore, Chicago and Los Angeles.

Church of England, Canada: Toronto.

AUXILIARY AND SPECIALIZED ORGANIZATIONS

Biblical Research Society, Los Angeles, Calif. — literary work.

Emeth Publications, Inc., Whittier, Calif.

Million Testaments Campaigns, Inc., Philadelphia, Pa. — publication of New Testaments in various languages.
Christian Jew Hour, San Antonio, Texas — radio ministry.
Message to Israel, New York, N. Y. — radio ministry.
Messianic Messenger to Israel, Inc., Waco, Texas — radio ministry.
Hebrew Christian Witness, Calgary, Alta., Canada — radio ministry.
Hebrew Christian Alliance of America, Chicago, Ill. — fellowship of Hebrew Christians.
Hebrew Christian Congregations: Baltimore, Chicago, Detroit, Miami, Philadelphia, San Francisco and Tampa.
Fellowship of Christian Testimonies to the Jews, Philadelphia, Pa.
Bible Institute of Los Angeles, Los Angeles, Calif. — Jewish missions course.
Moody Bible Institute, Chicago, Ill. — Jewish missions course.

BIBLIOGRAPHY

GIDNEY, W. T. *History of the London Society for Promoting Christianity Amongst the Jews.* London: S.P.C.K., 1909.
THOMPSON, A. E. *A Century of Jewish Missions.* New York: Fleming H. Revell Co., 1902.
Jewish missionary magazines published by various missionary organizations.

The mansions of the bayou country impress tourists and leave them without a proper understanding of the spiritual and material needs of Cajuns who live off the beaten track. (Courtesy of United Air Lines.)

8

The People Called Cajuns

J. C. WELLS

IN ANY DISCUSSION of the Cajuns in southern Louisiana it seems best to differentiate between Creole and Cajun. These two words are used interchangeably by many people, especially those not too familiar with the Cajuns. They are very different in meaning and origin, however.

The word *Creole* was long used to describe the descendants of those who came to Louisiana from Europe, either French or Spanish. Generally these were the ruling class, the military, or those engaged in education. The word *Creole* represented the highest of whatever the subject was. It was the best in furnishings, the best in art and sometimes even in the field of literature. It certainly pertained to the cuisine of the day. Creole dishes were the best that could be served.

The *Cajuns* have an entirely different background. They are not a lowly type of people, as many think, but represent some of the finest families of France. The word *Cajun* is a contraction of the word *Acadian*. The latter term comes from the area in Canada in which these people lived for several generations before coming to Louisiana.

J. C. WELLS is a graduate of the Mississippi College in Clinton, Mississippi, and the Southern Baptist Seminary in Louisville, Kentucky. For fourteen years he pastored a church in Lafayette, Louisiana, in the heart of the Acadian country. Now for many years he has been superintendent of the Baptist City Missions in New Orleans, where he has assisted in the organization of forty-two new churches. He also directs three schools for underprivileged children.

In Transit

When the French settlers made their homes in Nova Scotia, or Acadia, the country was under French rule. They were then, and are now, a closely knit people. But in 1765 these people, who had lands and homes that their great-grandparents had built, were told to take an oath of loyalty to their English conquerors. They refused, and as a result they were expelled by the British. But where could they go? Some went back to France. Some remained to take the consequences. Still another segment went south. One group, who had heard of New Orleans on the Mississippi River, decided to move there and join those French settlers. This group probably consisted of some three thousand persons.

Eyes to the West

The Acadians who came by way of New Orleans divided into several smaller groups, but all turned to the west. Some went straight west, while others went around the mouth of the Mississippi River and came up the bayous. There in the marshy land, where few other people had ventured, was the ideal place for them. The crooked, quiet, slow-moving bayous would furnish food, a means of transportation and a highway on which to build their homes. They settled in groups, which later became the towns and cities of the area. Crude homes were built. Many were thatched palmetto, which grew in abundance. Community activities began. Priests came with the immigrants and soon established Roman Catholic centers of worship.

In building homes and boats, clearing lands and digging canals with crude instruments, the Acadians were brought closer together, for this had to be done by groups. This type of work led to the Saturday night get-together. The families that had worked together through the week would meet and "make merry" with crude musical instruments, many made out of reeds, together with those brought from Canada, principally the banjo and other stringed instruments. They not only played, danced and ate, but they exchanged news. Often visitors from nearby groups would join them and exchange news. For some time this was their only social life.

When they arrived, the different groups split up, some going up one bayou, others some miles away on still another bayou. Each developed a distinctive dialect.

Harnett Kane writes: "The Acadian speech through the years has become like its user, something to and of and by itself. It is a dialect, more accurately a set of dialects, that makes for an adventure in listening. For it has been compounded during three centuries in France, Canada and Louisiana out of isolation, resourcefulness, and a sense of humor. For generations the Acadians have been away from their native country, but along the curving paths of Louisiana's Acadia, the listener hears terms common in French villages of the late 1500's. Local peculiarities have appeared; some words have taken new endings, others have been extended or cut off, or sounds have been transposed. The Acadian (Cajun) will drop a word or several words whenever he can. It is a kind of French with a Southern accent of its own, of variations within variations."[1]

The Cajun, whether out behind the small barn removing the valuable skin from a little animal, or down by the boat house scraping the scales from the fish to serve as the evening meal, or mending his hooks, lines and nets in preparation for tomorrow's catch, used language that his neighbors understood. "I like that, yes," he'd say. Then the negative would come, "I don't like you, no."

The Cajun was very plain in his dealing with those who came to buy his wares or to sell him goods. Since he had been knocked about so long, he became very suspicious of new people or strangers. This attitude perhaps had much to do with the backwardness of these people. They lived to themselves, mixing with outsiders only when it was most needful. As they developed, the villages grew into towns and cities. However, in their growth and development they clung tenaciously to their language, customs, habits, and religion.

I again quote from Harnett Kane in respect to the language and practices in the bayou country. "A little girl once caught my arm and pointed, 'Look at my little dog, how he is cute.' A man explained how he was going to test his prowess in the water: 'I am going to

---

[1] *The Bayous of Louisiana* (New York: William Morrow & Co., 1943), p. 15.

take myself a mile swimming.' When I repeated a rumor about his part of Louisiana, he assured me: 'That is not true, no.' "[2]

The Cajun mixes his English with French or most generally with one of the much used dialects. If he is conversing with you and he comes to a word for which he does not have a French word, he simply supplies an English word.

With the coming of modern conveniences the Cajun living in the bayou country has developed a new language or dialect, a mixture of French (Cajun), English, Spanish and some German. The oil industry, with all its complications, from scouting for oil to refining the crude petroleum, has done much to change the language, customs and habits of the bayou people.

Life Today on the Bayou

We must keep in mind that the bayou country was the original home of the Acadians in Louisiana. There are more than 450 of these bayous in Louisiana, the largest number in the southern part of the state.

The most used in the early days was Bayou La Fourche. This is called by many "the Broadway of the Cajuns." It is located about sixty miles to the west of New Orleans and served as the highway and outlet for trade for many years for many people. Plantation homes were built on its banks to accommodate the social elite. Beside these homes were the humble Cajuns' houses each with its little landing wharf. This "street" is more than thirty miles long. On its banks have grown villages, towns and cities. Today, instead of the little piroque (small one-man boat), large oil barges are seen floating down the bayou, making their way to the gulf and on to the big refineries. Barges with oil field supplies, steel, etc., from the East push their way upstream to the oil fields.

Much of the land first settled by the Cajuns is now growing sugar cane. Louisiana produces more cane sugar than any other state. Many Acadians still live on the big farms where they help to cultivate and harvest the cane. Among these are many who do not speak English. These people live in the coves, in the hinterland, on the smaller bayous near the marshes. The majority speak only a French dialect. This proves to be a problem for those who desire to help them. Many of these people have not been even as far

---
[2] *Ibid.*, p. 16.

away from home as New Orleans. Thousands living there cannot write their names.

The Cajun and the New Day

The development of the Acadians has been most inspiring. At first they were looking for a place where they could live to themselves. They came in contact with the outside world only when it was necessary in selling or buying. Occasionally a boy or girl from a more prosperous family would go to a college or university in the East, or even in Europe. This percentage increased as the years went by. Now the state's second largest tax-supported school is located in Lafayette, in the heart of the Evangeline country. This school did much to break down the barrier, insofar as the outside world was concerned. Many of the state's finest schools are in this area.

The Cajuns now constitute more than 20 per cent of the population in the state. There are more than 700,000 people of French extraction living in southern Louisiana. Many have gone out of the area occupied by the early Acadians into every walk of life. They are in large universities as scientists, in the halls of Congress as senators and representatives and in other places of governmental responsibility. In the field of religion, one denomination can count several pastors of leading churches, college professors and executive secretaries high in the esteem of the public.

Once the barrier was crossed and other people were permitted to go in, the Acadian's vision of life went beyond the cane field or the fishing village. Life began to mean more than the skins of a few muskrats, a few fishing boats, or even a few acres of sugar cane. From the mud and grass marshes of the bayou country of southern Louisiana, from the communities, towns and cities located on the banks of the commercial Bayou La Fourche, or the winding, beautiful Bayou Teche, from the prairie lands where the Acadians and others captured the wealth therein by pumping water from the bayous and irrigating the soil for rice, a people with a new vision are rising and they are making their imprint on the state, the nation and the world.

Many interesting things have come out of the experiences of the Cajuns. For example, the state of Louisiana requires six signatures on every marriage certificate before it is recorded with the court.

Not only that, but it must be signed in jet black permanent ink. In the early days when the land was divided, allocated or bought, it was divided by the French measurement of land, the arpent. To help everyone get a place along the bayou, the lines were not run to make squares, but the Acadian was given a small narrow frontage, broadening out as he went farther back from the bayou. A block of land might have seven or eight sides.

The Cajuns are known for their cuisine. In the early days they had to be resourceful, living from the bayous and the fields. Hence they learned to use as a regular diet such things as crayfish, crabs, shrimp and other bayou fish. Out of this have come dishes that are now known around the world. This cuisine is now served in the leading hotels of New Orleans and other places on the coast.

These people have been like a rose bud. The bud was closed when they lived in the marshes for many years; but finally the warmth and sunshine of other people and the tender mercies of the heavenly Father caused it to burst forth in an affluence of beauty and fragrance felt around the country.

The Religious Life

The Acadians came originally from Catholic France. When they moved to Louisiana the priests went with them. They built churches and began church schools in the early days. For many years they would not allow any other religion. With the coming of new industries and new people, the Cajuns began to realize that there were some good people outside their own clan. They started to mingle with others.

As social life developed, religious life also underwent some changes. Young people began to intermarry. Slowly the barrier was lowered. Evangelical denominations pushed in. Sunday schools were established, sometimes in homes, sometimes in the courthouse, sometimes in the park and occasionally on the bank of the bayou. Chapels were erected. Churches were organized.

Many of the Cajuns became Christians and united with evangelical churches. They were eager to read the Bible. They had not had that privilege before. They were happy with this newly found faith in Christ.

Today there are hundreds of churches in the bayou land and the

Evangeline country, many of the churches the most beautiful in
the state. There are many French (Cajun) ministers today. With
its wealth, its beautiful moss-covered oaks, its mild and balmy
climate and its fast-growing Christian faith, the Cajun land will be
God's country of tomorrow.

Other Groups Need the Gospel

Two other classes of people in the Evangeline country need attention. Both are suffering from the lack of good educational and
religious opportunities. They are the French Indians and the descendants of Negro slaves.

After the war between the states, an unusual thing took place
among the ex-slaves. Much of southern Louisiana had become the
"glory of the South." Many large grants had been made. Many
wealthy men had come from the East and purchased large tracts
of land, building palatial plantation homes. These sugar cane plantations were tilled by Negro slaves. No provision had been made for
their spiritual welfare, except to let them sit in the white churches
in a special place. When the war was over, however, slaves were
free. Friends from the North gave the Negroes Bibles. Schools
were begun. The Negroes read their Bibles, organized churches,
built houses of worship, and have grown so fast that in the city
of New Orleans one denomination of Negroes has over 250 churches
today. These churches have developed some of the finest ministers
of the land.

Along the coast line of southern Louisiana we find another group
of people difficult to classify. When the French traders came to
Louisiana during French rule, they discovered a profitable trading
ground. Along the coast lived a tribe of Indians known as the
Houma (hu-mah). Since these Indians were good trappers, the
French traders made their way to their territory and established
trading contact. It was a profitable business for both. Then the
territory passed into Spanish hands and Spanish traders took over.
When the United States bought Louisiana, American traders established more trading posts and shipped through the New Orleans port.

While the trading was going on, the life of the Houma tribe was
changing. Many of the French, Spanish and American traders
settled along the coast to promote their business. They married

Indian girls and established homes. Then others, Portuguese, Filipinos and Puerto Ricans, went into the Houma territory and traded. Many of these also married Indian girls. From this there has developed a mixed race, of which there are more than 4,000 today. For the most part they are fishermen and trappers.

The tribal lines of the Houma Indians have been lost. The offspring of these mixed marriages were not allowed to attend the white schools, hence the majority of the adults cannot read or write.

Evangelical groups have now gone in and built schools for the children. As a result their status has been raised considerably. Several church schools are at present in operation. The state is also building schools for them.

What Must Be Done?

While it is true that many denominational churches have been established in the bayou country, there is still a large segment of people not being reached with the gospel. The older people living down on the bayous, out in the caves of the cane fields, down near the gulf, speak very little English. They trap, hunt, fish and work in the cane fields. Thousands of these can be reached only in the French or a dialect of French. One way of doing this is by radio. Eleven stations now carry the message by transcription, sponsored by the Southern Baptists, and many of the people have been won to the Lord.

Then there is the large, sadly neglected Indian group, ostracized from all others because of mixed marriages. Some Christian work has been done among them. Sunday schools have been established as well as some churches. The work, however, is limited. While some restrictions have been lifted, there is still a great need to help them get established as American citizens. But greater still is the need to love them and bring to them the hope of salvation.

There are the young people, the business and professional men who are floundering and can be reached only through personal evangelism.

The "fringe" people, whose occupation is largely fishing or trapping, the majority of whom are illiterate, are still a neglected people. There is need for Christian teachers who will live with them, teach them how to read and write, and show them that God loves them.

French missionaries especially are needed who will go out among the people, in the interior as well as on the bayous, bringing to all the message of salvation.

BIBLIOGRAPHY

KANE, HARNETT T. *Bayous of Louisiana.* New York: William Morrow & Co., 1943.

————. *Deep Delta Country.* Boston: Little, Brown & Co., 1944.

MANT, ST. A. *History of Louisiana Baptists.*

Louisiana, a guide book. Compiled by Federal Writers' Project and WPA.

Mississippi Gulf Coast. Federal Writers' Project and WPA.

The Mormon Temple and statue of Joseph Smith, Salt Lake City. (Courtesy of United Air Lines.)

9

Is Mormonism Biblical?

GORDON H. FRASER

History and Development

MORMONISM HAD ITS GENESIS in the supposed visions of Joseph Smith in Palmyra, New York. On September 21, 1823, the angel Moroni is supposed to have appeared to Smith and directed him to a spot on a nearby hillside where he would find, buried in a cement chest, golden plates on which were inscribed the record of the people who inhabited the American continents in olden times. This record would disclose the "restored gospel." Smith was indicated by Moroni as the prophet by whom the message would be revealed to the world.[1]

On the third anniversary of the vision, Smith was permitted to remove the plates together with a device called by Smith the Urim and Thummim, which consisted of prisms mounted in spectacle frames, by means of which Smith was enabled to translate the "reformed Egyptian" characters in which the message was written.

On March 26, 1830, the first edition came from the press,[2] whereupon Smith announced himself as "Seer, Translator, a Prophet, an

GORDON H. FRASER first came into touch with the Mormons in 1932 while doing missionary work under the American Sunday-School Union in western Washington. Since then he has had numerous contacts with the Mormon Church in eastern Idaho, Utah and Arizona. These contacts include presidents of two of the sects of Mormonism. He has had personal interviews with many who have been delivered from Mormonism and with several authorities on Mormon doctrine who are still Mormons. He is author of the book *Is Mormonism Christian?* published by Moody Press. Mr. Fraser is also founder and president of Southwestern School of Missions among the Indians.

[1] *Pearl of Great Price*, p. 89.
[2] Printed by E. B. Grandin, Palmyra, N. Y.

Apostle of Jesus Christ, and Elder of the Church through the will of God and the grace of your Lord Jesus Christ."

The church was organized April 6, 1830, in the home of Peter Whitmer at Fayette, Seneca County, New York, with six members: three Smiths, two Whitmers and Oliver Cowdery, who had served as Smith's scribe. Smith and Cowdery ordained each other as the spiritual leaders of the church, and then laid hands on each other to impart the gift of the Holy Ghost. Orson Pratt, an early Mormon theologian, wrote of this event as follows:

> Thus was the Church of Christ once more restored to the earth, holding the keys of authority to bind, to loose, and to seal on earth and in heaven, according to the commandments and revelations of Jesus Christ.[3]

Soon after the founding of the church, Oliver Cowdery and a new convert, Parley Pratt, were ordained to carry the new gospel into the west. They soon found their way to the home of Sidney Rigdon in Ohio and presented him with a copy of the Book of Mormon. Rigdon feigned shocked amazement at the appearance of a "new Bible," but within a few hours had heralded it as a new revelation. Within a few weeks his entire congregation had been "converted" and baptized into the new sect.

Because of the reputation of the Smith family, the church was unable to thrive in Palmyra or Fayette. Soon after the addition of Rigdon's flock the entire church moved to Kirtland, Ohio, where headquarters were established and a temple built.

Missionaries were now sent throughout the country and a party pressed westward into Missouri. They reported excellent opportunities for colonization. In July, 1831, Smith and a party went west to investigate and, seeing the beauty and fertility of the country, Smith announced by means of a "revelation" that here, in western Missouri, Zion would be built and God's kingdom established in the earth.[4] The "gentile" Missourians felt otherwise. Almost immediately, trouble began to brew.

By September Smith was again in Kirtland, Ohio, busily engaged in getting a party of settlers off to Missouri to claim the country in the name of the Lord.[5]

---

[3] T. B. Stenhouse, *Rocky Mountain Saints* (London: Ward, Lock & Tyler, 1874), p. 33.
[4] *Doctrine and Covenants*, Sec. 57.
[5] *Ibid*, Sec. 64:26.

The next few years were spent by Smith in Kirtland, developing the theology of the church and devising what was called the "Order of Enoch." This had the semblance of a communistic society, which if it had succeeded would have placed all temporal goods in the hands of the church. The church had grown too large and too varied in its membership for this plan to succeed and the idea faded.

A bank was organized with Smith and Rigdon as the managing officers. The state authorities declined to give a charter for the bank, so it was organized as the Kirtland Safety Anti-Banking Society. One hundred and fifty thousand dollars of currency was printed, including Joseph Smith's famous three dollar bill.[6] There were no appreciable assets to back the currency and it was soon selling for twelve and a half cents on the dollar.

It was discovered by certain inquisitive souls that an array of cardboard boxes lining the shelves of the banking office, and each labeled $1,000, contained nothing more valuable than sand, shot and old iron.[7] Smith staved off disaster for a while, but because of threats of violence he and Sidney Rigdon left Kirtland on horseback between dark and dawn on January 12, 1838. They headed for Missouri, never again to return to Kirtland.

The first whispers of polygamy were heard about this time. This, together with the financial dealings of Smith, made the Mormons unpopular and another move was indicated.

Meanwhile matters had grown worse in Missouri. Smith and his associates spent considerable time in jail on various charges. Finally, after much feuding and considerable bloodletting on both sides, the "saints" were driven out of Missouri.

A new start was made by the church on the Illinois side of the Mississippi. Nauvoo was built and established as Zion, and a new temple was started but never completed.

Matters were never harmonious in Nauvoo. During the five years that the church remained there, abuses and scandals increased. Factionalism developed, principally because of polygamy, which was being promoted secretly but denied openly. A faction that had a sharper moral conscience brought the issue to the surface by the publication of an opposition newspaper, the Nauvoo *Expositor*.

[6] Fawn M. Brodie, *No Man Knows My History* (New York: Alfred A. Knopf, Inc.), pp. 195-198.
[7] *Ibid.*, pp. 196, 197.

Smith was incensed at being thus exposed within his own camp and ordered the press destroyed and the type melted. This was done before a second issue of the paper could be printed, whereupon the state authorities stepped in and ordered Smith's arrest. Smith managed to hide out for a period of weeks, but finally gave himself up and was placed in jail at Carthage, Ill., on charges ranging from disorderly conduct to murder.

A mob stormed the jail on the afternoon of June 27, 1844, overpowered the jailers and broke into Smith's cell. A gun fight ensued in which Joseph's brother, Hyrum, was instantly killed and another companion, John Taylor, wounded. Smith, to whom a revolver had been smuggled, fired into the mob, reportedly killing three and wounding two others before he was fatally injured by his assailants.[8]

The Mormons by now had become completely unwelcome in Illinois, as they had been earlier in Ohio and New York State. With their prophet dead, they became temporarily demoralized. Several new prophets arose, each armed with a supposed vision, claiming to be successors to the prophet Joseph. Each got a small following and five of these sects still survive, each claiming to be the true church.[9]

Brigham Young had himself elected president of the church, and dispensing with the necessity of a revelation or a vision, organized the church for its trek westward to Utah. The celebrated "hand-cart march" of the "saints" has been overglamorized by the Mormon historians. Actually it was a debacle of major proportions, in which the poorly equipped and poorly advised migrants perished by the hundreds along the way. It has been estimated that probably one-half the marchers either died of starvation or returned east in disgust. Others continued west and left the church as soon as they were able to do so, joining non-Mormon wagon trains that were bound for Oregon or California.

A hardy group survived and established the church in the valley of the Salt Lake. Brigham Young, ruthless but capable, and surrounded by a small group of devoted henchmen, forged the church into an almost irresistible religio-political organization that in turn had a complete hold on the commerce and banking of the area.

---

[8] *History of the Church* (Mormon), IV, 617, 618. John D. Lee, *The Mormon Menace*, p. 195.
[9] Gordon H. Fraser, *Is Mormonism Christian?* (Chicago: Moody Press), pp. 9-11.

Polygamy was now completely unrestrained and the last of Joseph Smith's "revelations," Section 132, was made the law of the church in this regard.[10]

Young died in 1877, but he was capably succeeded by three presidents who had come west with Young and had been companions of Joseph Smith. These were Lorenzo Snow, John Taylor and Wilford Woodruff. Utah was denied statehood because of the practice of polygamy, and finally Wilford Woodruff issued a "manifesto"[11] suspending the practice.

With the suspension of polygamy the church grew more rapidly until it achieved its present success.

The church is governed by a president and two co-presidents or counselors. The president presides over a quorum of twelve apostles, who in turn are assisted by a quorum of seventy. The church is divided into "stakes," which are geographical divisions, each ruled by a president, his counselors, twelve apostles and seventy. The stake is divided into "wards," each with its president, counselors, twelve and seventy. There is also a system of patriarchs descending in the same order. Their office is to dispense blessings on those who merit them.

At the age of eight children are baptized, at twelve boys become eligible to the office of deacon (the Aaronic priesthood), at eighteen they become eligible to the Melchizedek priesthood. They are then elders and can embark on their tour of duty as missionaries.

It is the plan of the church that every man have an office. When the ward grows to the point where all offices are filled (approximately 250), the ward divides and a new congregation is formed on a geographical basis.

Missionary Efforts

Very little effective missionary work has ever been done among the Mormons. During the early days of Mormonism, 1830-1870, the evangelical bodies were kept busy founding churches as the frontier moved westward. The Mormons were left strictly alone as being unreachable. Then, as now, the churches were satisfied to keep their members from joining the aggressive Mormons.

---

[10] *Doctrine and Covenants*, Sec. 132.
[11] *Ibid.*, following Sec. 136.

In 1869 the army marched west to suppress the Mormon threats of rebellion, to give protection to "gentiles" living in Utah, and to prevent such Mormon depredations as the Mountain Meadows Massacre, which had occurred in 1857.[12]

An army chaplain, Rev. Norman McLeod, was invited to hold services for the few Christians in the Salt Lake area. Sunday schools were started at the army camp and in the city. Dr. John Robinson, an Army surgeon, became superintendent of these two efforts.[13]

McLeod went east to secure missionary support. During his absence Dr. Robinson was waylaid and clubbed to death and a warning sent to McLeod not to return.[14] The work was continued by the U. S. district attorney Major Charles Hempstead. The Sunday schools were later absorbed by the Episcopal Church which, in 1867, established the first formal worship in the territory under the direction of two clergymen, Thomas W. Haskins and George W. Foote.

The Episcopalians had little success with the Mormons, but did maintain a foothold for the Christian forces in Salt Lake. A later clergyman, Bishop F. S. Spalding, made a lasting contribution to the enlightenment of the public in his publication of the paper, *Joseph Smith Jr. as a Translator*,[15] which is a potent exposé of the ridiculous claims of the Mormons' sacred book, *The Pearl of Great Price*. This Joseph Smith claimed to have translated from papyri found on an Egyptian mummy purchased from a traveling showman named Chandler.[16]

In 1869 two Presbyterian missionaries, Sheldon Jackson and Melancthon Hughes, held their first service at Corinne, Utah, and a church with nine members was organized in 1870. The Presbyterians in Salt Lake City pleaded for help, and in 1871 Rev. Josiah Welch arrived. He held services in a room over a livery stable.[17] This was the start of an aggressive missionary effort which resulted in the conversion of many Mormons and the establishment of over forty missions within a decade.

As the territory became populated by non-Mormons, the church

[12] *Schaff-Herzog Encyclopedia*, 1953 ed. VIII, 17.
[13] *Ibid.*, p. 20.
[14] *Ibid.*, p. 20; *Holy Murder* (Kelly & Birney), pp. 228–230.
[15] F. S. Spalding, *Joseph Smith, Jr. as a Translator*.
[16] Fawn M. Brodie, *No Man Knows My History* (New York: Alfred A. Knopf), p. 170.
[17] *Schaff-Herzog Encyclopedia*, 1953 ed., VIII, 20.

gradually transferred its efforts to the newcomers, so that by the beginning of the new century the missionary phase of their work diminished. The Mormons by this time had achieved a degree of respectability with the outlawing of polygamy and were experiencing tremendous growth. The tide turned against the Protestant churches, and of the more than fifty Presbyterian churches of the 1880's, not more than ten have survived.

The Baptists came to Utah in 1881.[18] While their testimony was a positive one, they had only nominal success among the Mormons. They have shared the fate of the Presbyterians.

The first and only extensive work directed solely toward the conversion of the Mormons was that of the Utah Gospel Mission. This was headed by John D. Nutting, who labored for fifty years in Utah and Idaho. Nutting and his associates worked through the country as itinerant missionaries using horse-drawn gospel wagons, and finally Model T Fords. These men worked in teams of two, adopting the tactics of the Mormons. Hence they were respected, if hated, and made considerable headway. It was difficult to recruit missionaries for this difficult work and with the retirement of Nutting the work was finally discontinued.[19]

One hardy character of this period, probably either an associate of Nutting or one of the Presbyterians, has become a legend. He was Rev. Duncan McMillan, who preached with an American flag draped over a dry-goods box for a pulpit, with his Bible on one side and a six-shooter on the other.

At the present time only two organized efforts are being directed toward the conversion of the Mormons. One of these, the Utah Christian Tract Society, has as its directors Mr. and Mrs. Arthur Budvarsen and as its field missionaries Mr. and Mrs. Einar Anderson. All are converted Mormons.[20] The other is the Christian Tract Society, directed by Mr. and Mrs. Harry McGimsey.[21]

Both societies major in a printed-page ministry, using highly specialized literature. The Utah Christian Tract Society has a special ministry in reaching those who are in danger of being ensnared in the Mormon cult. They carry on an extensive correspondence

18 *Ibid.*
19 *Light on Mormonism* (Utah Gospel Mission).
20 Utah Christian Tract Society, Box 725, LaMesa, Calif.
21 Christian Tract Society, P.O. Box 1311, Phoenix, Ariz.

work both with Mormons and those threatened by Mormonism. Mr. McGimsey's work is in literature distribution carried on by personal contact. Together with volunteer workers he covers the Mormon Church conventions in Salt Lake City and other Mormon gatherings wherever possible. His teams also do concentrated visitation work in the solidly Mormon towns of the mountain area.

Methods of Dealing with Mormons

In approaching evangelistic work among Mormons, two distinct needs must be considered. Each of these calls for different methods and preparation.

The most urgent need is that of salvaging those who are in the process of being indoctrinated by the Mormons. Since most of these are members of Protestant churches, it will be seen that this is largely the task of local pastors and their personal workers.

The urgency of this need will be evident when one realizes that some 15,000 Mormon workers have, at all times, an estimated 500,000 inquirers under weekly indoctrination.

These inquirers are usually the infrequent attenders at church services, and their defection will often remain undetected until it is too late. They are often attracted by the sincerity and friendliness of the Mormon missionaries and will come to their defense when approached by their pastor or a Christian worker. They will also usually insist that the Mormon instructors be present at any interview, which makes it necessary for the Christian worker to be prepared to deal not only with the defecting church member but with a shrewd, ruthless and calculating Mormon teacher who is a past master in the art of argument and evasion. The Mormon worker is trained in the knowledge of the doctrines and phraseology of the denomination involved. This is a deliberate tactic that is studied carefully in the Mormon training program.

As soon as Mormon missionaries are detected in a given area, the churches should immediately be alerted, as the missionaries are never sent into an area unless the church estimates that a Mormon congregation can be recruited. They always seek to proselyte their members rather than to draw them from the unchurched population.

If possible the evangelical churches should join in a campaign to alert their members and to instruct their workers in methods of dealing with the problem. If possible, a worker thoroughly familiar with Mormon doctrine and practices should be asked to hold instruction classes. A canvass should then be made to ascertain which of the members are being visited by the Mormons. Suitable literature should be distributed liberally throughout the area. Such literature is available from the tract societies mentioned.

In dealing with Mormons themselves there is no substitute for persistent, repeated calling on individuals and families. It may take months of such calling to win an individual from Mormonism. Since this is the method used by the Mormons, it is the only method they will respect. It is usually purposeless to get them to attend public services.

Suitable tracts will often arouse their interest and gain an opening, but these must be followed by personal visitation, since the average Mormon is so completely insulated against "gentile" doctrines that he will obstinately resent the suggestion that there is any "gospel truth" other than his own.

It is impossible, in the space allotted, to go into a detailed discussion of the lengthy process of dealing with the various types of individual cases. In lieu of this, the Christian worker should make a thorough study of the Christian doctrines for which the Mormons have a corresponding doctrine, bearing in mind that the Mormon has a carefully worded statement, in the language of orthodoxy, to cover each of his doctrines.

The worker should be thoroughly familiar with the Mormon sacred books,[22] bearing in mind that when a Mormon quotes "scripture" he will blend Bible verses with quotations from his own scriptures.

The worker should be familiar with the gross discrepancies of the Mormon books to realize that their books are contradictory within themselves.[23] This is a vulnerable point with the Mormons.

The worker should be familiar with the history of Mormonism.[24] The Mormon is very proud of his history, but in the case of many Mormons, this is due to the fact that he has had only the Mormon version of the stories of Joseph Smith and Brigham Young.

---

[22] *The Book of Mormon; The Pearl of Great Price; Doctrine and Covenants.*
[23] Gordon H. Fraser, *Is Mormonism Christian?* (Chicago: Moody Press), pp. 17, 19, 37-39.
[24] Fawn M. Brodie, *No Man Knows My History* (New York: Alfred A. Knopf).

If the Mormon can be made to question the veracity of his sacred books and the impeccability of his prophet, he is half won.

There is much literature on the subject, but unfortunately it has not been produced by the Christian press. A small start has been made in this field by Christian writers. The bibliography appended will serve as a guide. Since the Mormons make it a practice to seek out and destroy books unfavorable to them, it is a good habit to accumulate a small library on the subject for future reference. Some volumes have now become almost unavailable because of this practice of the Mormons. This is true of library books as well as those in used bookstores. The writer and his associates are accumulating a library of Mormon paraphernalia so that it may be available for research.

BIBLIOGRAPHY

Helps for Christian Workers

FRASER, GORDON H. *Is Mormonism Christian?* Chicago: Moody Press, 1957.
Light on Mormonism. Cleveland: Utah Gospel Mission.
SPAULDING, F. S. *Joseph Smith as Translator.* Private printing.

History of Mormonism

BRODIE, FAWN M. *No Man Knows My History.* New York: Alfred A. Knopf, Inc., 1945.
EVANS, JOHN HENRY. *Joseph Smith, An American Prophet.* New York: The Macmillan Co., 1933.
HOWE, E. D. *Mormonism Unveiled.* Published by author in 1840. Rare.
KIDDER, DANIEL P. *Mormonism and the Mormons.* 1842. Rare.
LEE, JOHN D. *The Mormon Menace.* Printed privately. Rare.
LINN, WILLIAM A. *Story of the Mormons.* New York: The Macmillan Co., 1902.
Holy Murder, The Story of Porter Rockwell. New York: Kelly & Birney, 1934.

Mormon Works

Doctrine and Covenants. Salt Lake City: Deseret Book Store.
History of the Church of Jesus Christ of Latter Day Saints, 8 Vols. Salt Lake City: Deseret Book Store.
Pearl of Great Price. Salt Lake City: Deseret Book Store.

King Follett Discourse. Salt Lake City: Zion's Book Store.

SMITH, JOSEPH. *Book of Mormon*. Salt Lake City: Deseret Book Store, 1920.

Commencement of the college division of the School of the Ozarks, Hollister, Mo. These young people of the Ozark mountains have earned all of their expenses at the School of the Ozarks, and most of them return as Christian citizens to live and minister among the people of their home communities.

Children's homes are an important feature of many mountain mission works. Here boys and girls of the Dessie Scott Children's Home, Pine Ridge, Kentucky, enjoy a recreation period.

10

The Highlanders

GARLAND FRANKLIN

T HE HARDY AMERICANS of the fascinating Appalachian and Ozark Mountain areas have a common origin. In the beginning they were Scotch-Irish Presbyterians, English Nonconformists, German Lutherans and French Huguenots. Since the predominating element was Scotch-Irish we will refer to them as such in this chapter. They settled not only in the southern highlands, but also in the Ozarks as they pushed on in their westward march. These elevated areas are highlands and their homogeneous people will be referred to as highlanders.

Immigration of Highlanders

In the eighteenth century thousands of Protestant Scotch-Irish came to this country from the north of Ireland. Caused by economic pressure and religious persecution, this movement resulted in what is referred to as the "transplantation of Ulster."

Settling at first in the region of Philadelphia, many eventually

GARLAND FRANKLIN was born in Knott County, Kentucky, where he lived as a boy until after the death of his parents. Leaving the mountains, he went to high school in Bedford, Ohio, and graduated in Mason, Michigan. During a return visit to Kentucky he was converted, and then had a greater desire than ever to secure an education. After two years at Northern Baptist Seminary, he entered Wheaton College and was graduated in 1931.

The call of God back to the mountains came unmistakably while pastoring a church in Glen Ellyn, Illinois. When Mr. Franklin arrived in Kentucky, others joined him in the work and Scripture Memory Mountain Mission was formed, of which he has been director until recently. He has also had a vital part in the National Home Missions Fellowship.

pushed south and west where more individual freedom could be found.

The Scotch-Irish, being used to a hilly terrain, found their way down the Great Valley of Virginia. They came for the most part by caravans on pack horses, oxcarts and mule teams. The great Appalachian region, often referred to as the Southern Mountains, extends over portions of nine states: Maryland, Virginia, West Virginia, Kentucky, Tennessee, North Carolina, South Carolina, Georgia and Alabama.

This elevated region is approximately 700 miles in length and about 200 miles in width. Even though the population is constantly shifting because of the economic situation, recent figures show that no less than seven million people live within the confines of this vast terrain.

In the beginning, these adventuresome people were hunters, explorers, fighters — and finally settlers. They found the land uninhabited except for the roving Indians and the roaming wildlife. Here was a virgin forest with untold wealth in timber and with coal in abundance beneath their feet. Yet their first interest was game.

It was these same Scotch-Irish who afterward continued their westward advance across the Ohio and the Mississippi Rivers into the Ozark country. While there are topographical similarities between these elevations, there are also some contrasts. The hills of the Ozarks are not as high as the mountains of Appalachia. They have more gentle slopes and yet breath-taking declivities, gems of scenic beauty. This stretch of territory extends through southwestern Illinois, southern Missouri, northern Arkansas and eastern Oklahoma. It is roughly estimated that the population in the Ozarks is now about 1,500,000. This country is sometimes referred to as the "Ozark Empire," meaning it is a little world in itself representing independent thought.

Isolation of Highlanders

Surrounded as they were by an almost impenetrable wilderness and by high mountain walls, the Scotch-Irish were hemmed in for generations both in the Appalachians and the Ozarks. For over 150 years there were scarcely any decent wagon roads. The creek and the road were wedded. When the creek was not in the road, the road was in the creek. Communications were non-existent except for the grapevine telephone. News passed along was distorted.

Under these conditions life slowed down; social intercourse was limited; schools were few if any, and far between. The literacy of the Scotch-Irish gave way to illiteracy. There was potential for a high degree of education, character, and leadership, yet the opportunity for development was wanting. The descendants of the Scotch-Irish were educated in everything except books. Circumscribed life resulted in close intermarriage and inbreeding, which in turn affected life's potential.

The following description of the people of the Ozarks has equal application to the people of Appalachia: "Up to about fifty years ago, well within the lifetime of persons now living, the Ozarker was self-contained and self-independent. He ground his own corn. His women spun their own thread, made their own clothes. He distilled his own whiskey. Crude furniture was made by whittling, and chairs were seated with twisted withes of willow or untanned oxhides. Houses were built by unskilled labor, and I have seen and spent hours in a four-room log cabin with two massive stone chimneys built by unskilled mountaineers as late as 1932. Bedspread coverlets there were elaborately made out of patchwork pieces or woven. Many days in the year were spent in the woods near-by, restocking the scanty larder with squirrels, rabbits, deer or possums. The life of the Ozarks was wild and primitive, but not without its savor."[1]

Isolation and neglect led to further decline. Lack of employment may have accounted for much self-employment in moonshining and bootlegging. Dram drinking, which leads to drunkenness, has often been the occasion for festering wounds to break open between neighbors. The best marksman remained, while his enemy went to a premature grave. The mountaineer in the absence of protection by law has often been left to defend himself.

These non-conformists were people of principle but they were cut off by natural barriers; consequently they were neglected mentally, physically, and spiritually. Even though the light of the gospel grew dim, they never departed from their faith in God and the Bible as His Word. "There is no infidelity native to the Appala-

[1] John Gould Fletcher, *Arkansas, A Look Around the Land* (Chapel Hill: University of North Carolina Press, 1947), pp. 7, 8.

chians. An infidel is an imported monstrosity. The only heresy is that of conduct. Men believe in the Bible as the only infallible rule of faith and practice."² This is also true of the native Ozarkians.

Independence of Highlanders

Since the early settlers were largely on their own, living in seclusion and solitude, they depended on no man. Every man carried his own gun, which was as common a weapon as his barlow knife. He fought off his enemies — both man and beast. He grew his own corn, beans, potatoes and tomatoes on his semi-vertical farm. Some farms, especially in the Appalachians, "are so steep that you can look up the chimney and see the cows coming home at evening time." These mountains have isolated and divided people. Each valley has its own bias, traditionally, politically and religiously.

The mountaineer loves his mountains. Here, regardless of struggles, he has found liberty, leisure, and life close to nature. His environment has developed in him an utterly independent spirit. Individualism is so strong it is difficult to rally the public in a cooperative effort.

Modern Communications Enlighten

With the coming of modern roads and more rapid transportation, geographical and psychological barriers are beginning to dissolve while people mingle more frequently and freely. As horizons are lifted the mountaineer's world is being stretched. Tourists, radio, and more recently television have brought their evils but also their education.

Advancement of Highlanders

In the final analysis, no man lives to himself. When he must do so out of dire necessity, he suffers inestimably in every phase of his life. While there has been some decline, there are encouraging signs upon the horizon. Education has been made available for every youth capable of receiving it. Depleted farms fail to produce body-building foods or adequate quality and quantity, but supermarkets have come in, bringing fresh vegetables and supplies. With over-population in many sections and general unemployment, the problem is where to find money to purchase the necessary food.

---

² Samual Tyndall Wilson, *The Southern Mountaineers* (New York: Literature Department, Presbyterian Home Missions, 1906), p. 23.

Lack of food, particularly of the right sort, causes malnutrition, leads to disease and mental apathy.

The economic dilemma has been so serious at times that the government has had to feed a starving society. Certain sections of the Appalachians have become the number one nursery of the nation. This very practice, if continued, will change a self-reliant people into beggars and dependent mendicants. There should be some other way out.

The people of the Ozarks, having more moderately sloping farms, can do more cultivating and cattle raising. While they do not have coal in abundance, they do have beef, chicken, sheep, turkey and dairy farms. Many small industries, finding a non-violent, fair labor climate, have moved in, thereby giving employment. This provides a supplementary income to small farmers. Ten sheep can be maintained as cheaply as one cow. Mountain cliffs and coves provide an ideal habitat for sheep.

Both areas have superb scenic beauty with moderate climates. These, coupled with the man-made lakes or dams, are bringing more tourists, especially into the Ozarks. Many elderly people from nearby cities and elsewhere are building homes in this area.

The mining of bituminous coal in the southern mountains has brought a certain amount of prosperity. There have, however, been strikes causing coal shortages, which have forced industry to find other kinds of fuel. This has had a crippling effect on the coal industry itself. The violence occurring during strikes has made it difficult, if not impossible, for industries to come in. Men will not invest their money in an environment where they may have their factories blown up overnight.

All of this has led to an exodus from the mountains. Capable school teachers, ambitious young couples, enterprising youth are leaving these sections for areas of better employment. Only when better economic conditions are created can this outflow of choice manhood be retained for our mountain society.

Evangelization of Highlanders

The rugged Scotch-Irish were largely Presbyterians. Presbyterians have always emphasized education, both for the ministry and among the mountain people. Their standards have been high, their accomplishments many in the founding of academies, colleges and

churches. From a recent annual report of the Board of Church
Extension, Atlanta, Georgia, we quote:

"Every Presbytery having territory within the Appalachian and
Ozark Mountain areas is seeking to provide a more adequate spiritual ministry for its mountain people by organizing Sunday schools
and establishing churches where needed, and by providing evangelists, ministers and pioneer workers to carry on the work. In the
early days of mountain missions many schools were established
in isolated communities for the training of children. In time most
of these schools were taken over by the state. The mountain schools
which remain, though few in number, are providing an opportunity
for more than a thousand boys and girls to prepare for Christian
leadership in every walk of life."

The Presbyterians, however, seemed to lack the emotional warmth
and fiery evangelistic spirit that appealed so much to a people
seeking freedom from the formalism of the established church.
Even though the Presbyterians had strength, they were destined to
be outnumbered by the Baptists and Methodists who were soon
to follow over the pioneer trail.

After the Revolutionary War Baptist preachers began moving
west into Tennessee and Kentucky. At times whole congregations
came along. Before long there were new churches and associations
springing up in the West. In time they made such headway that
they won many of the Presbyterians to their Baptist belief and
practice. Baptists stood for education, but they also believed a man
could be saved on Saturday night, receive a call to preach and
begin on Sunday morning. They have become the most numerous
of any denomination in the highlands as well as in the South generally. Their method and objective are expressed by J. Edward
Cunningham of Campton, Kentucky:

"We seek to establish a church-centered mission program, whereby a stronger church seeks to promote missions throughout the
entire area. We dream of the time when every person living in the
mountains can attend a Baptist church or mission if he so desires.
One of our major goals has been accomplished in that we have a
strong Baptist church in every county seat town; however, some
of these are still not self-supporting."

"Methodism was a comparatively late comer to America and

arrived still later in the Appalachian mountains."[3] According to history, about one-third of all the Methodist preachers in America in 1784 were laboring in North Carolina. One of these was Francis Asbury, a pioneer itinerant preacher to most of the people in Appalachia.

One of the older native groups, especially in Kentucky, is the Old Regular Baptists. They sing without accompaniment; the preacher as a rule lines off the stanzas while the congregation joins with him in the singing. During the song the preacher and the Christians often move about shaking hands and embracing one another.

When all this subsides it is time for the "preachin" to begin. Each preacher defers in favor of the other half dozen on the platform until someone is finally prevailed upon to commence. While they are deliberating, the audience will have a spell of whispering and visiting between themselves. The service, however, has not been interrupted.

Now the preacher is ready to begin, in a low tone of voice. He has no particular text or theme. He will "tetch" upon a little of everything from Genesis to Revelation. When once he feels inspired he may run his words together so that they are no longer discerned, but this is the climax of the "purty meetin." Before he has finished a fellow preacher leads out in another song, usually about loved ones who are beckoning us from heaven's golden shore, and another round of hand clasping begins. The meeting has only started. You see, the Old Regulars don't have weekly worship services in each one of their "meetin' houses." This is the monthly meeting time. Beginning on Saturday as a rule they will wind up Sunday noon.

While there has been much good accomplished through the Old Regulars, who bear down hard on sin, repentance, forgiveness and judgment, there is much to be desired. They have neglected their youth, since they believe that children must first grow up before they can be converted. Sunday schools and youth meetings are frowned upon. There is opposition to missions, as well as to an educated and financially supported preacher. As a friend said, "The people of the mountains want preaching without responsibil-

---

[3] W. D. Weatherford, *Religion in the Appalachian Mountains* (Berea: Berea College), p. 19.

ity." They are not to blame, for they have been taught to "sit" rather than to "serve."

Some of the native religious groups are very emotional and fanatical. These seem to appeal to the less intelligent and more unstable. Even though a law was passed in Kentucky in 1940 forbidding the handling of venomous snakes in connection with religious worship, the practice is still carried on, despite snake bites, horrible deaths, arrests, fines and imprisonments.

Only in the last twenty-five years have Catholics made much headway in the more isolated mountain districts. Recently they have been buying up hospitals in small cities, ministering to the sick, opening parochial schools to educate the young, and establishing Catholic churches. Catholic images and pictures are sometimes sold in most unexpected places and are frequently found in Protestant homes where religious sentiment is desired.

In spite of all that has been done, "the percentage of church members is below the general average, being variously estimated from 20 to 30 per cent. While there is an indigenous ministry, it is inadequate both in numbers and in training. The churches have never been self-supporting according to an adequate standard and are fast losing their power to hold the people, particularly the youth. There is an obvious need for well-trained persons to be sent across the barriers from the stronger churches to the mountain people, to evangelize and train them with the aim of strengthening the ministry and developing strong self-supporting churches. The four million unchurched in the southern mountains constitute probably the largest single home mission field."[4]

Indigenous Leadership Needed. Only as pastors and other Christian leaders are developed from among the people, and churches supported by their congregations assume the task of evangelism, will there be promise of success.

Having labored for twenty-five years in the Ozarks, the Rev. Floyd Hitchcock, who has the daily broadcast "Faith of Our Fathers," writes: "Here in the Ozarks we have many church houses, but very few churches which are well organized and functioning as churches should. The union church idea is very prevalent

[4] H. C. Goerner, *America Must Be Christian* (Atlanta, Ga.: Missions Board of Southern Baptist Convention), p. 75.

here. This free-for-all idea, however, does not protect them in their property rights or from the danger of heresy and false doctrines, which often creep in.

"After years of experience here in the hills, my observation is that what we need more than anything else is a trained native leadership made up of native converts who will make real sacrifice in an effort to reach their own people with the gospel.

"This presents a real problem, however, because when native converts need training they have to leave the Ozarks to get it by going to some Bible school in Kansas City, St. Louis, Chicago, Philadelphia, or somewhere else; and by the time they receive their training they have their sights on bigger things and more productive fields and we lose them from the Ozarks completely. The other danger is when trained workers come to us from the outside, they do not understand the people here in the Ozarks and say and do things which disqualify them for the work they are striving to do." To those who are acquainted with the situation it is apparent that these observations apply equally and in every particular to the Appalachian area as well.

Reaching Young People. There are an ever increasing number of interdenominational workers entering these mountain fields with a vision to reach youth. They have found a "great and effectual door" open in the public schools, where both whites and colored are contacted. Chapel services, consisting of cheerful singing, special music, followed by a visual aid lesson or an interesting Bible story, are held. The children are attentive and responsive. They can hardly wait until the Bible teachers come again to tell them more from God's Book. A worker visiting schools regularly may have from one to two thousand children as his parish.

Realizing the need for a closer personal touch with these promising youngsters, many faith organizations have developed camps where the children can go each summer and receive a week of Bible instruction. In many instances children earn their way by memorizing selected Bible verses. Scripture portions, Christian story books, and plaques are among the first awards, but the grand prize for the child is a free week at camp. Through learning "the way of salvation" verses the children are prepared for an intelligent decision for Christ as the evangelistic message is given in camp.

Children like camp, talk about it to their classmates and are
eager to memorize more verses so as to return. Christian teaching
is given to those who know Christ with a view to discipleship. As
a result of these repeated camp experiences there is, on the part of
some, an evidence of Christian growth. Out of this number there
are those who, if encouraged, become counselors and soul-winners
in camp. Disciples are in the making. From this sifted-down group
will rise up choice young people who go in for Christian training
and out into Christian service. These are splendid indigenous
workers now serving the Lord among their own people in the highlands. Still others have heard the faraway Macedonian call and are
serving on foreign fields.

Bible conferences are being held on these same camp grounds for
the upbuilding of the spiritual life of Christians. Outstanding Bible
teachers are secured, vital messages given, so that Christians are
beginning to see what Christ can do in and through their lives as
they surrender all to Him.

An Example. The work of Scripture Memory Mountain Mission
might be used as an example of this type of ministry, which is
being carried on in various places in the southern mountains.

The work of this mission, while not limited to youth, has largely
centered around the young. From the beginning, schools have been
visited, children have memorized Bible verses and have received
awards, including a Gospel of John, a New Testament, a story
book, a Bible, and a week at camp. Children in these rural areas
still have time to memorize God's Word. There has been great
interest and response, with hundreds getting through to camp.

Camp Nathanael, nestling on the banks of Troublesome Creek,
has been developed from a cow pasture into a campus. In this
scenic and serene setting many children, young people and adults
have been taught evangelism, principles of Christian living and
missions.

Monthly Bible conferences for various age groups are scheduled,
as well as two general Bible conferences annually. "The Voice of
Camp Nathanael," a weekly broadcast, has been beaming the
gospel to the people of this area for years.

As many as fifty vacation Bible schools are conducted simultaneously with the summer camps. A youth leadership conference

for upper high school and college age trains camp counselors and future leaders. Back in the rural communities, Sunday schools and churches are established and related ministries carried on.

As a result, many have been won to Christ, witnesses have gone out, young people have dedicated their lives to Christ for Christian service and, after training, have entered either home or foreign missionary service.

Realizing the need for keeping young people in their native environment for training, some Bible schools have been raised up in the South. Among these are the Southland Bible Institute in Kentucky, the Appalachian Bible Institute in West Virginia, and the Carver Bible Institute for Negroes in Georgia.

All of this, however, is no substitute for the indigenous church and its importance. Unless denominational and interdenominational workers alike keep the New Testament standard ever before them, they will never turn out New Testament products. Without these stalwart Scotch-Irish being transformed into veritable epistles of Christ, the mountaineers will still remain unevangelized and unenlightened in the gospel.

BIBLIOGRAPHY

CAMPBELL, JOHN C. *The Southern Highlander and His Home-Land*. New York: Russell Sage Foundation, 1921.

FLETCHER, JOHN GOULD. *Arkansas, A Look Around the Land*. Chapel Hill: University of North Carolina Press, 1947.

GOERNER, H. C. *America Must Be Christian*. Atlanta: Missions Board of Southern Baptist Convention.

JOHNSON, MONTE. *The Presbyterians in Religion in the Appalachian Mountains*. Berea, Ky.: Berea College.

JUSTIN, WINSOR. *The Westward Movement*. Boston: Houghton, Mifflin and Co., 1897.

LODGE, HENRY CABOT. "The Distribution of Ability in the United States." *Century Magazine*, September, 1891.

WEATHERFORD, W. D. *Religion in the Appalachian Mountains*. Berea, Ky.: Berea College, 1955.

WILSON, SAMUEL TYNDALL. *The Southern Mountaineers*. New York: Literature Department, Presbyterian Home Missions, 1906.

A rural church in Vermont

11

The Rural People

C. J. REDIGER

The History of Rural Missions

RURAL MISSIONS are not new. A study of the religious history of the American colonies indicates an ample amount of gospel preaching, at least in the established outposts. A strong sense of mission seemed to grip these early preachers.

"Pastors of parish churches felt an obligation to itinerate at intervals among remote settlements. [These] zealous preachers visited Cape Cod, pushed their way into the granite hills of New Hampshire, and traveled the inlets and rocky shores of Maine."[1]

The weakness of the pioneer ministry, however, was their lack of emphasis on the local church. The same author declares: "The people of the frontier were not without occasional preaching when the itinerant preachers came among them, but they lacked the church to conserve their emotion and make it fruitful."[2]

C. J. REDIGER, a native midwesterner, has had an unusual ministry. After serving a number of years as pastor of the Canton Gospel Tabernacle, he resigned to enter the ministry of rural missions. The Rural Home Missionary Association was the outgrowth of the labors of Mr. Rediger and his wife. From its founding in 1942 until 1958, when he left directorship of the mission, the work grew to the point where sixty missionaries were serving in fifteen states.

Mr. Rediger received his Bible training at the Chicago Evangelistic Institute, took some schooling at Brown's Business College in Bloomington, Illinois, and finished the business managers course at LaSalle Extension University.

[1] H. C. Rowe, *The History of Religion in the United States* (New York: Macmillan Co.).
[2] *Ibid.*

147

This deficiency was somewhat remedied by the spiritual leaders of the early nineteenth century. Various denominational societies united in a rural missionary enterprise. The Massachusetts and Connecticut Missionary Society, for instance, sent out two hundred missionaries and established four hundred churches. The American Sunday School Union was founded in 1817. The Congregationalists, Presbyterians, Reformed and the Baptists all formed a home missionary society reaching into the rural areas of that day. Thus a concerted and positive effort was made to conserve the fruit of gospel preaching by establishing Sunday schools and churches.

While the church continued its rural missions ministry throughout the closing years of the nineteenth century, the driving power which marked its early history was largely lost and the movement continued, with a few exceptions, by the sheer force of momentum. Consequently, the hinterlands of America were again largely left in the shadows by the year 1900.

With the dawn of the twentieth century, a new concept of rural mission activity began to develop. Independent and interdenominational rural mission agencies were born. The founders of these societies saw hundreds of rural communities where the spiritual needs were going unmet. There seemed to be no hope that these people ever would be reached short of a positive and unique effort in their behalf. Thus a new generation of Christians were awakened and challenged by the Spirit of God, and heard again the call of America's rural areas.

For purposes of this discussion, the term *rural* is used to describe all open countryside and villages up to 2,500 in population. With this as our starting point, we ask the question,

Why Rural Missions?

The simple answer is, to meet spiritual needs! The basic rural need is spiritual. While it is true that in some areas material needs are involved, it must be clearly stated that mission work is more than charity. The primary task of the rural missionary, therefore, is to touch those not being reached by the true gospel of God's saving grace.

The field of rural missions includes communities without an established church or with closed churches, both large and small.

It includes people of all ages: children who have never been to Sunday school, neglected teen-agers, careless and indifferent adults, and the bypassed shut-ins.

Sometimes the people in these communities could go to a nearby town to attend church, but since their parents lack interest the children receive no spiritual training or benefits. Only as the rural missionary comes into the area with the gospel do the people, both young and old, encounter an active witness for Christ.

The importance of the local church is recognized by home mission organizations, but though self-supporting churches may not be organized, the rural missionary still ministers to the needs of the people. His job is to reach those who are not being reached by any other group, regardless of cost or time involved. This means that he must evangelize. But he must follow evangelization with instruction. The convert must be thoroughly established in the Word of God to prepare him for spiritual life and service. As a result of this program, when a soul is saved, a life is also recruited for God's service.

A Closer Look at the Spiritual Need

A survey made by the Rural Bible Mission, Inc., of Kalamazoo, Michigan, of thirty counties in the state, showed over 50 per cent of the population did not attend any church or Sunday school — Catholic, Jewish or Protestant. It has been found that thousands of American villages are without an active church, and hundreds more are closing annually.[3]

The partial cause for this condition is the recent population shift to the cities. American farm population reached a peak about 1910.[4] Since then, farm population has dropped steadily. Because of this transition from country to city, rural churches have suffered serious losses in their effectiveness.

Another factor in this problem is urbanization. The consolidation of public schools also affects rural work tremendously. Naturally, people respond to this social development. For example, as rural children are brought to the consolidated or "town" school, they take on something of the attitude of their urban cousins. These customs

---

[3] *Why Missions in America?* (East Lynn, W. Va.: National Home Missions Fellowship), tract.
[4] The Christian Rural Fellowship Bulletin No. 202, New York, N. Y., p. 1.

and ideas may or may not be conducive to their spiritual development.

Various solutions have been proposed. Major denominations[5] are endeavoring to solve the difficulty by establishing a centralized church, or urging residents of such churchless communities to go elsewhere. In fact, some encourage the members of weak churches to close their doors and unite with the congregation of another church. To keep open the doors of a weak rural church is considered a waste of time and effort.

Another suggestion is the larger parish method. Under this plan, all churches within a given area are brought together on a purely voluntary basis, their resources are pooled, and the responsibility for their spiritual leadership is placed in the hands of a central staff. This staff works through the local leadership of each church and serves the needs of each within the limits of the available resources.

Still another plan is the group ministry. According to this idea, a bishop or board selects a number of ministers to co-operate in meeting the needs in one particular area. Each carries on his own pastoral duties, but also works with the other ministers in the task of redemption in the community.

Centralization of the rural church as a solution to its problems is suggested by both the liberal and conservative.[6] Regardless of these proposals, however, the need is not met, for the average rural community will not submit to these plans. Since most rural people are rather traditional, they prefer to remain in their own communities for their religious activities. It can be logically argued that they are at fault. But we must remember that when a certain tradition is established, it takes years to change it. Regardless of our personal feelings in relation to these facts, the simple conclusion remains unchanged. Rural people will not easily be herded together in larger town churches.

Some have suggested that, if they will not change, they ought to be left alone. This has indeed been done, and the results are evident. The experiences of home missionaries have shown the tragic fruit of this course. But they have also shown the encouraging response from rural people when we *refuse* to leave them alone.

---

[5] *Rural Life in the United States* (New York: Alfred A. Knopf, 1949), pp. 119, 120.
[6] *New Churches for a New America* (Wheaton, Ill.: National Association of Evangelicals).

The Importance of Rural America

Rural America, under God's blessing, has been a blessing to America. In years past, 85 per cent of the preachers and missionaries have come from rural areas. More than 48 per cent[7] of our preachers and missionaries have come from communities of less than 1,000 in population. Over 14 per cent have come from towns of 1,000 to 25,000 population. Out of sixty-three college presidents questioned, fifty-three were born in communities of less than 2,500. Seventy per cent of city church additions by transfer and 70 per cent of the board members of city churches have been from rural areas. These rural communities have been the backbone of American life.

This indicates that rural people are basically substantial and reliable. The reason is because rural life has consistently been more rugged than city life. The rural citizen is also something of an individualist. He thinks and acts for himself. It is true that some rural people tend to be lethargic and slow. Yet a good social program in the rural church, conducted on levels that meet scriptural standards, can help correct this deficiency, and can also help to retain something of the unique character and tradition of the countryside.

The Character of Rural Missionary Work

There is a difference between rural missions and other types of Christian service. First, compare the nature of the ministry in a small rural mission point to that of an established pastorate. The established church has a church schedule, a church board, and an operating program. This is not true in the small mission station. They have nothing. There is no live, interested, spiritual group of Christians, neither is there any machinery with which to work. This basic difference is tremendously important.

The work in a neglected rural community is carried on in different ways, depending on the policy of the mission doing the work. First, there are those missions that work toward a more or less permanent goal. Organizations such as the American Mission for Opening Closed Churches, Rural Home Missionary Association, Oak Hills Fellowship, Village Missions, and others enter into a needy com-

---

[7] Edwin Hunter, *The Small Town and Country Church* (Nashville: Abingdon-Cokesbury Press).

munity by placing a worker there who will serve as its spiritual leader. There are variations among the different groups, but the aim is somewhat the same.

The workers under these and similar boards begin in a closed church or some other available location. Since the goal, in many cases, is to establish a full church program, the missionary is very careful to lay a good foundation. To carry on a total program, mature Christians will be needed to assume places of responsibility, but these often must first be converted and trained.

The question of finances must also be faced. People must be taught to give, but this cannot be done until they have entered into a proper relationship with the Lord. This means that rural work is truly missionary work, for it must be paid for from the outside until it is able to carry its own responsibilities.

But there are other types of rural mission programs in addition to that of establishing rural churches. Representative societies of this other kind are the Rural Bible Crusade, Children's Bible Mission, Rural Bible Mission, "Go Ye" Mission, and others. Missionaries under these boards go into the public schools with a Bible memorization program, or conduct youth services in centrally located places.

Sunday schools which do not develop into churches are also a means used by some groups, especially the American Sunday-School Union. These organizations also conduct a summer camp program, where the children touched during the school term can be brought into closer relationship with the gospel of Christ. Many thousands are won to Christ by such organizations.

Here again the nature and character of rural work must be kept in mind. Many of these missionaries are living in communities that would appear outwardly to be typically American, yet they are ministering to woefully ignorant people concerning their one most important need — their relationship to God. It is indeed *mission* work.

Locating Needy Communities

It is most encouraging and interesting to observe how God has met the spiritual need in rural America through various agencies. The American Sunday-School Union discovers areas of opportunity through surveys, and by requests for spiritual aid from rural people themselves. The correspondent from the Oak Hills Fellowship reports that fields are located "by observing souls with compassionate hearts who, in some cases, could do nothing about the needs themselves, but who encouraged other missionary agencies and individuals to enter." The general secretary of the Rural Bible Crusade, Wheaton, Illinois, writes: "Men and women of spiritual burden and vision were quick to see the need and spiritual neglect in 'closed door' communities." The director of the Rural Bible Missions, Kalamazoo, Michigan, reports: "As evangelists were called to various areas to hold special services, they saw the many, many unreached people, especially the children. There are perhaps many ways of locating needs, but this was the way our mission saw the need."

Some twenty years ago, with a burden on my heart for the spiritually neglected rural areas, I resigned from an active pastorate to give myself to this work. Since I had been reared in a rural area myself, I felt a special call to minister to these people. Visiting a number of rural schools with another Christian worker, I found that a large percentage of the children did not attend Sunday school or church. Investigation revealed this to be a national condition. In addition to local areas, other needy communities were found by personal investigation, or "leads" from some individual. Because of a special burden for a certain section, I would often drive into the area, stopping every five miles to inquire about church conditions. Many needy communities were discovered in this way and a permanent work was started. These are a few examples of how spiritual needs in rural America are found.

Rural Missionary Methods

Rural mission organizations use differing methods — methods which are in harmony with their call and type of ministry. Since most such missions carry on a specialized type of ministry, various programs are used.

Those missions which specialize in children's and youth work conduct a program of Scripture memorization, either through the schools or otherwise, coupled with public school visitation where this is permitted, plus a strong daily vacation Bible school and camp program during the summer. Awards are usually given for the memorization program, ranging from a Gospel of John for the first verse, to a free week at camp for the maximum number of verses in the program.

The American Sunday-School Union, the oldest of the home missionary organizations, has a long history of ministry in rural America by means of Sunday schools. The missionary starts the work, then seeks qualified lay help in carrying it on under his supervision.

Organizations which are primarily concerned with establishing rural churches proceed on yet another course. These groups, after deciding on which rural community to enter, will either seek to open a closed church, should there be one available, or will go about starting a work that can be developed into a church. Some mission groups buy a closed church property outright, while others seek only the use of it on a temporary basis until the local people can themselves obtain it. The missionary workers are engaged by the mission board, and are urged to move into the community itself, or as close by as possible. Much tact and spiritual wisdom are needed to undertake such a work. Local interest must be created, for without this little can be done. Step by step the foundation is gradually laid; then as God enables, the local body of believers is formed into an organized church.

The mission groups which focus their attention on founding rural churches are, however, also interested in the corresponding ministries of daily vacation Bible schools and summer camps. A total program is encouraged, one that will meet the needs of all age groups, both young and old. Thus the adults are won to Christ now, and the children are reached and trained for future leadership in the church as well.

Rural Missions and World Missions

Rural missionaries and rural mission organizations are quick to agree that their work is merely a part of the over-all program of world-wide missions. The two cannot be divorced. The home base must make progress if it is to remain strong, for not to progress is to go backward. And home missions, to escape stagnation, must have an outlet! This scriptural outlet is "to the uttermost parts of the earth." Home missions thus can be a most effective "feeder" for foreign missions.

Some Christian leaders do not see the logical value of a strong home missionary program, fearing perhaps that home missionaries wish to be totally independent of foreign missions. But such is not the case. Rural missions seek only that percentage of resources which will enable the work to proceed apace with the foreign program. Is this asking too much?

God has so definitely led in home missions that the effects have been felt around the world. I feel safe in saying that virtually every rural mission board encourages a strong foreign missionary appeal. Young people, taught in the Word, come in contact with returned missionaries, or missionaries under appointment, and are called by the Holy Spirit into varied phases of Christian service. Missionary agencies and mission leaders unite in giving credit to the value of home missions in the foreign missionary program of the church. Here are a few reports.

A mission executive writes:

> From a little rural church in northern Minnesota we have received a number of able missionaries and several able pastors. . . . We find rural folks healthier, more willing to sacrifice, and more accustomed to the rough life of mission fields.

Reports from other boards follow:

> If we do not get these farm children under the sound of the gospel so that they can be saved, missions in general will suffer. We feel rural missions is a "must"!

> Today there are young people serving in the foreign missionary movement who attribute their life dedication to the influence of Scripture memorization.

> The light that shines farthest, shines brightest at home. Rural missionaries often become foreign missionaries, having proved themselves on the home field.

> It is our policy to build a vital and active missionary program, both home and foreign, into each church where we have ministered.

> Practically all our fields have a world-wide missionary budget, most for foreign missions.

Yes, home missions helps foreign missions. Not only are recruits found as a result of home missionary labor, but funds are also

channeled into the foreign missionary program. Every penny given
to rural missions pays dividends. The slogan, "In the interest of
foreign missions, build up home missions," is a valid one.

Consider also the result of the home missionary program in the
number of lives redeemed. We are apt to think lightly of the conversion of a child or young person, because our age looks for more
dramatic and spectacular results. But who can evaluate the importance of the following incident? In one rural community, the
workers won several young people to the Lord. But one young lad,
considered the "bully" of the neighborhood, declared that he would
not be a "sissy." No Sunday school and church for him! And he
kept his distance — for a while. But as others of his friends responded
to the gospel, he too felt the call of God and yielded to the Holy
Spirit. The change in his life was so great, that the teachers
marveled.

The benefits which community residents derive from an active
ministry of the Gospel cannot be estimated. One young girl expressed her feelings in this way: "We do not receive spiritual help
at home, at school, nor from the closed church. We are timid to go
elsewhere for help. If we go wrong, we are criticized, but very few
will do anything to help us spiritually."

The community life as a whole is benefited by an active rural
church. When a church is closed, the effect is seen in the moral and
spiritual conditions in the local area. When it is reopened, improvement is seen. FBI reports indicate that religious training de-
ters crime, but one need not go to the FBI for proof. Illustrations
abound everywhere. Communities are healthier and happier and
more law-abiding as a result of the home missionary and his ministry.

The Rural Missionary Worker

Rural missions could not be carried on without workers. Invariably students ask, "What are the qualifications?" It must be
recognized, of course, that various boards have different qualifications in respect to details. However, some of the basic qualifications
of the rural worker are:

1. He must be called to rural work. It is not enough just to have

a call to "Christian service." The leading of the Lord must be specific.

2. He must be prepared. Much harm has been done to the dignity and quality of rural work because of a lack of preparation.

3. He must be dedicated to his task. It will not do to enter the rural field simply for the purpose of gaining experience so as to be fitted for a better paying position later on! God may indeed use some workers in the rural field, then later place them in a more prominent position; but this ought not be the chief reason for entering the rural field.

4. He should have a rural background, if possible. Farming communities differ greatly from city communities. The culture and customs vary.

5. He must be industrious. If his people get the impression that he is lazy, his ministry will have little effect.

6. He must prove that he appreciates his people. Some from the city look down on rural people, and the rural people suspect this as the attitude of most rural workers. This must be disproved.

7. He must be friendly, but must carefully avoid undue familiarity. He must maintain friendly yet controlled relationships.

8. He must learn to intermingle with his people, not only in week-end services, but through the week as well.

A word should yet be said about the worker's attitudes. First, he must realize that he will not touch a great many lives, but he will touch the few with greater effectiveness. The Christian worker, as he remains faithful, "loves his way" into the hearts of his people, and eternity alone will reveal the influence such a ministry exercises.

Rural missions have little to offer from a financial standpoint. In most cases, partial support must come from off-the-field sources, either through contributions by friends and interested churches, or by subsidization by the group or denomination under whom he is working. Most rural missionaries live modestly and sacrificially for the sake of the gospel.

Should you work in rural missions? By all means — if God has called you. If God has called you, He will see you through to the end of a glorious ministry. Do not become discouraged.

The Future of Rural Missions

If all gospel churches would follow the Lord's command and reach into the surrounding areas near their own town or city, many unchurched rural areas could be cared for. Qualified members within these established churches could carry on services in these needy places.

However, since this is not being done, rural missions must expand their efforts. What then of the future? Note the following report from a leader in one evangelical denomination: "As people move to the cities, and as they improve the roads, more and more areas are without the gospel." A director of a mission board writes: "I am convinced that the needs of our particular ministry are so vast that all the boards engaged in this work are hardly scratching the surface. Churches are closing much faster than they are being opened, and the church in America is indifferent and unmoved by these needs." Another one states: "If our population continues to shift from rural to urban, a great many presently organized churches will close, and the remaining population will need mission work to meet its spiritual needs."

Rural missionary work is with us and has become a part of God's world-wide program. There are no evidences that circumstances which bring about the need are changing. Therefore, we urge all Christians to keep praying for rural missions and to support them in a yet greater way. We must continue reaching rural America for Christ.

What will be the spiritual future of this Eskimo child in Alaska?
(Courtesy of Arctic Missions, Inc.)

12

The Forty-ninth State

JOHN GILLESPIE

JUST THE MENTION OF THE NAME ALASKA causes a multitude of ideas collected in childhood to pass through one's mind. We heard that it was a land of ice and snow and great cold, with Eskimos, igloos, long winter nights and long summer days. We may picture a barren wilderness inhabited only by wild animals and a few natives here and there. Just how many of these ideas are true, and what of the missionary picture in our forty-ninth state?

The Land

The name *Alaska* comes from an Aleut word meaning mainland or great land. It is a land of magnificent scenery — steel blue glaciers, snow-capped mountains, giant forests, rippling streams and crystal-clear lakes. It is a land of wide extremes in temperature, for since it is one-fifth the size of the continental United States, the temperatures vary according to location. The average temperature for the entire territory is from about 58 degrees in summer to 18 degrees below zero in winter.[1] However, the temperature has been known to reach 100 degrees in summer at Fort Yukon and 78 degrees below

---

JOHN GILLESPIE left with his wife for the field of Alaska in 1941. Through direct village evangelism and homes for children, directing Victory Bible Conference Grounds and pastoring the Church of the Open Door in Anchorage, Alaska, for ten years, Mr. Gillespie has had ample opportunity to work and fellowship with missionaries and Christian leaders of various mission groups and denominations. As general director of Arctic Missions, Inc., he has traveled extensively throughout Alaska. He is thus in a position to appraise the past, present and possible future ministries in this new state.

[1] *World Book,* I, 172, 173.

in winter at the same place. Much of "cold Alaska" is very little different in climate from our northern states.

Daylight during summer and winter also varies from the southern tip to the northern coast. At Anchorage one can read a newspaper at midnight a few days before and after June 21, while in winter, just before and after December 21, one might turn the lights off at 10:00 A.M. and turn them on again at 2:00 P.M.

Alaska was purchased from Russia in 1867 for $7,200,000. It has paid for itself many times over in its rich natural resources. A great deal has been written of Alaska's gold and other valuable minerals, of its furs, forests and fishing industry. Much of its climate and industry is similar to that of the Scandanavian countries and for that reason many of those people became its first settlers.

The People

In 1960 Alaska's population numbered 226,000 and showed almost 57 per cent increase over the preceding ten-year period. This total includes Eskimos, Indians, Aleuts and whites. With the coming of statehood the white population will no doubt increase at a rapid rate. Better medical care for the native people is also causing their population to increase. The white people have come from every state in the Union, with a larger proportion of young people perhaps because of military service or allied work. It is a new country and its ruggedness appeals to the youthful, adventurous spirit.

The Eskimos inhabit the northern part of Alaska, particularly above the Yukon River and down the coast into the area of the Kuskokwim River. They are a happy, round-faced, dark-skinned people with almond-shaped eyes, which give a hint of a possible Oriental origin. Their many tribal customs and their folklore need to be studied if one is to understand the people. The Eskimo language has many dialects, but there are sufficient similarities for people of several villages to understand each other.

Formerly they dressed entirely in fur and skin clothing, however, they now use at least some factory-made garments. The parka is the best known piece of native clothing and has frequently been adopted by white people for winter wear in the Arctic. These long-hooded outer garments are often made of beautiful furs, extravagantly trimmed with intricate fur designs.

Native transportation is by umiak (walrus-hide boat) or dog
team. However it must be remembered that modern transportation
has reached into Eskimo country and they are quite familiar with
the airplane that links them with the larger cities.

Contrary to popular opinion, Alaskan Eskimos do not live in
an igloo made of ice or snow. Their homes are often built of sod
and scraps of wood. In recent years, however, since government
projects have come in, some of them live in wooden houses provided through the government.

The Aleut is a branch of the Eskimo,[2] but neither can understand
the language of the other. Their general territory is the Aleutian
chain. Yet about 500 of them live on the Pribilof Islands, where they
work for the government in the fur-sealing operations. The Russian
hunters first came to the Aleutian Islands in the late 1700's and
their influence is felt more among the Aleuts than in any other place.

There are more than 14,000 Indians in the central valleys in the
interior of Alaska and in the southeastern section. Originally they
were hunters and fishermen, but as is the case with the Eskimo and
Aleut many of them have taken up the white man's trades and work
for the government or in the canneries.

Schools have been provided in most of the villages of Alaska for
many years and practically all, except the very old people, understand and speak at least a limited amount of English.

Originally the religion of the native Alaskans was animistic and
there was much fear of spirits. The first influences of the Christian
religion were brought by the Russians with their occupation of
the territory. In many cases the native beliefs have become integrated with those taught by the Russian Orthodox Church or the
Roman Catholic Church. When the native dances are held in the
villages it is possible to see how very real their native superstitions
and fears are, even though there is a thin veneer of civilization. On
the other hand, when the people become a part of the white community these things are not readily evident in their lives.

The Early Churches

In a study of missions in Alaska a map of the state is helpful.
The number of villages and the size of type on some maps would
indicate large settlements. But a name on an Alaskan map some-

[2] *Ibid.*, p. 208

times marks only a deserted village or mining camp, or one which is occupied only at certain seasons of the year. It may mean only a cabin and a cache, or a roadhouse and a few additional buildings. At other times such a name may indicate a sizeable settlement. It is necessary for the prospective missionary to proceed with caution and endeavor to discover the real facts.

The first Russian Orthodox church was established at Kodiak in 1784 by missionaries who accompanied the fur traders. During the nineteenth century they established churches along Alaska's coast line, from the distant Aleutians to Prince William Sound and south to Juneau and Sitka — which is the present seat of their work in Alaska. They also established work at the mouth of the Kuskokwim and Nushagak and along the Yukon River.

Their method has always been the same. They baptized the people, administered the sacraments, and gave little or no instruction. At present there are villages in the Aleutian area where there is no church other than the Russian Orthodox, and there are numerous instances of persecution of those stalwart souls who dare to attend a gospel service.

In 1862[3] Father Seguin arrived in Fort Yukon from the interior. The Roman Catholics were not well received in the beginning, largely because they did not believe in polygamy. Seven years later another Catholic missionary joined him, and in 1888 Father Robaut and three sisters of St. Ann began a boarding school for native children at Holy Cross on the Yukon. Holy Cross has been one of the centers of Catholic work for many years, though they are found in many villages, and, of course, in the larger cities. There are a number of villages in the far western area which are entirely Roman Catholic.

It is always extremely difficult for a Protestant missionary to begin work in such a village because of the deep-seated fear in the hearts of the people of the priest and the church. At present the Catholics are building a large center in the region of Copper Center and are moving part of their work from Holy Cross to this area.

Protestant Missions

Captain Adolph K. Etholin,[4] a Finn and a Lutheran, came to the

[3] A. H. Savage, *Dog Sled Apostles* (New York: Sheed & Ward, 1942), p. 28.
[4] H. L. Foss, *Lutherans at Work in Alaska*, p. 7.

territory in 1840 to head up the work of the Russian American Company. Shortly after he assumed the office, he began the building of a Lutheran church at Sitka, for he had brought a Lutheran pastor by the name of Sidnyeuss with him. When the United States government took possession of the territory in 1867, a small parcel of ground in Sitka was set aside for the use of the Lutherans forever. This church was used from time to time by Protestants and Catholics until it fell into disrepair. The little organ used at that time is, however, now in the Alaskan museum.

A Presbyterian evangelist, Rev. Edward P. Hammond,[5] entered the territory soon after its purchase. He visited Fort Wrangell and Sitka in 1875. About this time a military officer from Fort Wrangell sent a letter to Rev. A. L. Lindsley of Portland, Oregon, requesting that missionaries be sent to Alaska. In May, 1877, John C. Mallory, a member of the First Presbyterian Church of Portland, went to Alaska and began a school, but was unable to do much because of ill health.

Dr. Sheldon Jackson became concerned about the need, and the first permanent work was begun in Alaska when he visited the territory in 1877. While passing through Portland he met Mrs. Amanda McFarland, a widow of a Presbyterian missionary to New Mexico, who was willing to serve in Alaska. She and Dr. Jackson arrived in Fort Wrangell on August 10. They found many of the natives involved in witchcraft and sorcery. Some were hostile and painted. Mrs. McFarland stayed to open a school for native children. She was the first missionary, and the first woman, to be sent by the Presbyterian Church to Alaska.

Dr. Jackson did much to educate and evangelize the native people. Through his efforts stations were established at Fort Wrangell, Sitka, Cape Prince of Wales, Point Hope and Point Barrow. He was also largely responsible for the establishment of reindeer herds, which were initiated into the northland as a helpful measure for the Eskimo people. Dr. Jackson later became the government's general agent for education in Alaska. He began the industrial school at Sitka, which is now known as the Sheldon Jackson Junior College.

At present Presbyterian missionary activities deal with three

[5] Clifford Merrill Drury, *Presbyterian Panorama* (Philadelphia: Board of Christian Education, 1952), p. 397 ff.

main groups: three tribes of Indians in southeastern Alaska —
Tlingits, Haida, Tsimshians; the Eskimos, who live above the
timberline along the bleak Arctic coasts of western and northern
Alaska; the white people. The board now lists seventy-five different
projects, and as of 1961 had fifty ministers and thirty-two churches
as well as other workers. Through the years the Presbyterians have
used boats and more recently planes in the work in southeastern
Alaska. They fondly call these the Presbyterian navy. An airplane
is part of their equipment in the north.

Churches Agree on Division of Responsibility

Dr. Jackson,[6] realizing that the territory was too large to be
reached by one denomination, called for a conference with the
secretaries of the Methodist, Baptist, Episcopal and Presbyterian
boards. They located on a map the areas where missions were
already established and those areas still unreached. They recognized that the Church of England in Canada had been working
along the Yukon River for sometime. These different denominations
at that time assumed the responsibility for missionary effort in
given areas. The Episcopalians planned to work in the Yukon area
and northward. The Methodists began working in the Shumagin
and Aleutian Islands and on the Alaska Peninsula. The Baptists
were assigned Cook Inlet and Prince William Sound. The Presbyterians had already been laboring in southeastern Alaska. Dr.
Jackson knew of the success of the Moravians with the Greenland
Eskimos so suggested that they begin along the Kuskokwim River.

As the mission leaders went about raising funds for their work,
interest was created. By 1887 other groups had begun, including
the Friends (Quakers) at Douglas Island and at Kake, and the
Swedish Evangelical Covenant Church on the Seward Peninsula. By
1890 the Congregationalists were at Cape Prince of Wales.

When the Rev. John W. Chapman[7] began working with the
Indians at Anvik on the Yukon River in 1887, the Episcopal Church
had its beginning in Alaska. Point Hope and Tanana were also
reached by Episcopalian missionaries. Rev. Peter Trimble Rowe[8]
became the first bishop of the Episcopal Church in Alaska. The

[6] Florence Hays, *Arctic Gateway* (New York: Friendship Press, 1940).
[7] James Thayer Addison, *Episcopal Church in the United States, 1789-1931*.
[8] Thomas Jenkins, *The Man of Alaska* (New York: Morehouse-Gorham Co., 1943),
p. 90.

emphasis of this church has been medical care for the people, the baptismal font and the administration of the sacraments.

Bethel on the Kuskokwim River became the center of operations for the Moravian Brethren. It is to be remembered that as early as 1732 Moravians sent Hans Egede[9] to Greenland to work among the Eskimos, and soon afterward they were teaching the Indians of North America. Early missionaries of this group landed in 1884 near the mouth of the Kuskokwim, where they spent their lives ministering to both bodies and souls of the people. Pastor Drebert, a member of this group, has been successful in translating portions of the Bible and a hymnal into the Eskimo language. They have been faithful in the distribution of literature through the region. At Bethel at present the native converts usually take charge of the morning meetings in the Eskimo language. In Sunday school and other services the English language is used with interpreters.

The first missionary trip of the Friends (Quakers) took place in the latter part of the nineteenth century. Their vessels were used in the Bering Sea, through the Bering Straits and into the Arctic Ocean. They settled at Kotzebue and have been faithful in their ministry to the Eskimos. They have established a native school and trained native leaders. Their printing press, located at Shungnak, farther north than any other, is turning out gospel material for their work. The Friends also maintain an airplane which keeps them in touch with the people.

Since the first Swedish Covenant missionaries landed on the shores of the Seward Peninsula, they have faithfully ministered to the people in that area. Along with numerous others, they have a church at Nome. One of their largest works, however, is located at Unalakleet, where they have a church and high school for the Eskimo children. Here they begin training young people to be the spiritual leaders of their people. For some years they have had native pastors in the field and they are endeavoring to teach the people to support them. They have a number of other stations, including a children's home at White Mountain. During the winter, a conference is held for the Eskimos, to which they come by dog team from miles around. It was said of the first missionary at

[9] Robert Hall Glover, *The Progress of World-Wide Missions* (New York: George H. Doran Co., 1942), pp. 80, 81.

Unalakleet, "When he came, there were no Christians; when he died, there were no pagans."

The first Lutheran church in the territory at Sitka has already been mentioned. In 1940 a new Lutheran church was dedicated on the site of the first church founded one hundred years before. When the effort to raise reindeer in Alaska began, the Laplanders engaged to teach the Eskimos the art of caring for the reindeer wouldn't come to the territory without a Lutheran pastor. Rev. T. L. Brevig came and ministered to their needs for many years.

Three groups of Lutherans have work in Alaska.[10] The Evangelical Lutheran Church maintained Teller Mission for more than sixty years and also labored at Teller Town and Shismaref. A plane is used in connection with their work in that area. This group, as well as the United Lutheran Church of America and the Lutheran Church (Missouri Synod), has churches in some of the larger cities. An independent Lutheran group operates a children's home at Cordova.

The Woman's Home Missionary Society of the Methodist Episcopal Church sent its first missionaries in 1886. Rev. and Mrs. J. H. Carr went to the Shumagan Islands, and in 1890 Miss Agnas Saule went to Unalaska as a school teacher. She immediately saw the need for a children's home and before the end of the first year she had taken several children into her own home. It was through her influence that the Jesse Lee Home (named for a pioneer missionary) began at Unalaska. For many years it served the needy children in that area and then in 1925 it was moved to Seward. At the present time the Methodists have churches at some points in the Aleutians and Cook Inlet area and as far north as Nome. They also maintain a large church in Anchorage.

The American Baptist Convention began a work on Kodiak Island after the territory was divided and has maintained a church in the city of Kodiak and two children's homes nearby. They also operate a missionary boat, the *Evangel*, for the purpose of reaching the area. In addition, the group has a work in Cordova, begun in 1950. Actually, the American Baptist group, by mutual consent, assumed the responsibilities of the church here begun by the Presbyterians years before. They have also assisted in the hospital

[10] Foss, *op. cit.*, p. 8.

work of Cordova. Here also they have a Christian center for youth. Very recently the American Baptist Church has begun work in Anchorage.

In the years following the beginning made by the eight original denominations in the territory, the picture has changed considerably. The fact that the native children receive training in English at schools provided by the government has had its effect on missionary work. The white population has grown by leaps and bounds, and with the growing population have come many other denominations for the purpose of starting their own churches. These include Pentecostal, Nazarene, Assembly of God, Church of God, Church of Christ, Salvation Army, Southern Baptists, Baptist Mid-Missions, Conservative Baptists, General Conference Baptists, Plymouth Brethren and a number of others. Many, if not all, have work in Anchorage, and a number also have churches in other communities of the state. A few of these have been concerned about the people in Alaska's back country. In addition to those groups mentioned, there are also most of the sects and isms to be found in continental United States. This adds up to a confusion of voices both in the city ministry and by radio to other parts of the state.

It would be impossible to enumerate all the various evangelical works, just where they are working and what they are doing. But mention should be made of the work of Child Evangelism; the Overseas Christian Servicemen's Centers, Inc., which maintains a servicemen's center in Anchorage and uses the radio to broadcast the gospel. A number of good gospel broadcasts are to be heard in the state but others have been dropped because they did not pay for themselves.

Faith Missions

Four faith missions of an interdenominational nature have been working in Alaska for a number of years. These groups labor primarily in the villages and with the native people.

The Slavic Gospel Association (formerly the Russian Gospel Association) began work in 1939, when Walter Covich went to the territory. He was soon followed by other excellent missionaries who have ministered in difficult places. Originally their work was especially slanted to the people of Russian descent; however, it is not limited to this group. Their work has been in the Kodiak Island area and on Cook Inlet. Mention should be made especially of the faithful labors of single young women in villages dominated by the Russian Orthodox Church and of the converts in those places.

In 1939 Vincent Joy came to the territory under the auspices of Central Alaskan Missions. The Lord has blessed the efforts of this group especially in the Copper River area, where the effect of the gospel has been clearly seen in the lives of old people as well as young, in the work of the native gospel teams as they witness to the saving grace of God, and in the one-week summer Bible conference, which is conducted by the native people themselves. It has been a joy to hear the testimonies of those who have been claimed from a life of sin and debauchery. Central Alaskan Missions also maintains Faith Hospital, which is staffed by Christian doctors and nurses. This has been a blessing to both natives and whites and to the missionaries of other groups to which their help has been generously offered.

In 1935 Dr. W. E. Pietsch made a survey trip into Alaska. On his return to the States he formed the Alaska Evangelization Society and this group was officially incorporated in 1937. They are presently occupying two stations on Cook Inlet, one in the Bristol Bay area and two in the interior. They also are burdened for the native people in their areas, and though many times the work has been difficult, the Lord has blessed their efforts.

Independent Missionaries Organize

Between 1934 and 1951 a good number of excellent independent missionaries came to the field. Each was burdened for an unreached area where mission groups were not working. Being independent, they were isolated from mutual Christian fellowship and the advantages of a co-ordinated work. Most of them had been burdened for the organization of a group which would bind them together and co-ordinate their efforts in the field, as well as provide care and missionary continuity. On the advice of Christian leaders in the States, such as Dr. John G. Mitchell of Multnomah School of the Bible in Portland, Alaska Missions, Inc. (later changed to Arctic Missions, Inc.) was formed in 1951, bringing together twenty-one missionaries, most of whom had been on the field from ten to eighteen years.

Since its beginning the burden of the group has been the continual outreach to new unevangelized villages. New missionaries have been added and new villages occupied, until the group now numbers more than fifty working in three main areas: the Yukon and Innoko Rivers, the Lake Iliamna and Bristol Bay area, and along the rail belt. Some of the villages have been opened recently in spite of strong opposition. In such cases it takes a long time before real fruit is seen. Through faithful witnessing in other villages both old and young have been won and some of the young people are presently training for full-time Christian service.

John Gillespie and a board of directors made up of Christian businessmen and veteran missionaries chart the course of the mission from the field office in Anchorage. They also maintain a home office in Portland, Ore. This group has recently become a member of the Interdenominational Foreign Missions Association.

No history of missions in Alaska would be complete without a bit of detail on some important independent projects. Children's homes have long been a means of reaching the lost for Christ. One of the first of these was begun by Miss Blanche Nason at Valdez, known as El Nathan Home. At one time it housed almost one hundred children, but a devastating fire in 1946 made it necessary to send some of the children to Matanuska Valley under the leadership of Rev. and Mrs. Kenneth Hughes. They had been given sixty acres of virgin land for this purpose. After clearing it, they built up one of the largest homes in the state. It is known as Lazy Mountain Children's Home because of its location.

This type of work has been carried on by various groups, but at any location and under any circumstances it is difficult. Because of the tremendous liquor traffic and the apparent inability of the natives to cope with it, many children have had to be taken from their parental homes by the government agencies. Tuberculosis has frequently caused the death of one or both parents, thus leaving the children hopeless and ofttimes helpless. These children are placed by government agency workers in the Christian welfare homes.

Discipline problems are great because most of the children have had none in their former homes. The children are not in these homes by their choice. As a result all kinds of conflicts, misunderstanding and mental fears plague them from time to time. Here also, however, can be seen some shining examples of God's grace in the hearts and lives of the boys and girls.

Camping Programs

Another method of reaching the people of Alaska for Christ has been through summer and winter Bible camps. Various denominations have used the camping program for their own people. The largest interdenominational camp ground in the state is Victory Bible Conference Grounds, Inc. Begun in 1947, this camp provides a summer program for all ages and a winter camping program for young people. It is here that a large interdenominational missionary conference is held each year. Some leading Bible teacher is brought in each year for the purpose of instructing and encouraging missionaries and Christian leaders. The Lord has blessed this camp in its program of evangelism for all ages and races.

Mission Work Present and Future

Let us now consider the present and future aspects of the work. It is true that Alaska's population will continue to grow rapidly. As more land is opened for homesteading, the populated areas will spread. There will be a continuous need for the same types of work known in any state. There must be churches wtih an evangelistic slant and a Bible-teaching ministry. The prospects for children's and young people's work will grow with the population. Doubtless the government will continue to maintain the large military bases in the state and there will be a continuing need for work with service personnel. Gospel broadcasts and other reliable methods of preaching Christ should be used that everyone may have an opportunity to hear the claims of the gospel.

These methods will serve for city and urban communities, but what about the many little native villages which dot the landscape in the interior far from roadways, and which can be reached only by airplane or perhaps by boat? Missionaries who have worked in the state for many years do not expect statehood to make any major difference in these places.

How is work carried on in these villages and what kind of life must the missionary live? He must first realize that the villages are small (from under 100 to perhaps 300 in the largest villages) and widely scattered. The next village may be many miles away. He will probably find a native store in the village which will provide a few staples, but he will, no doubt, decide that it is more profitable to buy his groceries for a year at a time and have them shipped in by boat during the short summer period.

Weather will play an important part in the missionary's life. He must be equipped with warm clothing and must be willing to do hard physical labor part of the time. It may be possible for him to burn oil for fuel, but in most places it will be wood — many cords of it — which must be cut in the woods, hauled to his home and sawed into stove lengths. His water may come from the river or lake — and in winter he must chop a hole in the ice, lower the buckets and then carry the water to his home. Perhaps, instead of water, he will cut chunks of ice from a lake and haul them like cord wood to his home where they will be placed in a large drum and melted for water. He will even need to haul snow in the same manner.

In many villages the missionary will find that the dog team is an indispensable means of transportation. A dog team, however, means additional work, for the missionary must spend part of his summer cutting and drying enough fish so that his dogs will have food for the winter. The dog team is used not only for hauling the necessities of life, but as a means whereby he can visit with his people as they go on their trap lines. The dog team also provides a point of mutual interest between the missionary and his people. By living with them in the village he is sharing the experiences they have from day to day.

The missionary must get used to the idea of complete isolation for several weeks each fall and spring at the freeze-up and break-up periods. During these times it is impossible for an airplane to land on the rivers because of the ice floats. If he or his family should become ill during this period, it will be virtually impossible to get to a doctor or hospital for medical care. During the trapping season and again during fishing season he may find that his village is nearly deserted. He will, therefore, have to plan ways to reach the people while they are at their fish camp or on the trapline.

One contemplating missionary service in the interior of the state may feel he will hire native labor to do much of his work so that he can spend more time in actual teaching. Yet he will find that the native people are very much aware of the average wage scale in the cities and set their prices accordingly. Most missionaries find that it is beyond their budget to hire help except in extreme emergencies. The missionary may also find that the education of his children is a problem. Where the native schools are crowded, he may have to teach his children himself. Even if they are allowed to go to school through the eighth grade, he will not find a high school, except in a large community.

A missionary entering some villages may be welcomed by the people, but in others he will meet all kinds of opposition. The people may be quite sure they do not want a missionary. Where the missionary is welcomed, he may soon be able to hold classes for the people. If, however, there is strong opposition, he will have to follow a different method. He will have to visit in the homes of the people and seek to be of help in any possible way. He must take every opportunity to serve them and win their friendship. He may be called upon to perform all kinds of services, from binding up their wounds and burying their dead to writing out orders to the catalogue stores and generally advising them in such areas.

The missionary must also realize that he has much to learn from them. He must be teachable. The native may not be cultured in the ways of the white man, but he has no equal when it comes to living in the frozen north. The Christian worker may not be able to hold any services for a long time, but in the process of living with the people he will have opportunities to winess. In being all things to all men he will win some, though it may be several years before any strong converts are seen.

He will also learn that a show of hands in response to an invitation at the close of a gospel service may mean little. There will be little or no change in their lives. He will probably decide that personal contact is best, for he will be better able to explain the implications of being born again. He will no doubt find that it is necessary to spend many hours in personal counseling with each convert that he may grow and mature in his Christian life.

Alaska *is* a mission field, but to the individual contemplating missionary service in Alaska may we suggest a word of caution. A great volume of propaganda is being published to draw settlers to the new state. A multitude of Christian workers are feeling the need to start their own work in this inviting land. Let the prospective Christian worker carefully gather and glean the facts concerning the country and the actual needs. There is much yet to be done, but it will be done only by those who are genuinely called of God and equipped for the task.

Workers chosen of God for the task are needed, but let us be very certain that the glamour of the land and its close proximity to the other forty-eight states do not approximate a call.

BIBLIOGRAPHY

DRURY, CLIFFORD MERRILL. *Presbyterian Panorama*. Philadelphia: Board of Christian Education, 1952.

FOSS, H. L. *Lutherans at Work in Alaska*.

GLOVER, ROBERT HALL. *The Progress of World-Wide Missions*. New York: George H. Doran Co., 1942.

HAYS, FLORENCE. *Arctic Gateway*. New York: Friendship Press, 1940.

JENKINS, THOMAS. *The Man of Alaska*. New York: Morehouse-Gorham Co., 1943.

McGINNIS, F. *Methodists at Work in Alaska*.

SAVAGE, A. H. *Dog Sled Apostles*. New York: Sheed & Ward, 1942.

World Book Encyclopedia. Chicago: The Quarrie Corporation, 1947.

A Buddhist Shrine

There are more Buddhists than Christians in Hawaii. Do we
consider our fiftieth state a mission field? (Courtesy of Northwest Orient Airlines.)

13

Hawaii—Land of Sunshine

ROBERT C. LOVELESS

ON THURSDAY, March 12, 1959, the Congress of the United States passed legislation that assured the admission of Hawaii as the fiftieth state of the United States of America. This climaxed a series of events that began as far back as 1778 — almost as early as the American Revolution. For it was on January 18, 1778, that Captain James Cook of the British Navy discovered the Hawaiian Islands, naming them the Sandwich Islands after John Montagu, Earl of Sandwich and sponsor of Cook's expedition.

There are seven inhabited islands in the archipelago. Hawaii (southeasternmost) is the largest, while Oahu (containing Honolulu) is the most densely populated (450,000 out of a total population of 632,800).

History

When Cook made his discovery he found semitropical isles populated by about 300,000 Polynesians, who it is thought came to the islands at least a thousand years ago in large canoes. These probably came from other Pacific islands.

ROBERT C. LOVELESS was educated at Wheaton College, Illinois, receiving his M.A. degree in 1948. In September of the same year he went to Hawaii to assume the pastorate of the Kaimuki Evangelical Church (Congregational), which post he held for ten years. In September, 1958, he left the church to assume the presidency of the Honolulu Christian College.

Loveless is also president of the board of the Christian Broadcasting Association and past president of the Evangelical Ministers Fellowship. In 1959 he served as chaplain to the 139th Meeting of the Territorial Association of the Congregational Churches.

Missionary activity did not commence in the islands until forty-two years after Cook's discovery. However, two striking events that took place in the interim, it would seem providentially, paved the way for the missionary invasion.

The first of these was the conquest and unification of the islands by Kamehameha I in the year 1795. The islands up to that time had been ruled by regional chiefs. After a ten-year struggle, Kamehameha gained control of his own island, Hawaii. Then this Napoleon of the Pacific quickly conquered the other islands.

The other significant event was in 1819, just one year before the arrival of the missionaries. Kamehameha II in that year by official act abolished the established Hawaiian religion with its ceremonies and taboos. This seems to have been done for vicious and selfish reasons, probably to remove the inconvenient strictures of the religion. However, it proved to be a most providential step as far as the missionary movement was concerned, for it created a vacuum which was to enhance greatly the early spread of the gospel.

The missionaries, Congregationalists commissioned in Park Street Church in Boston, boarded the brig *Thaddeus* on October 23, 1819. Under the leadership of Hiram Bingham and Asa Thurston they arrived in Kailua, Hawaii, on April 4, 1820. These missionaries with their families, together with other missionary families who were to arrive in later stages, endured great hardships. Some of them were to lay down their lives for the advancement of the missionary cause.

Besides the immediate establishment of the church, which had in fact been organized in Boston, they began to reduce the language to writing and to translate the Scriptures into the Hawaiian language. This translation was completed in 1839. Much of the early educational program of these devoted educators was right out of the Bible, the primary available work. The church very quickly made itself felt in a social way, partly through the conversion of some of the royalty — notably Keopuolani and Kaahumanu, wives of Kamehameha. By 1825 the Ten Commandments had been officially adopted as the basis for civil law. This was not without considerable opposition from sailors and officers from the "civilized" countries who resented the consequent tightening of restriction on liquor and sex.

One of the most famous of the conversion stories is that of Princess Kapiolani. Her witness is notable, for it was she who went up to the very rim of the seething volcano Kilauea. This she did in the name of Christ in violation of one of the long-standing and most feared taboos of the Hawaiian people.

The work for the most part progressed slowly and steadily. In marked contrast to this is the Great Awakening in 1836-38 and a period of revival in 1860-61. Prominent in the former was Titus Coan, sent out in 1831 by the American Board. On a single Sunday in 1838 Coan baptized 1,705 converts at Hilo. Out of these revival movements grew outthrusts of missionary effort to other islands — notably the Gilberts, Marquesas, Marshalls and Carolines.

By 1864, the Hawaiian Islands were regarded as Christianized. The mission was withdrawn and full supervision of the work turned over to the indigenous church. Dr. Rufus Anderson, distinguished executive of the ABCFM, in his evaluation of the Hawaiian mission in 1870, regards as "mistakes" the slowness to ordain native ministers and to turn over full leadership to them. This developed something of a patronage mood in the Hawaiian church, vestiges of which prevail even to this day.

In addition to the direct contribution of the Christian missionaries, there were other outstanding factors in the development of the fiftieth state. Kamehameha III stands out as the Hawaiian monarch during whose reign many of the most important social and political reforms were activated. In 1840 a constitution was adopted, patterned much after the Constitution of the United States. Missionary William Richards, who had been released from his ministerial duties to serve as an adviser to kings in matters of jurisprudence, had a hand in its framing.

In 1843, Hawaii was recognized simultaneously by the United States, Britain and France as an independent government.

In 1848, Kamehameha III initiated a major land reform known as the Great Mahele. Up until this time all land had belonged to the king and the people were regarded as tenants. The Mahele caused many of the lands to be deeded to common people. One development from this program, which still has a great impact on island life today, was that many of the chiefs and common people sold their lands to Caucasian immigrants, who thereby acquired

enormous estates. The term "the Big Five," common in contemporary Hawaii, has reference to such estates.

Toward the end of Kamehameha III's reign a series of immigrations began that were to change the entire ethnic complexion of
Hawaii. This was made necessary because of the demand for
laborers on the sugar plantations. Many of the Hawaiians had died
through disease, and those who remained were not disposed toward
this kind of work.

The major immigrations took place as follows: Chinese in 1852;
Japanese in 1868; Portuguese in 1878; Puerto Ricans in 1900;
Koreans in 1903; and Filipinos in 1906. Many of these workers
graduated from plantation jobs to other positions in the community — some more rapidly than others. The result is a community
characterized by cultural exchange, intermingling of the races,
and intermarriage. Although it would be an overstatement to indicate that there are no racial problems in Hawaii, it is quite true
that integration is more advanced here than anywhere in the world.

The breakdown of racial proportions in Hawaii's population of
632,800 is approximately as follows: Japanese, 40 per cent; part
Hawaiian, 17 per cent; Caucasian, 15 per cent; Filipino, 13 per cent;
Chinese, 7 per cent; pure Hawaiian, 3 per cent; Puerto Rican, 2
per cent; Korean, 1 per cent; other, 2 per cent.

In 1891, during the reign of Queen Liliuokalani, there was an
attempt to turn the clock of history backward toward the days of
the strong monarchy. The revolt was unsuccessful, however, and
rather brought about in 1893 the establishment of Hawaii as a
republic with Sanford B. Dole as the first president. This was
followed by the annexation of Hawaii as a territory of the United
States in 1898, with Dole appointed as the first governor. Hence
the lines of political development were set toward the day when
Hawaii would ratify a state constitution in 1950 and be admitted
as the fiftieth state of the union in 1959.

Culture, Customs, Spiritual Condition

The original religious pattern that served as the challenge to
initial missionary effort was animistic, with generous mixtures of
taboo, fetishism, and human sacrifice. Though this religion was
discontinued before the beginning of the missionary enterprise, it

was not totally eliminated from the minds of all the Hawaiian people. Those who work among the Hawaiian churches still find superstitions which seem to have their roots back in the old animistic culture.

Later immigrations from the Orient brought, as might be expected, a large influx of oriental religions. Most prominent of these is Buddhism, today claiming upward of 150,000 adherents in Hawaii. Largest of the Buddhist sects is the Hongwanji, a syncretic product of the mingling of Buddhism and Nestorian Christianity in Japan. This has brought about many interesting parallels between their teachings and Christian doctrine. These need to be understood for evangelism among these people.

Roman Catholicism became established in the islands as early as 1839. Entrance was finally gained after an earlier unsuccessful attempt in 1827. Much of the success of Roman Catholicism seems to be attributable to its stress on education and the establishment of parochial schools. The growth has been further enhanced by the immigration of people from Roman Catholic countries. They have grown until they number at least 125,000 nominal adherents.

Another significant religious group in Hawaii is the Mormons, or Church of the Latter Day Saints. This group appeared in Hawaii as early as 1858. It celebrated its centennial by the dedication of a five-million-dollar college campus. Their appeal seems to be largely to the Hawaiian people (though not exclusively), who figure in the church as one of the "lost tribes." Present figures indicate a Mormon population of better than 15,000.

Besides these, every conceivable oriental and occidental sect has some sort of headquarters in Hawaii.

As has already been pointed out, the earliest Protestant missionary work in Hawaii was carried on by New England Congregationalists. The Episcopal Church also was here very early, reflecting English influence, just as the Roman Catholic Church gained entry through French political pressures.

The Second World War was a time of major social and religious upheaval on the Hawaiian scene. Because of political considerations, the United States government placed severe restrictions on all citizens of Japanese ancestry and closed all the temples. This was a blow that threatened to inundate the Buddhist movement in

Hawaii. During this time many young people of oriental extraction became restless about their religious loyalties and there was a
tendency to listen to Western religion.

This was a time, as might be expected, of significant Protestant
growth. The older groups made advances, and newer groups came
in: Methodist, Lutheran, Baptist, Disciples of Christ, Church of
Christ, Assemblies of God, Nazarene. The Salvation Army, which
had first come at the invitation of the Congregationalists in 1896,
played a large part during the war. The Presbyterians were not
represented in Hawaii until 1959 because of a comity agreement
between the Congregationalists and Presbyterians.

The movements of modernism and liberalism, which had such
devastating effects on mainland Protestantism in the last half
century, were reflected in Hawaii. As these influences became
entrenched in many of the seminaries, it was inevitable that the
effects would be felt far and wide in the church. Hawaii was no
exception.

Since the war, however, there has been a very heartening resurgence of evangelicalism. This has been partly through the entry
of new groups with an evangelical message, notably Baptist, Christian, Assemblies of God, Nazarene, and evangelical Lutheran
groups. There has been also a marked revival of evangelicalism in
some of the old line denominations, especially the Congregational.
In this oldest group in Hawaii, there has been the most amazing
development of an evangelical movement that has seen some of its
largest churches "converted."

Another heartening factor is the growing tendency toward
evangelical co-operation across denominational lines. This is ob-
served in such projects as Hawaii Youth for Christ, Child Evangelism, the Honolulu Christian College, the Christian Broadcasting
Association (KAIM and KAIM-FM), the Inter-Varsity Christian
Fellowship, Interschool Christian Fellowship, the Evangelical
Ministers Fellowship. This development can be attributed in a
significant measure to the contribution of Christian schools on the
mainland where many of its leaders were trained.

Prospect

It should be pointed out that today, almost a century after the
so-called Christianization of the Hawaiian Islands, there remains a

monumental challenge to Christian evangelism. The expected
decline of Buddhism did not materialize. When restrictions were
lifted after the war, a period of marked Buddhist resurgence began.
New temples were built and an effort was made to reach the youth.
A rough estimate of the religious breakdown of Hawaii's 632,000
population might be: Buddhist, 150,000; Roman Catholic, 125,000;
Protestant, 40,000.

This challenge takes on its own peculiar dimension of urgency
in the light of Hawaii's admission as a state. Here is a field within
our United States that in many ways is comparable to a foreign
mission field. This is true although Hawaii has acquired a veneer
of Western culture.

It is to be prayerfully hoped that the next ten years will see a
marked growth and consolidation of evangelical effort in Hawaii.
This will necessitate the expenditure of lives and money considerably beyond the present rate. It would seem that this could be most
effectively done through the strengthening of existing works, rather
than through the multiplication of organizations. At any rate,
individuals and organizations that have a burden for Hawaii would
do well to consult evangelical leaders in the formulation of their
plans that there may be a measure of brotherly strategy in the
attempt to claim these islands for our Lord Christ.

BIBLIOGRAPHY

BINGHAM, HIRAM. A Residence of 21 Years in the Sandwich
    Islands. Canandaigua, N. Y.: H. D. Goodwin, 1855.
BRADLEY, HAROLD WHITMAN. The American Frontier in Hawaii.
    Stanford: Stanford University Press, 1942.
COULTER, JOHN WESLEY. The Pacific Dependencies of the United
    States—Hawaii. New York: Macmillan Co., 1957.
LIND, ANDREW W. Hawaii's Japanese—An Experiment in Democ-
    racy. Princeton, N. J.: Princeton University Press, 1946.
Missionary Album. Portraits and Biographical Sketches of the
    American Protestant Missionaries to the Hawaiian Islands.
    Honolulu: Hawaiian Mission Children's Society, 1937.
RESTARICH, HENRY BON. Hawaii From the Viewpoint of a
    Bishop. Honolulu: Paradise of the Pacific, 1924.
World Book Encyclopedia. Chicago: The Quarrie Corporation,
    1947, Vol. 8.

The center of Quebec City with historic Chateau Frontenac. Christian tourists visiting this famous city seldom realize how little Protestant work exists here. (Courtesy of The Province of Quebec Film Bureau.)

14

"O Canada, Terre De Nos Aieux"

(Land of Our Forefathers)

ARTHUR C. HILL

PROBABLY NO OTHER WHITE PEOPLE in the Western Hemisphere are so definitely North American as the *Canadiens*. They have lived as a nation in the St. Lawrence River valley for more than four hundred years and are as firmly established on the soil of Canada as they are emphatically removed from any European attachment. The *Canadiens* do not speak of "the old country" as do other North Americans of European descent. They are *Canadiens*, and nothing else.

Many of the most adventurous spirits of France came to Canada during colonial times. They explored the northern half of the continent as far west as the Rockies, and as far south as the Mississippi River system, but never had the people to settle this vast area. Later, much of the drive behind the zeal for exploration came from

ARTHUR C. HILL was born in London, Ontario, in 1907. He was graduated from the University of Western Ontario in general science in 1929 and in medicine in 1932. He was the first student president and first Canadian secretary of the Inter-Varsity Christian Fellowship of Canada (1933-34). Since 1935 he has been practicing medicine in Sherbrooke, Quebec.

Dr. Hill was president of the Quebec division of the Canadian Medical Association from 1942 to 1943 and has held other similar positions since. He has also been active in the Gideons, IVCF, and as Sunday school superintendent at Grace Chapel, Sherbrooke, Quebec. He is currently editor of the *News of Quebec* and chairman of the executive committee of the Christian Brethren in the province of Quebec.

the fanatical, and often heroic, desire of the Jesuit missionaries to bring more and more Indians under the Roman cross.

At the beginning, Canada also received many Huguenot settlers fleeing from the persecutions in France. It seemed, indeed, that at one time New France might be settled largely by French Protestants. The government would have been happy to turn over the "few acres of snow" to these non-conforming citizens of France, but the coming of the Jesuits changed all that. As they became more and more powerful in New France, they determined that it should be solidly Roman Catholic country. Protestants were refused permission to land at Quebec, and soon there were practically no Huguenots left in the colony.

The expanding French empire soon came into conflict with the English-speaking settlers of the middle and southern Atlantic coast. After almost two hundred years of strife, sometimes violent, at times almost quiescent, the French cause was defeated. Following Wolfe's victory over Montcalm on the Plains of Abraham, Quebec City and all of Canada passed into British hands.

After the fall of New France in 1763, the French aristocracy were given the option of returning to their homeland. Most of the *seigneurs*, the businessmen and the higher clergy, left Canada, never to return. The *habitants*, who numbered 65,000, were abandoned by their natural leaders and seemed to face inevitable absorption into the 1,500,000 English-speaking people of North America. In fact, this was what the victorious British confidently expected.

But they had not taken into account the tremendous fecundity of the *Canadiens*. During the next few decades the birth rate in Canada rose to over sixty per thousand, a record never equalled in any country during recorded history. The *Canadiens*, deprived of their leaders, turned to the parish clergy who had remained as their national champions. Often the curé was the only educated man in the parish, and he soon assumed a place of far greater importance to the *habitant* than he had under the old régime. Thus began the complete control over the lives of his parishioners which the Roman priest has maintained ever since. The *Canadiens* became a fast-multiplying, tightly knit national group under the leadership of their clergy.

Then the American Revolution broke out, just ten years after the fall of Quebec. The *Canadiens*, people and clergy alike, feared much more their hereditary enemies to the south than they did the British under the wise governor Sir Guy Carleton. So instead of joining the thirteen colonies, French Canada remained loyal to the British Crown and thus insured that they would not be absorbed into the great English-speaking majority in North America.

The Canada of 1765 to 1800 was overwhelmingly French-speaking and Roman Catholic. Successors to Sir Guy Carleton were not so wise as he and attempts were made by some extremists to suppress the French language in Canada. These proposed to put all schools under Protestant control and even to have the governor appoint Roman priests to their parishes. The sharp contention that arose over these efforts to Anglicize Canada has never really disappeared. The mutual distrust that still exists between the English and French-speaking peoples of Canada dates from this period.

However, it was evident to cooler heads that guarantees must be given to the *Canadiens* to secure to them their own language, their freedom of worship, French civil law and so forth. Successive acts of government did give them these guarantees. Thus during the war of 1812 the *Canadiens* made common cause with their English-speaking countrymen to repel the invasion from the United States and "keep Canada British."

These guarantees of language, freedom of worship, French civil law and provincial control of education were all incorporated into the British North America Act in 1867, whereby Canada became a nation.

Quebec Today

The 65,000 *Canadiens* of 1765 have, by means of their unusually high birth rate, now grown in numbers to over five million. They not only represent 85 per cent of the population of Quebec, but they have expanded by the hundreds of thousands into eastern and northern Ontario, northern New Brunswick, and the industrial cities of New England.

They are a hard-working people who will accept rigorous conditions of living far more readily than most of their Anglo-Saxon

neighbors. For many generations their culture was largely that of
the agricultural *habitant,* with a small intellectual elite. Those who
achieved an education were far more interested in the learned
professions and politics than in industry and engineering. As a
result, the twentieth-century expansion of industry in Quebec has
been financed by English-Canadian, American and British capital.

The *Canadien* complains that he has become a hewer of wood and
drawer of water in the land where he should be master. The French
language universities of Quebec, however, are now training many
more engineers, business specialists and scientists, so that we may
expect to see a gradual improvement in this situation. In the meantime, this feeling of restricted opportunity in his own province adds
to the sense of grievance which has characterized the *Canadien's*
thought and attitudes for many years.

French Canada is perhaps the most solidly Roman Catholic area
in the whole world. The population is not only nominally but
actively loyal to the Roman system because of the historical background. Their nationality, language and religion are bound together
so tightly that they honestly believe that a *Canadien* who is converted to Protestantism is a traitor to the whole *Canadien* way of
life. This makes it very difficult for evangelical Christians to live in
small towns and villages, where the word of the parish priest can,
and often does, prevent a man from finding employment and his
family from buying food.

It is necessary to understand this background of the *Canadien*
in French Canada. We must see the reason why in Quebec he
enjoys official status for his language and his treasured institutions.
We must also understand why the Roman Catholic clergy have
become the leaders of their people, even in their cultural, professional and economic life. It is only when we have an understanding of his historic past, of which he is very proud, that we
can successfully present the gospel to the citizen of Quebec.

Protestant Witness in Quebec Through the Years

In spite of the efforts of the Roman hierarchy, there has always
been a handful of French-speaking Protestants in Quebec. In
Up to the Light, Dr. Paul Villard,[1] one of the most gifted leaders

[1] Paul Villard, *Up to the Light* (Toronto: United Church of Canada).

French Protestantism has ever had, has given a survey of the wide-spread evangelistic efforts of the nineteenth century.

There was a time when truly evangelical missionaries were sent into Quebec by the Anglican, Methodist and Presbyterian churches. The most noted of these evangelists was the great Father Chiniquy, whose *Fifty Years in the Church of Rome*[2] is so well known (but not so well read) in our day. At the height of Charles Chiniquy's influence there were some sixty French Presbyterian churches in Quebec. There are now three. These two statements show what happened in general to French Protestant churches in Quebec from about 1860 up until 1930.

Reason for Protestant Decline. There are two principal reasons for this tremendous decline. The first seems to be that, though the early converts from Romanism were people of deep conviction who formed strong evangelical churches, their children were often Protestant in name rather than by conviction. Growing up in an evangelical atmosphere, they were less aware of "the hole from whence they were digged." As evangelical fervor cooled, these *Canadien* Protestants often left Quebec to avoid persecution, or even married Roman Catholics and were absorbed back into the Roman church.

The second reason for this was the lack of French Protestant schools. The Quebec public school system is dual in character. One part is largely French-speaking and Roman Catholic and the other is English-speaking and Protestant. As there was no provision for the education of the small minority of French-speaking Protestant children, they had perforce to attend the English schools. All their education therefore was in English and they rapidly became Anglicized. Those who remained in Quebec were eventually absorbed into the English-speaking Protestant population and lost to the cause of French Canadian evangelism.

Shift in Emphasis in Preaching. During the fifty years before 1930 there took place a marked shift in emphasis in the preaching and activities of the major Canadian Protestant denominations. The social implications of the gospel were stressed, while the idea of personal salvation through faith in Jesus Christ passed into the

[2] Father Charles Chiniquy, *Fifty Years in the Church of Rome* (Toronto: S. R. Briggs, 1886).

background. All members of society, including Roman Catholics and Jews, were embraced as brothers, sons of one Father, and all (probably) on the road to heaven. This kind of thinking dulled the edge of Protestant evangelism in Quebec. Interest in Quebec fell off, and the flow of funds to Quebec missions dried up. There were few candidates for missionary work in Quebec; often none at all. The French Protestant churches in the province lost all sense of mission to their compatriots, so that within a generation or so most of them ceased to exist.

A large section of the population of English-speaking Canada had been born in "the old country" and was not Canadian in outlook. A strong imperialist sentiment in Ontario associated everything in Quebec with "Rome, rum and rebellion." There was little communication between the English and French-speaking Canadas on those levels where friendship and understanding flourish. Evangelical Christians in Ontario and other provinces did not escape this antagonistic attitude of mind, and so felt no compulsion to send the gospel into Quebec.

A successful evangelist must love the people he is trying to reach and they must feel that they can trust him fully. These conditions just did not exist. Quebec went without the gospel.

By 1930, the evangelical witness to *Canadiens* was at its lowest ebb. The fine days of Chiniquy and his immediate followers had passed. French Protestantism in Quebec was anemic. It had long since ceased to make converts from Romanism in any significant numbers. Indeed, it was suffering greatly from relapses to Rome, intermarriages which usually result in a return to Rome, and emigration of Protestant *Canadiens* to greener fields.

Resurgence of Gospel Preaching in Quebec

Shortly before the outbreak of World War II, evangelical Christians in both Canada and the United States began to take a fresh interest in the missionary needs of Quebec. Long accustomed to thinking of missions in terms of Africa, India, China and Latin America, it came as a shock to believers in North America that the neediest mission field in the world lay right at their doors. It was shown that while Angola (Portuguese West Africa) had Protestant missionaries at the rate of forty per million of the population, the

Congo over sixty missionaries per million of its people, and even China had fifteen per million, Quebec had less than ten missionaries per million of its French-speaking Roman Catholics. This figure remains at about fourteen per million even today. We found that we had been sending missionaries to the uttermost parts of the earth and had neglected our Samaria.

The interest was shown mostly among groups of evangelical Christians, often called the "evangelical sects" by the larger denominations. To these people, especially the Evangelical Baptists, the Pentecostals and the Christian Brethren, has fallen the task of evangelizing Quebec in the twentieth century. The return of many Christian young men and women from the services, and the consequent training of hundreds of them in Bible colleges and seminaries, has produced a supply of enthusiastic candidates for missions, some of whom have found their way to Quebec.

What is Going on Today?

The work carried on by the Grande Ligne (Baptist) Mission has been an exception to the usual rule. This mission was begun in a rough loghouse over one hundred years ago by a devout Swiss Christian, Madame Feller. The history of this mission makes fascinating reading. It contains stories of many heroic missionaries who gave everything they had to the Lord for the spreading of the gospel in Quebec. The school she founded developed into the Feller Institute at Grande Ligne (near St. Jean) and continues to render service as a school to this day. The evangelical fervor of the Grande Ligne Baptists, after being quiet for several decades, seems to be brightening up. Two or three churches report growing congregations and spiritual blessing in souls being saved and added to the church.

Perhaps the most active Baptist group in the province is the Fellowship of Evangelical Baptist Churches. Their oldest and most fruitful field of work is the gold mining area of northwestern Quebec. Their missionaries have been most aggressive in evangelism. Several of them have gone to jail for months at a time for preaching the gospel on the streets of these northern towns. They have finally earned the right to do this, though of course they still suffer many indignities.

During the last few years the Evangelical Baptists have opened up twelve new fields where until now there was no gospel testimony in French. Their effective force numbers eighteen missionary families, several of whom are *Canadien.*

In a letter from Pastor Ernest Keefe he says: "We have broadcasts in French from Noranda and four other stations in northwestern Quebec; also from Pembroke and Cornwall in (eastern) Ontario and St. Jérome in Quebec. There is a monthly television program in Noranda. Our aims are (1) to establish indigenous French churches, (2) train converts whom the Lord calls to full-time service, (3) provide education in the French language for the children, (4) produce literature like our monthly *Le Phare,* as well as tracts and booklets."

The missionary work of the Christian Brethren dates from about 1928. Their missionaries, few in number, carried on quietly for years, mailing out tracts, calling on interested contacts, and finally forming a few assemblies of Christians. After the war, their work received a great impetus from the arrival in the province of several young workers, some with Bible school and other good training. With these vigorous recruits, the work of evangelism has gone forward until now seventeen assemblies in all have been established. Their missionary force numbers nineteen families and three single workers, almost half of whom are of *Canadien* of French extraction. They have one French radio broadcast from the city of Granby and another from Timmins, in northern Ontario.

The third active evangelical group is the Pentecostal Assemblies of Canada, the French conference. For some years their work was more or less centered around Montreal, where they have two thriving churches and several smaller works. Recently their Bible school (Berea) has been graduating able young *Canadien* missionaries and they have branched out into other parts of the province. They now have fourteen assemblies. Twelve of them have their own church building or hall. Three other works are in the process of being opened. They have five weekly radio broadcasts: Sherbrooke, Cornwall (Ontario), Rouyn, Val D'Or and St. Jean. In 1961 their Bible school had ten men and four young women students. Most of the Pentecostal pastors and missionaries are *Canadiens.*

The United Church of Canada has four missionary pastors in Quebec, all of them *Canadiens*. These pastors care for five organized churches and hold regular or occasional meetings in half a dozen other centers. They have for many years conducted a French language boarding school at Pointe Aux Trembles. While caring for their own people, the United Church missionaries are not noted for aggressive evangelism.

Besides the above missionary enterprises, work among *Canadiens* is carried on to some extent by six other Protestant groups.

Other Evangelistic Agents

We are made increasingly aware of the importance of good literature in all our missionary efforts. Evangelical missions in Quebec have, on the whole, made intelligent use of literature and especially of the New Testament in an attractive edition.

Publications Chrétiennes Enr., Cap de la Madeleine, has recently strengthened the hands of Christian workers by producing first-class Christian literature of general interest and in very pleasing format. Pictures and colors are freely used. At present, the press issues two monthly papers. One, *Vie Ardente* (On Fire for God), is adapted to Christians, while the other, *Vers Minuit* (Almost Midnight), is for general distribution. In several communities, missionaries have placed localized editions of *Vers Minuit* in every home (four to five thousand copies) with encouraging results. This has proved more effective than sending out items by mail.

The Bible schools in Quebec should also be mentioned. These were originally founded to instruct *Canadien* Christians in the Word. Unfortunately, as we believe, most young *Canadien* Christians who feel called of the Lord to His work are too impatient to get going to take one or more years of study in a Bible school. As a result, most of the students at the Bible schools have been from the States and other parts of Canada. They wish to learn French en route to some French-speaking mission field (often not Quebec!). We hope and pray that more *Canadien* Christians will see the need for Bible school training in the years ahead. The oldest of the Bible schools is Bethel, situated near Lennoxville. At Athelstan is the Montreal Bible School.

These are both interdenominational and evangelical. The Pentecostal Bible school (Berea) in Montreal has already been noted.

There are now two orphanages in Quebec for the receiving and the Christian training of children who are orphaned, who come from broken homes or who for some other reason need a true home. The first of these, Le Flambeau Mission, is situated in the Eastern Townships near Knowlton. The second is in Sion Home, in Quebec City. Both these homes receive children from any group of society and are dependent upon the offerings of the Lord's people for their maintenance.

The Open Air Campaigners began work in Quebec in 1958, in fellowship with various local churches.

Suggestions for the Prospective Missionary

Religious liberty in Quebec is not what it is in the rest of North America. The government, local and provincial, is strongly Roman Catholic and is greatly influenced by the Roman organization in all its decisions. "In a Catholic state, the church will require that — if religious minorities actually exist — they shall have only a de facto existence without opportunity to spread their beliefs."[3] Recent court decisions in favor of the so-called Jehovah's Witnesses and the results of the persecution of Baptist and Brethren missionaries have aided the cause of freedom in Quebec. But the Roman Catholic Church makes it as hard as it can!

There is a great need in Quebec for French Protestant schools. About eight of these already exist, but most of them are small and many large centers have none. The main difficulty is the lack of teachers. The government is bound to build a school and pay a teacher's salary where there is a reasonable demand. Roy Langley, principal of Mansonville high school, has organized a branch of the Teachers' Fellowship (IVCF) to build up a pool of Christian teachers who can speak French.

There are many openings in Quebec for non-professional missionaries of all kinds — doctors, engineers, teachers, mechanics, etc. These must be people who are willing to identify themselves with the *Canadien* Christians and help them in their mission.

All missionaries intending to come to Quebec must plan to learn French *well*. These are an ancient people, proud of their language

---

[3] *Civilta Catholica*, Rome, April, 1948.

and traditions, and they do not enjoy *français fracture*. While *Canadien* Christians make the best evangelists, there will be a need for years to come of well-informed missionaries who can instruct converts and shepherd the churches.

It is well to remember that all evangelistic efforts in Quebec must aim at relating the convert to a local church. When a Roman Catholic leaves his church, he is immediately cut off from the services his priest and church have given him, that is, the registration of children, solemnization of marriages, conducting of funerals, etc. All these must be performed by representatives of a church which is recognized by the government. Hence there is no scope for the interdenominational mission in Quebec. It must also be remembered that the *Canadien* is a gregarious, friendly person who loves to visit endlessly with his family and friends. He *must* have a new church fellowship to take the place of the old.

Missions Working in Quebec

French Baptist Churches: Fellowship of Evangelical Baptist Churches, Verdun; Independent Baptist, Valleyfield; Grande Ligne, Montreal; Baptist Convention of Ontario and Quebec, Coaticook.

French Pentecostal Assemblies, Montreal
French Presbyterian Churches, Montreal
French Anglican Churches, Montreal
French United Churches, Montreal
Salvation Army French Corps, Montreal
Mennonite Board of Missions, Montreal North
LeFlambeau Mission, orphanage, Bondville
Sion Children's Home, Quebec City
Open Door Society, Sweetsburg
Bible Institute of Montreal, Athelstan
Bethel Bible School, Lennoxville
Child Evangelism Fellowship, Montreal
Christian Brethren Churches, Sherbrooke
Chrétienne publications, Cap de la Madeleine
Open Air Campaigners, Toronto
Teachers' Christian Fellowship, Mansonville

BIBLIOGRAPHY

History of Canada and Quebec

BOVEY, WILFRED. *Canadien: a Study of the French Canadians.* Toronto: J. M. Dent, 1933.

LOWER, A. R. M. *Colony to Nation: A History of Canada.* Toronto: Longmans, Green & Co., 1946.

MASTERS, D. C. *A Short History of Canada.* Toronto: Van Nostrand, 1958.

WADE, MASON. *The French Canadians, 1760-1945.* Toronto: Macmillan Co., 1955.

WRONG, GEORGE M. *The Canadians: The Story of a People.* Toronto: Macmillan Co., 1939.

Protestant Missions

CHINIQUY, FATHER CHARLES. *Fifty Years in the Church of Rome.* Toronto: S. R. Briggs, 1886.

Forty Years in the Church of Christ, 1898.

Mes Combats. Montreal: L'Aurore, 1946.

DUCLOS, R. & P. *Histoire du Protestantisme Français au Canada et aux États Unis.* Montreal: Libraire Évangelique, 1913, 2 vols.

The Huguenots in France and America. Cambridge: John Owen, 1843.

HILL, ARTHUR C. *News of Quebec.* Sherbrooke, Quebec, 1942-1959.

LAFLEUR, THEODORE. *Historical Sketch of the Grande Ligne Mission.* Montreal: Bentley & Co., 1885.

LINDSEY, CHARLES. *Rome in Canada.* Toronto: Williamson & Co., 1889.

VILLARD, PAUL. *Preparing the Way.* Pointe aux Trembles School, 1907.

Up to the Light. Toronto: United Church of Canada, 1928.

City rescue missions offer food for the body, food for the soul, and social rehabilitation.

15

Lights in the Cities' Jungles

WILLIAM SEATH

Rescue missions are the outposts of the gospel of Jesus Christ in the heathen jungles of our own country. For there are jungles, just as heathenish in America as any country in this world. It is no longer uncommon for men and women to enter rescue missions who have never held a Bible in their hands, who do not know that there are Old and New Testaments in the Word of God and who have never been in a public worship service and thus have no conception of Jesus Christ. To these and countless thousands of others who have lost the way, rescue missions carry a message of hope, love, practical help and, above all, the story of Jesus Christ as the Saviour of men.

Scriptural Background

The late Dr. W. E. Paul in his book, *The Romance of Rescue*,[1] places the beginnings of rescue missions in the third chapter of Genesis and says that "Adam was the first rescue mission prospect, for

---

WILLIAM SEATH, a Presbyterian minister, entered rescue mission work in 1920. He served as associate superintendent of the Union City Mission of Minneapolis, Minnesota, until 1931. From that time until February, 1963, he was executive director of the Christian Industrial League in Chicago. Since then he has been executive administrator of the League.

Dr. Seath is past president of the International Union of Gospel Missions and a member of the mayor of Chicago's Commission on Rehabilitation of Persons. For a number of years he has also been a member of the summer faculty of Houghton College, Houghton, New York. He does considerable writing and is called to speak all over the United States and Canada.

[1] W. E. Paul, *The Romance of Rescue* (Minneapolis: Osterhus Publishing Co.).

he went into sin in the characteristic way of the down and outer."
"The rescue mission deals primarily with poor people. . . . The
Bible uses the word *poor* with preventative and remedial measures
in the laws."[2]

The story of the pool at Bethesda in John 5 is probably the best
demonstration of a rescue mission program. The pool was in the
skid row of Jerusalem. It was at the back gate of the city, the sheep
market. It was where the sick, crippled, handicapped and unemployed congregated. It was here that merchants, farmers and
caravaneers came to secure men to work. Into this area the Master
came, selected the worst case present and performed the mighty
miracle of a complete restoration.

The Problem

The problem of dealing with the unfortunate, the crippled, the
handicapped and the aged has been one which has been faced since
the beginning of human society. There always has been and
always will be a segment of society which cannot live normally
and which by sheer force of circumstances is driven down into
the depths of degradation. The basic problem of the man and
woman of this type is *sin*. It can be disguised in any way men
desire, but the problem remains the same. There is only one cure
for sin and that is the *blood of the Lord Jesus Christ*. "The rescue
mission deals with this problem in such a way that these who are
lost can and will be restored to lives of active usefulness in a
society which can accept them on the proper level."[3]

In the ancient world the migrants or vagrants were usually runaway slaves who found refuge in the larger cities, especially Rome.
The Orient has always had thousands of these wanderers. No effort
was made to solve the problem. A coin tossed by the passerby was
the limit of assistance. In England, the problem of the transients
became so desperate that in 1603 King James I issued a proclama-
tion ordering that all vagrants be deported from the country.

"In America, the real transient movement of labor began right
after the Civil War. The natural result of war is a restlessness on
the part of men released from military service. At that time the

[2] C. E. Morey, *Rescue Mission Dynamic* (1958, unpublished).
[3] William Seath, *A Study of Rescue Missions* (Chicago: Chicago League Print Shop, 1952).

railroads began their great westward expansion; the era of large farms began; road construction took on new significance and the need for seasonal workers called for thousands of men."[4]

General Background in America

In America the rescue mission movement began about 1830, when a work was started to help the men sailing on the Great Lakes. It was known as the Western Seamen's Friends Society. This work was about one hundred years ahead of its time in program, for it operated Sunday schools, summer camps, nurseries, lodging houses, gave medical service and even legal aid. From this group the Bethel Mission, still doing a fine work in Duluth, Minnesota, was organized in 1873.

In 1872 the Jerry McCauley Water Street Mission was founded in New York City under the name of "The Helping Hand on Water Street." This mission, which is still operating in New York, was organized by Jerry McCauley, river rat, ex-convict, drunkard and loafer. His story is always an inspiration to mission men and women.

The term "rescue mission" probably began in Syracuse, New York, in 1888. Prior to this date, H. B. Gibband knew of places of shelter for runaway slaves which carried names such as rescue band and place of refuge. When Mr. Gibband opened a mission in Syracuse he utilized the word *rescue*. Seeing the success of these missions, other cities adopted the idea and the great rescue mission movement was under way, spreading westward until today rescue missions are an integral part of Christian service in nearly every large (and many a small) city. The rescue mission is the *church in action in an area where the organized church cannot function.*

As already mentioned, the real transient movement of men began after the Civil War. By 1926 there were approximately three and a half million transient seasonal workers — men who moved in well-defined patterns from one type of job to another, depending on the season. In 1926 these men began to feel the effect of modern machinery. Demands for farm labor were curtailed. The lumber industry used only a fraction of those needed previously. The natural ice harvest was a thing of the past. Only railroad work was

---
[4] *Ibid.*

left. Today the steady decline in the number of jobs available has become a matter of real concern to rescue mission leaders.

The depression of 1930-1933 created new and complex problems. Entire families became transient; other families were forced to seek help for the first time. The picture changed and new problems developed. There were calls for family work, children needed help, young people faced new and frightening situations.

One other factor which had a great bearing on the problem of underprivileged areas was that many churches moved out of what is now called the "inner city" to the suburbs, leaving vast sections entirely unchurched. The rescue missions were forced to move into this field. Today the denominations are increasingly aware of the needs of the inner city and much is being done to alleviate the situation.

Modern Trends

From a very humble beginning as rescue stations for men, mostly drunkards, rescue missions have grown and are still growing into one of the strongest branches of the Christian church. "The average valuation of missions is $40,000, with 125 missions having a total valuation of $20,000,000. The average budget for operations is about $54,000."[5] Within the last few years several missions have erected new buildings at costs in excess of $250,000. Others are spending up to $100,000 in remodeling projects.

The work of rescue missions is highly diversified. It includes meals, lodging, clothing, medical and dental clinics, employment service, baths and fumigation, family relief, work with courts, boys' and girls' clubs, gymnasiums, summer camps, day nurseries, children's homes, maternity homes, mothers' meetings, hospital and jail visitation, foreign language work, home visitation, counseling. Some have large industrial departments, alcoholic wards and farms. The old slogan was "Soap, soup, salvation." Today the challenge is "a complete rehabilitation of the whole man."

Originally the mission executive was a man who had come up from the gutter, a "twice-born man" who lacked training or experience, but whose testimony and desire to see others saved made up for the lack of formal education. These men and women are

---

[5] Charles E. Morey, *Rescue Mission Dynamic.*

still essential to the program of any mission! Their testimonies are needed to stir the hearts of the hearers and to demonstrate beyond a shadow of doubt that *"Jesus saves."* But more and more the need of formal education and good training becomes apparent. In one outstanding mission, six out of eight staff members have at least one degree. Missions now have doctors, dentists, sociologists, psychologists and case workers on their staffs who are competent to minister to the needs of the whole man in Christ.[6]

Rescue missions now minister to men, women, children, young people, the foreign born, migrants, ex-convicts, unmarried mothers and those who are not "down and out" but who do have personality problems and are referred to the mission by ministers and business people.

The Rescue Mission Organizations

There are many ways in which rescue missions are organized and directed. Some of them are:

One man control. This mission has no board, no control by any church. All property is held in one name. The disadvantages of this type of setup are apparent. There are very few of this kind.

Just an advisory board. This is similar to the above except that the executive selects an advisory board which has no authority.

Self-appointed and self-perpetuating board of directors. The board controls the property, appoints the executive, handles affairs of the mission. There are dangers in this type of setup.

A board of directors appointed by various churches. Sometimes the directors are named by the pastors, sometimes by vote of congregations. This is good, except that the board may become too large. In some cases these "delegates" form a corporation which elects a smaller board of directors. This is excellent.

Denominational control. There are two styles here.

1.   One denomination starts the work, a board is selected by the denomination and the mission remains under denominational control. The weakness of this is that other churches are shut out and the mission may develop into a church.

2.   One denomination starts the work, the board is selected by the denomination and then other denominations are invited to

---
[6] *Ibid.*

join and appoint directors. In this case ownership of the property remains in the one denomination, but all others share in the work, financing and control. This is an excellent method of operation.

Board under church auspices. A group of pastors and laymen start a rescue mission. An organizational committee is set up to complete the organization, including constitution, by-laws, incorporation. The board of directors is selected by this group, and so many elected each year for a specific number of years. Every director must be a member in good standing of a church (Protestant evangelical). In this program as many denominations as possible are represented and an effort made to have only *one* director from any one church. This is another excellent method of organization, as it assures support from all churches and centers control in the Protestant evangelical churches.

Types of Missions

There are many types of rescue missions, each one filling an important and unique place in the community. None can look at the other and say, "I am more important than you." In I Corinthians 12 we find the scriptural basis for this conclusion. All types are essential to a complete work of rebuilding broken lives.

The gospel mission. This type of mission confines its activities to preaching the gospel. Usually such missions operate in rented halls, hold services once or twice a day and two or three times on Sunday. They do not house or feed men, but sometimes give out tickets good for a bed in a nearby lodging house or a meal in a convenient restaurant. The theory back of this work is that if a man accepts Christ he will begin to look after himself. Many wonderful conversions are reported by this kind of mission. However, on the whole and with a few notable exceptions, such missions do not accomplish nearly as much as those with a more complete program.

The lodging house and meal type. Probably the most popular type of rescue mission is one which has free beds to offer and also to rent, and which serves meals, free and paid for. This sort of program can begin without too much capital investment. A lodging house or small hotel is rented, chapel arranged on the first floor, rooms rented to produce some income and the mission is under way on a partially self-supporting basis. Many missions which started in this fashion have grown to where they own fine fireproof buildings and have large programs. Care must be exercised to guard against too much stress being put on raising money to the exclusion of the gospel.

The mission giving meals and lodgings without charge. There are some missions which operate in the same manner as those above but they do not sell meals or rent beds. They are able to operate without this financial backing. The advantages of this type of work are many, as there are not the distractions which so often affect the other methods. Many of the finest missions in the country do their work this way.

The industrial mission. This is a mission with a sheltered workshop or occupational therapy department. As missions grew and developed, all sorts of things were sent in for distribution to the needy. Ultimately there was a surplus of material. Mission men put this material and unemployed men together and the industrial work was under way. These men (and now women) work these discards over into things of value which are either sold at low cost or given away. Some missions have fine buildings and excellent equipment. Some have large fleets of trucks and utilize fifty to a hundred or more men and women in this activity.

There are many advantages in this. Converts are given work during their early days as Christians. Money thus derived is used for the spiritual work. But great care must be exercised to keep from becoming commercial and stressing "production" rather than "salvation."

Many lodging house type of missions and industrial missions have fine *church homes* for both men and women, where complete rehabilitation work is done, including case work, counseling, psychiatric service, recreation, leading to a *"complete rehabilitation of the whole man."*

Specialized work for women. In the main it is not practical to house both men and women in the same building. The approach is different and the program must be geared to the needs of women.

Missions are now helping women occupy a very prominent place in the picture. Many of these have fine buildings, excellent equipment, well-trained workers. Others set up separate departments with homes for women away from the main headquarters. Some are able to care for mothers with children, and a few have facilities for caring for entire families. This is a highly specialized field and there is great need for adequately trained staff personnel who are thoroughly Christian. With the migrant problem increasing by leaps and bounds, this kind of mission work must be expanded to meet the ever-growing need. Maternity homes are run by numerous missions, especially in the South.

Specialized work for children and young people. As the work of rescue missions expanded, the problem of children within the area became acute. What could be done? Sunday schools were started, but this was insufficient. Children's missions were organized, and in rapid succession came clubs and weekday classes, summer camps, gymnasiums, craft work, medical and dental clinics, day nurseries, homes for abandoned children. The part played by rescue missions in preventing or overcoming juvenile delinquency can never be estimated.

In all this work the gospel of Christ must be the dominant factor. Once again, here is a field requiring the finest trained leadership. It is not easy. In fact, it is the most difficult of all rescue work, but the rewards in seeing the change in young lives makes it worthwhile.

A great many missions have some form of children's work along with programs for men and women. A survey of missions affiliated with the International Union of Gospel Missions indicates that about 80 per cent have Sunday schools and work with young people.

In addition to these general types there is work with alcoholics, including homes, hospitals and farms, family work, general farms and even Bible conferences.

Presenting the Gospel

The most important work of the rescue mission is the presentation of the glorious gospel of Jesus Christ and the winning of souls to Him. Unless this is uppermost, the work must fail.

There are many ways in which the gospel is presented. "The heart of the rescue mission is the gospel service."[7] Foremost is the *evening service,* which is usually conducted by a group from one of the churches. Many missions assign a certain night a month to a specific church. Either the executive or one of the staff is present to

---

[7] William E. Paul, *Rescue Mission Manual* (Minneapolis: Osterhus Publishing Co.).

assist, make announcements and care for the men after the service. The following suggestions will be helpful for the group:

The purpose of the service is to win men to Christ.

Groups must be in a spirit of prayer, anticipate results, be at the mission early, start and close on time.

The leader and song leader should not talk too much. Always remember that the audience is tired and should not be asked to stand more than once.

Never "talk down" to the audience; talk with them. Present Christ as Saviour; do not condemn or rain fire and brimstone all over them. Do not criticize another mission, preacher, denomination or religion. Be constructive. Preach Christ and Him crucified.

Maintain a dignity in Christ.

Refer all appeals for help to the mission workers.

Prayer meetings. Prayer is essential. Time *must* be found for the staff and workers to unite in prayer. No service should ever begin without prayer. All interviews and counseling sessions should close with prayer.

Street work. This is a vital part of the work of rescue, but it must be handled very carefully. Good, well-planned street work is one of the most effective methods of presenting the gospel. A few ideas:

Secure permit from police department.

Watch location. Guard against too much noise.

Use groups of from three to ten and have good music, vocal and instrumental.

Keep message and testimonies short and to the point.

Maintain a dignity in Christ. Never argue with anyone.

Hospital calling. Here is a great field of Christian service. Always work with doctors and nurses. Go from bed to bed quietly, men to men, women to women. Be brief and to the point. Keep your voice low. Watch the emotional factor. Carry gifts of tissues, gum, candy, razor blades and Scripture portions. Always check with the nurse before giving gifts other than Scripture. Always pray before leaving.

Jail work. The same rules apply as in hospital calling. Be very careful in all actions. Obey prison rules and co-operate with officials. Never violate the confidence of a prisoner but never take advantage of your permission to deal with him. *Never carry out messages* without the consent of authorities. When conducting services in prison, use small groups, the best possible talent, and guard against relatives or friends of inmates joining group. Be very conservative in dress. Be careful what you promise and always keep your promises. Investigate carefully both the family situation and the record of an inmate before committing yourself to any course of action.

Tract distribution. This is an extremely effective way of presenting the gospel. For best results use tracts clearly printed on good paper with language the non-Christian can understand. Let the message be of hope and salvation. Avoid sensationalism. Let the Holy Spirit direct in the distribution.

Many missions, after receiving permission, install tract cases in hotels and lodging houses and keep them filled. This is an excellent method of distribution. It is well to have tracts applicable to the Christian life for the new convert.

Other methods. There are many other methods of presenting the gospel, but we will mention only three:

Clubs and classes. Bible classes for converts, converts' clubs, mothers' clubs, and so on, are invaluable in preparing the new Christian for his or her place in life. Avoid doctrine.

Radio and television. Many missions have regular radio broadcasts. All that has been said regarding other methods applies here.

Churches and clubs. Churches, church groups, luncheon clubs are a fertile field for the skilled mission worker. Never take advantage of the audience by preaching at them. Tell the mission story and use lots of illustrations. Never apologize for the gospel. Close on time and remember that you are representing Jesus Christ.

Relationship of Rescue Missions to the Church

A survey of the missions affiliated with the International Union of Gospel Missions shows that 98 per cent are not churches. They work in complete co-operation with the local churches. Rescue missions channel their converts into the church. In one year four hundred converts were received into the churches of Grand Rapids, Michigan, from the one rescue mission. Forty-seven per cent of the member missions of the International Union of Gospel Missions received direct donations from churches. Eighty-seven per cent of all these missions are interdenominational.

The rescue mission receives financial support from the church, workers on a volunteer basis, members of boards and women's auxiliaries. It also secures groups to carry on services. To the church the rescue mission gives opportunity for service and the inspiration which comes from seeing the mighty miracle of the new birth in the lives of men, women, boys and girls.

The International Union of Gospel Missions

The IUGM, as this organization is commonly known, is an association of rescue and gospel missions in good standing with the Protestant evangelical churches and have endorsement by the various community organizations. Certain standards of membership are enforced.

The IUGM was founded in 1913, and has grown in numbers and effectiveness over the years. Today there are about 250 mission members with an individual membership of 1,000. A full-time executive secretary is available for counsel and guidance, as well as work in organizing new missions, making surveys, assisting boards and superintendents and caring for placement and employment. A convention is held in a different city each year. There are fourteen districts, each with its own organization, officers and program. There are also two metropolitan divisions, one in Chicago and one in Los Angeles.

The IUGM sponsors a training school each summer and has a fine "on the job" training program for those who are interested in this Christian service.

The Future

The great need in rescue missions is that of trained leadership. Methods of operation have changed during the past forty years. Executives and staff workers need training in personal counseling, public relations, financing, administration, psychology, case work, in addition to Bible and theology.

But these things must be properly balanced with a genuine new-birth experience plus a passion to see souls saved. There is only one reason anyone should go into rescue mission work and that is because he *cannot stay out of it*. The challenge is here! Let the Holy Spirit direct.

The rescue mission is the church in action in areas where the regular organized church cannot function. The message of the rescue mission is *"God loves and Jesus saves."*

Survey of Men Passing Through the Rehabilitation Church Home of Chicago Christian Industrial League[8]

Age	1961	1962	Marital Status	1961	1962
20-29	2.0%	7.0%	Single	39.0%	40.5%
30-39	23.0	26.5	Married	3.0	1.0
40-49	38.0	34.5	Separated	12.0	15.0
50-59	21.0	21.0	Divorced	37.0	35.0
Over 60	16.0	11.0	Widower	9.0	8.5
Group under 40	25.0	33.5	*Children*		
Group under 50	62.0	68.5	Yes	37.0	36.0
Group over 50	38.0	31.5	No	63.0	64.0
Birthplace			*Military Service*		
U.S.A.	98.0	96.5	World War I	2.0	2.5
Foreign	2.0	3.5	After World War I	5.0	3.5
Percentage of U. S.			World War II	39.0	40.0
born in Chicago	16.0	18.0	After World War II		
From Where			(Korea inc.)	6.0	13.0
East	9.0	12.5	None	48.0	41.0
West	2.0	4.5	*Physical Handicaps*		
South	38.0	29.5	Yes	17.0	13.5
North Central	49.0	32.0	No	83.0	86.5
Native Chicago	16.0	18.0	*Alcoholic*		
Foreign	2.0	3.5	Yes	81.0	76.5
Religion			No	19.0	22.0
Catholic	28.0	26.5	Uncertain	0.0	1.5
Protestant	67.0	72.0	*Time in League*		
Other	2.0	.5	Less than a month	30.0	50.0
None	3.0	1.0	1-3 months	38.0	31.5
Regularity of			3-6 months	13.0	6.5
Church Attendance			Over 6 months	19.0	12.0
Yes	17.0	15.0	*Education*		
No	83.0	85.0	Less than 8th grade	16.0	13.5
Occupation			8th grade graduate	36.0	27.5
Common labor	17.0	28.0	H.S. non-graduate	28.0	26.5
Skilled labor	45.0	16.0	H.S. graduate	10.0	24.5
Hotel, restaurant	11.0	19.5	College non-graduate	7.0	6.0
Sales	2.0	4.0	College graduate	3.0	2.0
Clerical, professional	7.0	5.5			
Misc. (semi-skilled)	8.0	25.0			
Railroad	1.0	2.0			

[8] Based on 200 case records.

BIBLIOGRAPHY

BRANTLEY, CLOVIS A. *God Can.* Atlanta: Home Mission Board, Southern Baptist Convention, 1946.

DEES, JESSE W. *Flophouse.* Francestown, N. H.: Marshall Jones Co., 1948.

HADLEY, SAMUEL H. *Down in Water Street.* New York: Fleming H. Revell Co., 1906.

MOREY, CHARLES EDWARD. "Rescue Mission Dynamics." 1958. Unpublished.

PAUL, WILLIAM E. *Miracles of Rescue.* Minneapolis: Osterhus Publishing Co.

——*Rescue Mission Manual.* Minneapolis: Osterhus Publishing Co.

——*Romance of Rescue.* Minneapolis: Osterhus Publishing Co.

SEATH, WILLIAM. *A Study of Rescue Missions.* Chicago: Chicago League Print Shop, 1952.

——*Personal Evangelism.* Chicago: Chicago League Print Shop, 1946.

——*The Master Touch.* Chicago: Chicago League Print Shop, 1954.

——"The Rescue Mission and the Current Social Disorganization." 1956. Unpublished.

WITHROW, PAT. *Soup, Soap and Salvation.* Winona Lake, Ind.: Rodeheaver-Hall-Mack, 1952.

Busy boys entertain themselves while their parents work in the California harvest field. Who will tell them of Jesus and His love? (Courtesy of Missionary Gospel Fellowship.)

16

Present-Day Vagabonds

MAX R. KRONQUEST

WE LOOK UPON the white migrating farm laborer as almost another race," quite frankly explained one man. And anyone who sees how these laborers are treated in the communities near which they chance to live for a time will agree that the statement is based on good evidence. Migrants, whether white or of some other color, are "outsiders" wherever they go.

As they move along the highways, their heavily laden cars or trucks crammed with mattresses, pots and pans, it is easily seen that these are not just campers or vacationers. When they go into the stores to buy, there is something about their manner and bearing that somehow seems to give them away. They are "different."

Who Are the Migrants?

Who are these migrants? Why do they accept a way of life that keeps them from having a sense of belonging in any segment of society?

The word *migrant* itself means simply one who moves from place to place. But we have applied the term to a vast number of seasonal farm laborers who do much of the back-breaking work of harvesting vegetable and fruit crops. Unlike the familiar hired man, they are not permanent residents of the community. Today's huge farms

Before his appointment in 1949 as director of the Missionary Gospel Fellowship, Inc., MAX R. KRONQUEST had a varied ministry in Santa Fe Prison, on radio and in coal mines. He also served as pastor for sixteen years in Nebraska, Colorado, Michigan and New Mexico. A native of Nebraska, Mr. Kronquest received his training at Rockmont College.

and orchards often demand a large task force for a brief, critical period when the harvest is ripe. As soon as the harvest is past, farmers can do without this extra help until the next time. A few weeks of work may be all that any one harvest will provide.

This need has produced a class of "rootless Americans," the migratory farm laborers. Unskilled workmen with only the labor of their hands to sell, pressed by economic necessity, they seize the one opportunity that seems to offer a little cash to meet the present need. When one crop is harvested, they move along to another place where another harvest may be ready to begin. If things go well they may be able to get in several months of work. It is poorly paid work, and one has to travel a long way to get it, but at least it is something.

Why do people become migrants? One missionary who works among them says: "In the early days Americans became migrants because of destitute circumstances. Now the second generation are migrants because they know nothing else." Another declares: "They are migrant because of lack of education, insufficient work in local areas, alcoholism, crop failure and unstable nature." An executive of a large denomination believes: "Americans do migrant labor because they do not have other trades or means of livelihood. Foreign groups do it as a means of getting started in this country, with expectations of progressing into other more desirable types of work."

In other words, this type of temporary farm labor depends on the weaknesses and misfortunes of men. Fortunately it represents only a small portion of the whole farm labor force in the country. But even so, it involves many hundreds of thousands of people over most of the country.

The racial composition of this migratory labor force has varied from time to time. There was a time on the West Coast when employers thought they had a permanent supply in the Orientals, such as the Chinese, Japanese and Hindus. But most migrants do not stay migrant if they can improve their position. So these found other employment, the Japanese becoming particularly successful in truck farming.

In the thirties a very large element in migratory labor was the "Okie." This was a name applied not only to displaced farmers and laborers from Oklahoma, but also to those from other parts of the "dust bowl," such as Arkansas, Missouri and Texas. The economic depression, coupled with the prolonged drought and disastrous dust storms, forced many families to take to the road with what little possessions they had, in the hope of making a new start somewhere else. Their plight was vividly pictured in John Steinbeck's famous novel, *Grapes of Wrath*.

But most of the "Okies," too, are no longer migrant. They have found their way into more rewarding occupations. Their place has been taken by other depressed segments of the population, mainly Mexicans and Negroes.

The Negroes, who are mostly in the East and South, are American citizens. The Mexicans are of three types. Many are also American citizens who have long lived in the Southwest and are particularly numerous in the Rio Grande Valley of Texas. These are often called Texas-Mexicans. Then there are the "wetbacks," Mexicans who have slipped across the border illegally by the hundreds of thousands to find employment in the more favored United States. Some have been deported, but many more have successfully avoided deportation and provide much of the cheap labor in the fields. The third group are Mexican nationals who have been legitimately brought into the United States to supplement the labor force. The governments have agreed on the terms of their employment, and they are supposed to be returned to their own country at the conclusion of their contract.

Where Do the Migrants Live?

Migrants can scarcely be said to have a home. Of course those who come as contract laborers from such places as Mexico and Jamaica are returned to their own country when the work is done. But those who are Americans are free to settle where they will during their months of unemployment. However, they are seldom in any place long enough to qualify as voters, nor are their children likely to get much in the way of consecutive schooling.

Migrants are commonly thought of in connection with California. Perhaps this is because of the "Okie" rush and the greater amount of publicity given to the problem in that state. Yet Texas employed far more migrants during the 1960 season, and Michigan ran not far behind California in the number employed.[1] New York, Kansas, Florida, Oregon, Washington follow in that order. These were thirteen states that employed more than ten thousand domestic migratory workers each. So the problem is very widespread.

In almost all the states where they are employed, it can be said that the people want the migrants to be present when the harvest is on, but they want them to be gone when the harvest is over. As field hands they are needed, but as people they are not wanted. Some of them do stay around during the off-season period, especially where the climate is mild, but local authorities would prefer that they did not.

Some migrants get from place to place in their own dilapidated trucks or jalopies. These are the ones who make up their own itineraries and hire out as independent workers. Unless they go back to the same places year after year, they are taking a great risk. The harvest may be delayed or it may be too small to provide much work.

Many workers sign up with crew leaders or labor contractors. All the arrangements are made by the crew leader, including transportation. This plan gives the worker more assurance of employment, but it is open to a number of abuses. The worker has very little protection against a dishonest or unreliable crew leader, though a few states and the federal government are trying to remedy the situation.

The transportation provided by the crew leaders often consists of heavily loaded trucks or buses unfit for carrying people. By staying off the main thoroughfares they can often avoid the inspectors. But if they are stopped and the conveyance is taken out of service, the workers are left stranded. In many cases no rest stops are made, no matter how long the trip. There is an Interstate Commerce Commission regulation that calls for an eight hour rest stop after each six hundred miles or less, but it is extremely difficult to enforce. Besides, where could these homeless and penniless travelers stay?

Housing while the harvest is on is a somewhat different problem. Neither the worker nor the employer is likely to be interested

---

[1] The figures for domestic workers alone are 80,800 in Texas; 63,200 in California; 54,100 in Michigan, according to the Bureau of Employment Security, United States Department of Labor.

in permanent-type housing for such a short period. Yet many of the makeshifts that are used are a serious threat to the morals of the workers and to public health. In some areas the shelters, row upon row, are a bit larger than a single-car garage, with side flaps for air and light. These are usually the old federal camps, with the shelters arranged in a circle. There is a public toilet and bath to accommodate roughly each fifty families.

The federal camps provide a center building for civic meetings, shows, dances, camp weddings, etc. A few have a sewing room and some have schools. A central laundry can be used for a very small fee. Public showers and toilets, outside faucets and garbage cans are scattered around the camp.

Today farm organizations or the county usually operate these old federal camps. They charge a set amount for rent, regardless of income. In California, low cost government housing is going up alongside the camps. These developments provide better quarters for migrants and others, who pay rent according to their income.

Living conditions in private camps are often more deplorable than in the old federal camps, though some states and enlightened employers have been taking steps to remedy the situation. Many have no laundry facilities or showers provided, and outside privies often serve more than a score of families. Once a liquor store replaced a gospel tent where Sunday school was being held by evangelical Christians.

These camps are often very large affairs. It is necessary to realize that the major employers of migrant labor are not small farmers but large companies with very extensive holdings. One such "farm" is forty-five miles long, while another has 150,000 acres of tomatoes to be harvested. Caring for crops on such a large scale calls for an army of workers. And since they are paid according to the amount they gather, they want their housing close by.

Because so many camps are very temporary affairs, it is impossible to calculate just how many there are in the country. On the west side of Fresno County, California, there are over six hundred camps with from fifty to two hundred families each. It is estimated that the West Coast has more than two thousand camps. For many of the migrants a succession of camps are "home" for a considerable part of the year. Others are able to stay longer in a single area.

The government estimates the total migratory labor force at about 500,000 and their average income at about $900 per year. This means that a half million Americans are averaging about $75 per month. But of even more concern than the economic handicap is the fact that they are deprived of many of the rights of American citizenship. They seldom live in one place long enough to qualify as voters. They have only recently begun to be included in the Social Security program. Most of the federal and state legislation for the benefit of laborers either exempts farm labor from its provisions or restricts them to permanent residents. The President's Committee on Migratory Labor reported in 1960 that the life of the migrant "is characterized by 'exclusion.'"

What of the Children?

Nothing is more distressing than the plight of the migrant children. Economic necessity and lack of training for better paying jobs force many adults to join the ranks of the migrants. If the children are to be rescued from such a life, there must not only be a desire for improvement, but also an opportunity for training. Yet the very circumstances of migrant life make this a most difficult thing to accomplish.

First of all, the economic necessity that drives the parents into migratory work makes them try to earn all that they can during the harvesting season. Even little children can earn a few dollars for the family's needs. Of course there are child labor laws. But these are hard to enforce when the growers are pushing the harvesting of their crops, or when the workers will simply move on to another area where enforcement is not so strict.

Then there is the problem of the schools themselves. Local school systems have neither the personnel nor the facilities to care for a sudden flood of non-tax-paying pupils, many of whom need special attention. This is presuming that the schools are willing to take them. But in many schools these pupils are definitely not welcome and are made to feel that they do not belong.

Besides, a migratory life breaks up any schooling into such small fragments that children are soon likely to be behind their age group in school. As they go into the upper grades this disparity becomes even more acute. Put with children much younger than themselves, they learn to resent school and quit as soon as possible.

Some of the states are struggling with these problems of schooling and are even providing special schools. But there is still much to be done. Meantime some of the young people are seeking an escape from their drab existence by entering into premature marriages. Of course they marry within their own circle, the social barriers being what they are. But this only makes it more likely that they will be unable to escape from migrant life.

Why a Special Work for Migrants?

From some of the things mentioned, it should be obvious that very few of the migrants will be reached by the ordinary ministries of the Christian church. Those ministries are based on a more or less stable population. The local church reaches people who are part of the community, who can look forward to church membership and assuming certain regular responsibilities that go with such membership.

The migrants cannot do this. They can receive from the church, but there is very little they can contribute to it. There is not even enough cohesion among themselves to form a migrating church. They are in a very real sense a home mission field.

Their spiritual destitution is not surprising, but it is deplorable. Some put it this way: "When they left home, they left their religion also." This seems to apply equally to white and Negro Americans of Protestant heritage and to Mexicans with a background of Roman Catholicism. Lack of a sense of belonging, long hours, inferior clothing, plus instability has taken heavy spiritual tolls. Widespread publicity of the book *Grapes of Wrath* has given them inbred complexes.

Many have really never heard the pure gospel message. Illiteracy keeps them from reading God's Word. Churches as a rule do not want them. Consequently adult indifference is rampant. One father's approach each week was, "You kids goin' fishin' with me or to Sunday school?" A few parents actually come to the center building door to call their children out of the services. The children themselves are soon aged and hardened by the vice and infidelity they sometimes observe in their parents. Yet missionaries among them report that in some areas the people beg them to come back every time they hold a service.

What Is Being Done?

The major denominational effort for the migrants is known as Migrant Ministry and operates under the National Council of Churches. It began its work in 1920 with a concern for the Polish and Italian migrants who were working in Maryland and New Jersey. Now its operations have been extended to thirty-one states. Even so they declare that they are contacting less than 15 per cent of the migrants. Six areas in Florida, for example, are not being touched because of lack of resources. In this one state they have eleven salaried workers plus twenty-five volunteers reaching twenty-two camps.

The Southern Baptists have taken a special interest in those of Mexican background. They have about a hundred of their missionary pastors among Spanish-speaking people spend part of their time each year ministering to the migrants. Couples with mobile equipment serve in each major flow of migration north and south.

There are also several non-denominational missions that minister to migrants. Perhaps the oldest is the Mission to the Migrants, with headquarters in Los Angeles. Their work began in 1935, although it was not incorporated until 1947. When hordes of displaced Americans began gathering in squatter camps adjacent to the harvest fields, postal clerk Ralph Blakeman began preaching to them along the highway. Others joined him in the work, and the operations were extended to Arizona and Oregon as well as California. The founder speaks of his work as being largely seasonal, with special attention being given to Mexicans and other foreigners.

The Missionary Gospel Fellowship, with fifty full-time workers, is doubtless the largest independent mission at work among the migrants. It began in 1939 with the efforts of Paul Pietsch in California and now has extended its work to Arizona, Oklahoma and Florida. The headquarters remains at Turlock, California. Much of its work is carried on in the old federal camps, though a few workers have been led to reach out to the private camps and to do open-air or itinerant work.

An interesting ministry in another part of the country is that of the Chapel Crusaders from Winona Lake, Indiana. Mr. and Mrs. E. C. Ralston have a trailer-house chapel with which they have carried on an itinerant ministry to young people since 1951. Working in southern farm labor centers (camps), they minister to people from Jamaica and the other British West Indies as well as to Americans. In the northern United States their work is among Mexicans. With one full-time helper and many who give part of their time, they have seen nearly a thousand conversions each year. They have reached as many as a thousand migrant youth in a single large camp, where schools are conducted in connection with the camp.

One of the newest organizations is the Migrant Missionary Fellowship of Pompano Beach, Florida. It was not organized until 1957, though the founder, Ken Thornton, had been giving full time to this work for some five years previously.

What Kinds of Ministry?

The needs of the migrants are many — spiritual, economic and social. And to some extent most of the missions address themselves to more than one of these needs. That is, even those who concentrate mostly on the spiritual needs do not refrain from offering material help as they are able, and they also give some attention to the social. For example, the Mission to the Migrants not only conducts open-air gospel meetings; it also distributes thousands of garments besides quilts, layettes, mattresses, etc. In Florida the Missionary Migrant Fellowship during a severe crop failure fed almost a hundred a day for three months. At Christmas nearly five hundred sacks of "treats" were given out along with Gospels of John. One farmer who disliked the colored people tried to order the missionary to stop giving out the "treats."

The major differences, other than doctrinal, are in the emphases. The Home Mission Council of the National Council of Churches, for example, is strongly impressed with the social needs. In some areas they sponsor extensive social betterment programs for a week at a time in each camp.

The independent missions, on the other hand, are firmly persuaded that the basic need is really spiritual. Many of the migrants after conversion find the necessary incentive to settle down to steady employment. Others, especially young people, gain a new outlook on life and a consciousness that the Lord can make their lives meaningful. One lad summed up his testimony at the end of a youth conference with these words: "If God could use that dummy (puppet) and the musical saw, He can sure use me some place."

But even with evangelism the approaches can be varied. The house-trailer chapel that carries along its own audio-visual equipment is specially effective with the young people. Open-air preaching is common, sometimes assisted by chalk illustration. Public address systems are useful in the open air and sometimes even films can be shown. Gospel recordings among the foreign born are a great help to the missionary who does not know their language. After hearing a recording in his own language, a Japanese tearfully announced, waving at the record player, "Today I am a new man!" Church and Sunday school services are often held in the center building. Of course there is the ever present need for personal evangelism. Correspondence courses for follow-up work have a special significance with the migrants, who are constantly on the move.

How One Mission Operates

In the Missionary Gospel Fellowship workers are assigned to "work" a camp. They establish Bible clubs, regular services, recreational and camp programs as the Lord leads. Because of varying conditions, camps even within the same county may call for a different pattern of work. However, some things are basic.

It is most desirable to have a community building in which to meet. This not only provides shelter, but shuts out many distractions. In the old federal camps the center building is the migrants' church house. If a center building is not available, a mess hall can be used. Even tents or shacks have been employed, or meetings are conducted in the open air, weather permitting. It has been found that the best message is a pure, simplified gospel message, illustrated by flannelgraph, chalk drawings, an occasional film or object lesson.

Sunday schools are invaluable. When possible, Sunday school teachers are enlisted from reliable local churches to assist the missionaries in the camps. This aid is also welcomed at other times, such as in vacation Bible schools or in the Christmas season. The Sunday schools do their best work of getting into the hearts of the people when they are allowed to express themselves. For children, the application of the lesson can be brought in through meaningful handwork. Encouraging them to make prayer requests touches the heartstrings. Many children ask prayer for erring relatives. Some come back later rejoicing in answers to their prayers.

Boys' and girls' clubs with craft and recreation are most profitable. In one camp where the manager required an evening of recreation, about two hundred youths came each week. Before long they were opening their hearts to the missionaries. The camp managers often are interested primarily in the recreational aspect, but dedicated missionaries have found that crafts and recreation are also an avenue to a better understanding of the young people and a greater spiritual influence with them.

In the Missionary Gospel Fellowship around three hundred register annually for the week-long youth conference that is held in the Sierra Nevadas for migrant youth from the camps served. Away from their usual environment, under daily teaching on Christian living, with cabin devotions and daily living with their counselors, taking Bible studies and hearing a missionary challenge, many have their lives transformed. Strangely, we have found more willingness to obey regulations and a greater appreciation of the high standards and purpose of the conference among the migrant youth than among the church youth. There are always problems, of course, but each time we have allowed church youth to register for the migrant conference camp, we have had complications and increased problems. There is a place for this sort of integration, but the summer camp does not seem to be the place for it.

Generally speaking, married couples make the most useful missionaries among the migrants. This is because they are often called on to help solve home problems. Single women can sometimes do excellent work among the women and children. Single men face some of the same problems that a single man has in the pastorate. Once a male missionary stood at the door inviting a migrant to church. The husband arrived home protesting, "Don't you be calling on my wife!"

Much of the success of the work depends on winning the confidence of the migrants, and in some cases that of the camp manager. For this reason it seems most desirable to assign a worker to the same camp for a number of years. He knows the situation and the camp manager, and presumably he has the confidence of the more permanent residents of the camp or of those who return to the same place year after year. Often when cults and other groups want to press in and take over the center building, the manager then assures them, "We already have a good non-denominational work functioning here in this camp." A steady, consistent program benefits everyone concerned.

Any missionary working among these people must have a good, sane working knowledge of the Scriptures, a heart able to endure hardness, and a persistent determination to keep on in spite of discouragements when the job seems thankless. As much as on any foreign field, there is a need for the Lord's call to this ministry.

What of the Future?

Shall we always have these migratory farm laborers? We hope not. No situation that capitalizes on the weaknesses and misfortunes of men should be allowed to continue. But the problem is a complex one. More and more the states and the federal government are taking an active role in trying to solve the problem. The tremendous amount of publicity given by press, radio and television has helped awaken the public to the plight of these "disenfranchised Americans."

Some of the measures now being taken are the regulation of the camps, the registration of crew leaders and labor contractors, the provision of continuous employment through the annual worker plan, the various attempts to reduce the need for migrancy by mechanizing harvest work, developing rural industries and diversifying crops, plus the programs for teaching the migrants so they can compete for more stable employment .These and all the measures that are being taken to ameliorate his present condition have their value. One day such migrancy may cease to be a major factor in our national life.

But this change is not going to take place this year or next year. Meanwhile the church is faced by the spiritual plight of these hundreds of thousands who are not normally within reach of its ministrations. They are a depressed segment of the population, and the world may look on them as a very unpromising mission field. Yet our commission to "go . . . preach" is not based on promise but on need. And needs they have many.

Large numbers of these workers are Negroes and Mexican-Americans. This must be kept in mind in planning work among them. The cultural background of a people and the character of the society among whom they commonly move has much to do with the methods by which they can most effectively be reached with the gospel of Christ.

And we must not forget the thousands of contract laborers, mainly from Mexico, who every year form a part of this migratory labor force. Their presence among us puts the foreign mission field on our front doorstep. Just as the earnings they take home play a major role in the economy of their home country, so the impressions they get of Christianity in the United States are likely to affect their relationship to it at home.

BIBLIOGRAPHY

Estimated Employment of Seasonal Hired Agricultural Workers. Washington: Bureau of Employment Security, U. S. Department of Labor, 1960.

FULLER VARDEN. *No Work Today! The Plight of America's Migrants,* Pamphlet No. 190. New York: Public Affairs Committee, Inc.

HANCOCK, RICHARD H. *The Role of the Bracero in the Economic and Cultural Dynamics of Mexico; A Case Study of Chihuahua.* Stanford: Hispanic American Society, 1959.

Migratory Labor in American Agriculture. Report of the President's Commission on Migratory Labor, Washington, D. C.

Report to the President on Domestic Migratory Farm Labor. Washington, D. C., 1960.

Selected References on Domestic Agricultural Workers, Their Families, Problems and Programs, 1955-60, Bulletin 225. Washington: Bureau of Labor Standards, U. S. Department of Labor, January, 1961.

Status of Agricultural Workers under State and Federal Laws. Washington: Bureau of Labor Standards. U. S. Department of Labor, April, 1961.

Ministering to those who have committed offenses against society.

17

Behind Prison Bars

ARVID OHRNELL

Punishment of evildoers is essential for the preservation of the human race. Unless evil is properly rewarded with punishment, it eventually corrupts all men. To this fact history bears fearful and conclusive testimony.

The Scriptures set forth the importance of separating the evil from the good, lest that which is good be enveloped by that which is evil. The Lord Himself said, "A little leaven leaveneth the whole lump." It is on the basis of this principle that penal institutions are not only justified in their existence but are an absolute necessity.

Evil has a way of propagating itself just as weeds have a way of taking over a farm unless definite measures are constantly taken to exterminate them. To allow the lawbreaker to mingle freely with his fellow men is to foster an increase in lawlessness. Only as the lawbreaker is punished commensurate with his crime can righteousness prevail.

The penal institution serves a twofold purpose. First, it provides a place of confinement, which in itself is punishment for the evil-

ARVID OHRNELL, who came to this country from Sweden in 1925, was chaplain of Washington State penal institutions at Walla Walla and Monroe for sixteen years. He is now serving as national prison representative in connection with the Home Missions Department of the Assemblies of God. In this capacity he ministers in various state and federal penal institutions, as well as county jails throughout the country. In addition to this, he handles applications for Bible correspondence courses and carries on extensive correspondence from his headquarters in Springfield, Missouri, counseling prisoners and their families.

doer, and prevents him from contaminating others by his contact with them. It should be stated here, too, that proper punishment has a cleansing effect even upon the lawbreaker himself. Secondly, the penal institution has somewhat the same effect upon society as a genuine Christian has upon a company of sinners. It does not necessarily always prevent every manifestation of evil, but it serves to keep it in abeyance. If evil is kept in abeyance for sufficient time, it tends to lose its force.

Perhaps the greatest threat to righteousness in our time is the leniency shown toward the criminal. When the threat of confinement and punishment no longer looms heavy over men's heads, evil is certain to wax worse and worse.

Types of Penal Institutions

Because we have different types of people of all ages, we must have different types of institutions. Children cannot be thrown in with hardened criminals who are without conscience or principles. That is the reason we have detention homes for young boys and girls.

The matron of a detention home should be like a real mother — without respect of persons, with a broad understanding of the problems of children and with love to win their confidence. The boys with habits should be watched and talked to in love and understanding. If possible, punishment should be avoided and confidence put in the child. Many times words of confidence will have more influence upon a child than a rod.

Secondly, there are boys' and girls' training schools in most states for children from twelve to sixteen. How necessary it is that children in the first period of youth have an opportunity to attend school. The brighter children usually are put in a class by themselves so that their learning will not be blocked by a high class of morons or by the slow and lazy.

The next class includes youngsters who have been convicted of a felony and are sentenced to a reform school. In some states reform schools are for those from sixteen to thirty-five. But the largest group includes those in the second period of youth, from sixteen to twenty. There generally are elementary and high school grades in every reform school. If possible, everyone completes the eight grades and the clever and more ambitious complete high school.

These young people also receive commercial training in the field of bookkeeping, shorthand and mathematics. Vocational training for work as barbers, printers, painters, tailors, shoe repairmen, plumbers, carpenters, brick masons, mechanics and farmers are available also. States which have a good training program for youngsters have less parole violators.

Then there are the state and federal institutions for hardened criminals or lawbreakers. All those in penal institutions are not criminals at heart. Many have had opportunities to live a successful life when they were paroled, but preferred to return to crime. There is need for a separation in the institutions between the lowest type of individuals and those who have seen their mistakes and are ready to repent.

Types of People Imprisoned

If we walk down the main street or through the business section of a busy town, we meet all kinds of people, young and old, from inhabitants of skid row to highest society. We will meet rich and poor, educated and uninformed, intellectual and moron, ambitious and down-and-outer, religious and infidel. All represent different classes and standings in society; all are passing from the cradle to the grave.

Inside our institution we meet men who post-dated checks. The businessman forgot he was going to hold the check until that date. The bank called the police, the law acted and the guilty one received a warning. The second time it happened it became a felony which resulted in a conviction in a superior court and a sentence to a state institution. Among that class of people we can also meet ministers and evangelists of the gospel.

Then we will find the alcoholics, a harmless class, but they have to be watched. They can make moonshine from potatoes and fruits. They are their own worst enemy. As soon as they are released they have to celebrate their freedom, and the few dollars they received when they left prison are soon gone. Under the influence of strong drink their subconscious mind dictates to them to write checks, and back they have to go.

We find many joyriders. They have a habit of stealing cars, sometimes under the influence of strong drink. They may steal an old car and receive a five-year sentence, depending on whether they are repeaters or not.

There are different types of sex offenders from rapists to sodomites. The sodomites are a problem in our institutions. They try to tempt the younger convicts into unnatural affections. They change from a masculine appearance to feminine in voice and actions.

The gamblers are a class by themselves. They cheat, steal and rob. They are dangerous and unmanageable.

The killers are often very peaceable. Many times they kill someone without any previous thought. In a state prison where there are around two thousand inmates, approximately two hundred are lifers. Some receive a life sentence because of being convicted more than twice, some for armed robbery, kidnaping, arson and murder.

We meet young and old, storytellers, habitual liars and those who have a repentant spirit.

The Criminal's Background

If we were to make a summary of the background of men in our institutions from the Atlantic to the Pacific, from the border of Canada to the border of Mexico, we would find frequently they have three things in common: (1) a poor education, (2) no trade, and (3) almost no religious background. The majority of persons have committed crime while under the influence of strong liquor. A man with a good education, no trade, no religious background and under the influence of liquor can easily get into trouble.

Of five thousand men interviewed in a West Coast state, 73 per cent had committed crime under the influence of liquor. Only one could tell how many books are in the Bible and only one know how many Gospels. One declared he had been attending Sunday school for ten years, but on being questioned he could not give the name of the church, the pastor or the Sunday school teacher. When questioned further he admitted, "I went only two or three times in ten years."

Of the five thousand men, 41 per cent came from broken homes and many from homes where some relative had been convicted. One young boy's uncle had been executed, his mother had died in a state prison, his father was a habitual criminal, his father's sister was in a state hospital and his only sister was among the feeble-minded.

But it is not only the lower classes that are uninformed about our Bible. We were reading the Bible in a state prison with a university student. He had been asked to read chapters 9 and 10 of the book of Hebrews. As he read about Moses and the candlestick, the tabernacle in the wilderness and the altar, he suddenly stopped and asked, "What is this about? Who was Moses? What about the tabernacle?" He continued, "I never read the Bible before. I don't know anything about it."

In a large Bible class, one of the members was a medical doctor who had transgressed the law. He went over the New Testament four times trying to find the book of Exodus.

I spoke to a man one night just before he was shot to death by the firing squad. His testimony was, "If I could live my life over again, I would attend Sunday school and by and by I could be a Sunday school teacher. I never attended church. The same thing was true of seven boy friends from childhood. They all died in the chair or were hanged. I am the only one alive and I am facing the firing squad!"

Kinds of Punishment

The Bible mentions many severe punishments for lawbreakers. God established capital punishment. Cain was marked the rest of his life from the day he killed Abel. In the forty years the children of Israel traveled through the wilderness, there was trouble in the camp from time to time, but the troublemakers always had to pay a high price for the mistakes they made. Pharaoh's baker in Egypt was hanged for his attitude in the palace. Aaron, the great high priest, and Moses, the greatest leader of all times, could not cross the Jordan into the land of promise because of disobedience to the Lord's command.

Even if a lawbreaker is not apprehended, the law of retribution is still in operation. "Whatsoever a man soweth, that shall he also reap." Many are in a living hell because of unconfessed sins. Many in state hospitals have lost their minds because they were afraid to confess.

The punishment for lawbreakers is not universally the same. In six states, arson is punishable by death. Armed robbery, habitual crime, rape and escape in connection with assault are punishable by death or a life sentence. A joyrider in many states receives five years. Bogus check writers receive up to fifteen years. In the Missouri State Prison we found a man who had been convicted twice before he came there. Under the influence of strong drink, he stole a sixteen-dollar watch and received a life sentence.

Sodomites who have molested small children can be sure of a stiff sentence anywhere, especially in California. In some southern states they can be executed for their deeds.

Some states still use old-style hanging as capital punishment. In Utah, firing squads are used, while in many other states the gas chamber and the electric chair are used to carry out the death penalty.

A man already incarcerated who does not behave himself can be punished in many ways. A common punishment is a few days, weeks or months in isolation with only bread and water. In many states the parole board has power to change sentences and release men, but a man must have a good record to be released.

What a blessing it would be if there could be segregation according to classification.

Life in the Prisons

Many times we hear people talk about the easy life inmates live inside modern penitentiaries and institutions. They have radios, movies, ball games, good food, books to read, a fine sports program, and they never have to pay anything for it. Yes, they have those things in some places, but not everywhere.

Who do you think have to work the thirty thousand acres of land in Louisiana connected with the state prison and the eleven state farms in Texas and all the farms in Arkansas? Who build roads in Tennessee and Georgia, and repair bridges in Florida, and make twenty-five thousand gunny sacks a day at San Quentin? Everywhere a great deal of work must be done by the inmates of the prisons.

Each inmate sleeps in a cell with from one to four others. They curse and swear over unjust action by the police and court witnesses. Everyone has made tremendous mistakes with the exception of the speaker; he is the only dependable one. Everyone else lies and persecutes him. He complains about the unfairness of the officers, about his bed and about the indigestible food. The governor and parole board are completely uninformed.

The prisoners have to go to bed at a certain time in the evening and awaken early in the morning. They march to the dining room to eat, and return to take care of the bed and clean up the cell. They walk to the factory or to other types of work. At noon they march to the dining room for lunch. After a little rest in the cell they are ready to go to work for the rest of the day. They eat supper, perhaps read a paper, and go to bed. The day is over.

They dress the same on Sunday as every other day of the week. In most prisons they have a movie, a ball game and a church service. The attitude of the inmates toward the religious activities in the institution depends on the chaplain. Some chaplains have only a handful of prisoners attending the services.

The greatest punishment for any man is losing his freedom, always being told what to do, and having to keep company with the lowest type of individuals.

The Need for Witnessing to Prisoners

I once listened to some students in a Bible institute give their testimonies. One young man felt called to Africa. "Amen" and "Thanks be to the Lord" were heard from students all over the room. He had consecrated his life to the Lord. A few were called to India and China and the reaction was the same. At last a young man testified, "I was born in the state of Idaho and lived there all my life until I came to Bible school. As soon as I receive my diploma, I am returning to Idaho to be a pioneer." Everyone was quiet. There were no amens or praise to the Lord this time. He was only going back to Idaho to be a pioneer. It is the same when it comes to jail work. Often this ministry does not appeal to people. It does not appear very glamorous.

A county seat we once visited had not had a service in more than fourteen years! The superintendent for that county jail informed us that he then had fourteen men locked up. In another county jail they had not had one religious service in twenty-six years. Many times police stations and city and county jails are fields ready for

harvest. Everyone serving time at Sing Sing and other large prisons
were locked up in a local jail when arrested. They possibly could
have been reached with the gospel then, if someone had visited
them.

The finest jail workers are those from the churches where the
real gospel is preached, where the pastor and all members believe
in salvation of lost sinners. When that type of people have jail
services they have a message to bring and they expect sinners at
the altar. The locked-up men can feel the warmth in the service.
The testimonies radiate life. Such a service makes a tremendous
impression on the audience. As a result souls are saved. If only one
or two inmates or a handful attend, the service should be conducted
with the same warm spirit.

I met a thirty-two-year-old man in a state prison convicted for
the first time. He had been under the influence of liquor and had
taken a car without the permission of the owner. Before he fell
by the wayside he had been arrested many times for being drunk.
After he was arrested and locked up all alone, a pastor from a local
church visited him and led him to the Lord. His testimony about his
childhood was, "I went to a Sunday school a few times, but that is
all. When arrested for being a thief, a pastor read about it in the
paper and came up to talk to me. It touched me and I gave my
heart to the Lord. He visited me and gave me instructions. Since
I have been transferred to the state prison, he has contacted me by
letter, and as soon as I am released I am planning to attend Bible
school." That man conducted a Bible class in the prison and many
came to the Lord.

How to Witness to the Prisoner

No one should try to work among the outcasts of society unless
he has had a real experience of salvation. He must have God's love
in his heart for that type of people. He must be patient and have
a vision.

Jail workers should never repeat what they are told by inmates
or be misled by any stories. Never take the witness stand or repeat
any statements against the court. Our duty is to proclaim the gospel
and lead souls to Christ. The police and the sheriff are to make
the arrest; the prosecuting attorney's job is to present the case to the

court. But the Christian jail worker should stay clear of the court. The law enforcement agencies will soon find out whether jail workers are dependable or not.

Working in city jails, police stations and county jails we find men just as they were when arrested. Possibly they are dressed in a pair of dirty overalls, with only one shirt and a pair of socks or maybe they will be in a worn-out suit. To be a successful jail worker it is necessary to dress up individuals who need suits and overalls. Most of the men in county jails have only one shirt. It does not require any special effort to make the announcement in a church about the need for shirts.

In a county jail where we held services, we talked with a colored man who looked like a dirty tramp from skid row. His knees stuck out of his pants when he walked and his toes stuck out of his shoes. We had him take a shower and paid for a haircut and a shave. We bought a suit his size in a pawn shop and found a shirt, a tie and a pair of shoes and dressed him up. He looked like another man.

A prisoner we never could talk to before, who had been behind the bars for twenty-one years and was now returning for life, came to the front and said, "What a wonderful religion you people have. Look at that colored man. I have been a member of a church all my life, but I have never before seen anything like this. I am sick. Doctors say I can live only four more years. How can I get hold of your religion?"

We told him to believe in Jesus and confess all his sins to Him. We helped him pray and instructed him in the Word of God and gave him a Bible. He was delivered by the power of God and confessed the name of Christ. He returned to the state prison and confessed Christ. About four years later he died.

As a chaplain for nine years in the state reformatory of Washington I always met newcomers with a warm hand. I invited them to come to the services as soon as they had been released from isolation. After they were dressed up and taken down to isolation, I would go down with a notebook and ask them whether I could do anything for them. Sometimes I would be requested to write a letter to a mother. I was to tell her that her son was in trouble, but that this would be the last time, and from now on he would be attending church. The one in the next cell might say, "Could you drop my wife a few words and tell her that I cannot write until I am released from isolation?" Maybe the next one had a sweetheart and wished me to inform her that she could expect a letter in about thirty days. Because we took a personal interest in every inmate, 45 to 47 per cent of the whole prison population attended services. Thirty sang in the choir.

It is possible to be a successful jail worker or a successful prison chaplain if you pay the price.

Does the Prisoner Respond to the Gospel?

During my many years as a prison chaplain I have had the opportunity to deal with about eighty or ninety men under death sentences. I have been present at thirty-two executions.

Of the thirty-two, twenty-seven men turned to the Lord, confessing all their sins, mistakes and crimes previously unconfessed. They died in peace without fear of death or eternity. The other five died with fear and trembling. One lost his mind and had to be tied to an emergency board. One was cursing the officers. Two were dragged into the execution chamber. One was joking and making fun of the officers. He had asked for a glass of liquor and it had affected his mind.

The first condemned man with whom I dealt was bold in denying his guilt. We prayed together almost every day for two months and nothing happened. At last I told him, "We have prayed together about fifty times and you are the same person. You cannot say that you are saved or are a child of God, and this is not like our Lord. If you killed that girl, confess it. If not, you will have to give account before the Lord one day. If you are guilty you will never receive peace with God until you confess."

He stood looking around for a couple of minutes before he stated, "I killed the girl. God have mercy upon me. What shall I do?"

He was told to make open confession in court and pay the penalty as a Christian should. He made an open confession in court. Before he was executed we had thirty hours of prayer and Bible reading the last three days of his life. With a prayer and a smile he took the last steps into eternity.

The last execution I witnessed was that of a wholesale killer. We had prayer together many times. During prayer from time to time a strong feeling was present. The man had killed many. On asking him about it, his answer was, "If I should make a full confession you would be afraid of me. You would not dare come back. You are my only friend and I would like to keep you until I die." At last he was persuaded he would not lose his only friend because of a confession, and he confessed fourteen killings and over three thousand robberies. Detectives and crime investigators from everywhere came to hear the confessions, checking and rechecking the statements made.

When time came for him to pay the penalty he said to the warden, "There are five steel doors between me and freedom. You know I cannot or would not try to escape. I am only asking you for this last favor. May I walk into the execution chamber with my friend and spiritual adviser and not with the guard?" It was granted. A few minutes later he was dead.

After Release, What?

Society is very much concerned about having a criminal convicted. Many times the county has to pay thousands of dollars to convict a single person and send him to a penitentiary where the state has to pay for his upkeep until the day of his release. If a convict is married, the state also has to take care of his family. The crime bill is tremendous, around $20 billion a year.

But what happens when a man is released? In the state of Missouri a person who has served his time receives $25 as "get" money. If the man has something or someone to fall back on he can make it. If not, it is almost impossible. A man released from one state prison lost seven jobs because of his record and every time he came to our home as the only place of refuge he had. At last he was able to locate a permanent job. He has now been working there many years and he and his family are members of a fine church.

Many times the daily papers carry a story that an ex-convict has committed a crime. What about the thousands of ex-convicts who have made good, are members of churches and live a useful life? That is a class you will never read about in the daily papers.

One young fellow who served time where I was chaplain was paroled to one county. His father, living in another county, died.

Without permission the ex-convict went home to his father's funeral. He was returned to prison on a parole violation because he left without proper permission. It is no crime to attend a funeral, but for him it was, because of his record. A man on parole cannot get married without permission, and in some states he cannot buy a car without permission.

In the many dealings I have had with incarcerated men I have found that if a man repents and lives an honest life for the Lord, the Lord can give him an open door when he is released. I have seen it happen many times. Christian men having a twenty-to-twenty-five-year prison record, who are without a trade and have a very poor education, have found jobs immediately upon release. God located the job before they were released.

One thirty-year-old man who served seven years for armed robbery and started studying theology was released with a ticket and a few dollars. When he arrived we learned a porter was needed in a Greyhound Bus station. When they asked him who he was, he answered, "I am a Bible student." The business manager said, "You are hired." They liked him so much that one month later they called asking, "Do you have another student you can send us? We need one more."

An ex-convict can make it if he is honest and receives help in time of need.

Our Responsibility

Many churches complain, "We cannot reach the unsaved. What shall we do about it?" Jesus said in Luke 14:23, "Go out into the highways and hedges, and compel them to come in." Jesus also said, "I was in prison, and ye came unto me" (Matt. 25:36).

In early times the apostles went to the temple to meet the people. There is no place in the Holy Scriptures where we read that we should rent a hall or erect a building and expect people to come. We have to go out on highways and byways and call sinners to repentance. The pastors and assemblies that are following the instructions from the Lord have success. *It is the responsibility of the local church to have services in jails.* The *Directory of State and Federal Correctional Institutions*[1] lists 419 different institutions

---

[1] Compiled by the American Correctional Association, New York.

with a population of 249,290 inmates in the United States alone. There is an overwhelming increase in the number of training schools for boys and girls, most of which are crowded beyond normal capacity. Even though there may be only one or two inmates, we should remember the attitude of the Lord toward individuals.

The members of the local church should see in prison work a great opportunity to proclaim the gospel to lawbreakers. They should also realize the importance of thorough preparation for the services. Only the gospel can change the hearts of lawbreakers. The gospel is the power of God for everyone that believeth.

I have noticed how young people especially make a tremendous impression on criminals. While I was chaplain in Washington, one day fourteen new inmates arrived. One of the young men had a face like marble. Without any change of facial expression he went down to isolation, after being dressed in a prisoner's suit with a number on his back. This young man had come from a very ungodly home. The superior judge wrote a letter to the institution stating that in his opinion the young man was already a habitual criminal.

This young fellow came to my office many times. He was afraid of people outside and wanted me to contact them and try to create a better understanding. One day we contacted a Bible school and asked whether some students would hold a service, which they did. When the service was over this young criminal came to my office saying, "A change is going to take place in my life today. I looked at every student who took part in that meeting. Not one looked like us criminals. It must be the type of religion they have embraced." He gave his heart to the Lord and about a month later he started to take part in our service. He became a fine Christian.

What an impression God-fearing people can make in a service! What a responsibility and a challenge! Born-again believers have a message to bring to defeated sinners tired of being slaves to destructive habits and false mirages. What an opportunity for the local church to point those on skid row and in prison to the blood-stained banner of the cross.

*　*　*

Many inmates actively study the Scriptures through the Moody Correspondence School. Some enroll in a simple gospel course which clearly presents the plan of salvation through which many have been saved. Others enroll in such basic courses as *First Steps in the Christian Faith, God's Will for Your Life, The Bible Says* and various book studies of the Scriptures. In addition to individual enrollments, there is often a class using one of the courses taught by the chaplain or even one of the inmates.

In a typical year more than 100 prisons are serviced by the Moody Correspondence School with about 5,000 enrollments. The courses are usually paid for by the inmates themselves or sponsored by some outside church or agency.

The showings of the Moody Institute of Science films have been effective too. More than 1,000 such showings were scheduled in a recent year.

THE EDITORS

BIBLIOGRAPHY

BERNARD, WILLIAM. *Jailbait: The Story of Juvenile Delinquency.* Garden City, New Jersey: Garden City Books, 1951.

FUCHER, HENRY PARK. *Prison Is My Parish.* New York: Fleming H. Revell Co., 1957.

HOGLER, J. ARTHUR. *The Treatment of the Young Delinquent.* New York: Philosophical Library, 1952.

Juvenile Delinquency — Interim Report of the Committee on the Judiciary U. S. Senate 83rd Congress — Report No. 61. Washington: U. S. Government Printing Office, 1958.

LINDNER, ROBERT M., LUHAR, EDWIN J. and SELIGER, ROBERT V. *Contemporary Criminal Hygiene.* Baltimore: Oakbridge Press, 1946.

Training Personnel for Work with Juvenile Delinquents. Children's Bureau Publications No. 348, 1954. Washington: U. S. Department of Health, Education and Welfare, Social Security Administration.

WHITEHEAD, DON. *The FBI Story.* New York: Random House, 1956.

World Book Encyclopedia, Vol. 13. Chicago: The Quarrie Corporation, 1947.

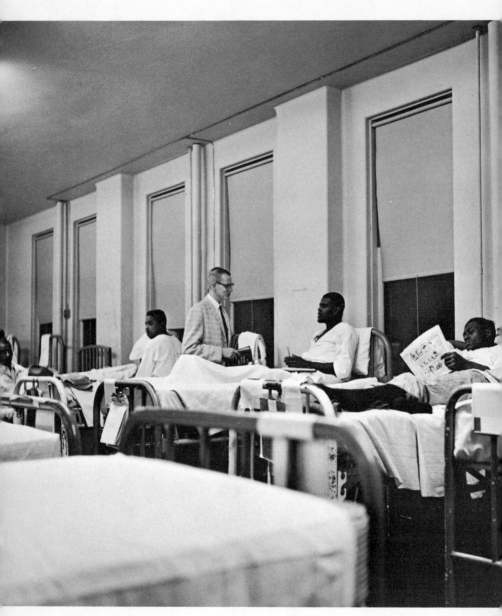

Visitation at Cook County Hospital, Chicago.

18

"Sick, and Ye Visited Me"

ALVIN BRAY

AMERICA IS MORE HEALTH MINDED TODAY than at any time in its history. Health insurance of some kind is a must. Bigger and better convalescent institutions are the order of the day.

To staff these institutions and medical centers demands an ever increasing army of trained technicians, doctors and nurses and provides for some of our most satisfying careers. People are now recovering from ills which only recently were considered fatal. Man's life expectancy has steadily increased throughout this present century. We indeed owe much to medical science. Strangely enough, however, the medical profession is beginning to recognize that the ministers of the gospel have done much to bring about this change and to feel that co-operation with the clergy is essential for an effective health program.

To many church leaders the sick calls have always been the most vital part of their ministry. They know sick calls must be answered promptly and repeatedly. But with the rapid pace of our day, ministers find they cannot possibly carry this important load themselves. This has led to the professional chaplaincy program which has done much to relieve the pressure. But here again the program has its limitations, and to meet the true spiritual needs of the sick remains a challenge that cannot be overlooked.

ALVIN BRAY is a graduate of Moody Bible Institute and for seven years was pastor on the northwest side of Chicago. Since 1949, he has been Protestant chaplain of Cook County Hospital in Chicago. He is also active in the Light Bearers Association, one purpose of which is to assist lay Christians in an active and productive hospital ministry.

Types of Hospitals

In general there are three types of hospitals — public, governmental and private. Public hospitals are directly supported in one way or another through taxation. They include municipal, district, county and state institutions.

Government hospitals are also tax supported but the central control comes from the federal government in Washington, D.C. These hospitals serve (1) the employees working for the government and their families; (2) those who have served or are serving in some branch of the armed forces; (3) the merchant marines who are working on ships at sea; and (4) those institutions engaged in some form of governmental research.

Private hospitals are not tax supported but represent private investment. Most of these are non-profit institutions, which means that all financial benefits accruing therefrom are reinvested in the institutions themselves in some acceptable manner considered beneficial to the public at large. Usually the name of the institution will identify its essential form of operational control.

Types of Hospital Ministry

There are two types of hospital ministry, Christian work done by the professionally trained and that done by laymen.

Since the beginning of American history the layman has worked side by side with his pastor in calling on the sick. In recent years the assistance of Christian laymen has unfortunately been discouraged.

In the main, the chaplaincy training program in public hospitals is controlled by the National Council of Churches. The governmental institutions have a chaplaincy program very similar to that of the armed services.

Private institutions fall under two categories, the religious and the non-religious. Religious hospitals are ministered by their own denominational chaplaincy training and placement program. The non-religious hospitals also, in recent years, are inclined toward a chaplaincy service which is supplementary to the pastoral preference calls. Even institutions which formerly frowned upon the chaplaincy service now look with favor upon it, because of the many patients who have no church connections and therefore no pastor to call on them, especially in times of spiritual need when very ill. They recognize that such spiritual aid will be beneficial in the patient's general well-being, even aiding recovery itself.

Times of Hospital Ministry

Non-visiting hours: Professional work of the chaplain and the minister, including that of the clinical training staff, is being done during non-visiting hours when the public is not present.

Visiting hours: Almost all layman's work is done during the regular visiting hours. This is the preferred time for non-professionals because the patients are now ready to receive visitors. They expect company and are more responsive.

A Basic Problem

At the beginning of this century there remained an open door to regular hospital visitation by all Christians. Scriptures were freely read, singing and praying were routinely expected and engaged in.

Unfortunately this door is not open today in many hospitals. The trend is to limit public services and visitation to a single representative Protestant or Catholic group or a professional chaplain specially trained for this type of service. While this has its advantages, there are also some serious disadvantages. The chaplain may be of another faith or from a liberal denomination. In the case of the latter, the chaplain may or may not be evangelical. This means that the spiritual needs of the patient are not always met.

Evangelicals and conservatives are now, however, forming effective hospital training programs which are being respected and recognized by hospital officials. In New Orleans, the Southern Baptists are forming a clinical training program for prospective chaplains. This program is offered in conjunction with the New Orleans Baptist Theological Seminary.[1]

Another excellent clinical training program is offered on an even greater scale by the North Carolina Baptist Hospital at Winston-

---

[1] Clinical Training Program for Chaplains, Southern Baptist Hospital, New Orleans, Louisiana.

Salem, North Carolina, in affiliation with Dr. Young's School of Pastoral Care.[2]

The Lutheran General Hospital of Park Ridge, Illinois, is offering clinical training even to non-Lutherans in conjunction with the Lutheran Theological Seminary in St. Paul, Minnesota.[3]

The Hospital Chaplains Association of America, Inc., is an interdenominational chaplaincy agency with offices in Downey, California, offering practical assistance.[4]

In the Chicago area, the Light Bearers Association, Inc., has been set up as an interdenominational laymen's agency for hospital work.[5] This will probably always remain primarily a laymen's work, but it is rapidly growing and will continue to need qualified, trained and spiritual chaplains. Plans are under way to extend the work of the Light Bearers to other states as needs and opportunities present themselves.

In anticipation of an even greater future challenge, the Light Bearers are now pioneering in three phases of basic training for workers:

1. Locating and approving Christian hospital workers. These workers are given credentials and are responsible to the Light Bearers. They serve in a way which avoids duplication and overlapping of Christian work in the wards.[6]

2. A basic training course is given in Christian counseling, introducing also suitable literature designed to meet the spiritual needs and problems of the patient. Certificates are issued on completion of the course.[7]

3. An organizational plan is being set up. Senior Light Bearers are approved workers who have taken the basic training course and have given at least one full year at the bedside of the sick. These are given further training and assist in organizing other Light Bearer units in hospitals and institutions.

[2] Clinical Training Program for Chaplains, North Carolina Baptist Hospital, Winston-Salem, N. C.
[3] Clinical Training Program for Chaplains, Lutheran General Hospital, Park Ridge, Illinois.
[4] Hospital Chaplaincy Ministry of America, Inc., 7605 Firestone Blvd., Downey, Calif.
[5] Light Bearers Association of Illinois, Inc., 1835 W. Harrison St., Chicago 12, Ill.
[6] *Christian Evangelism Through the Light Bearers.*
[7] The Christian Counseling Course.

Why Minister to the Sick?

Ministering to the sick offers one of the greatest opportunities of all Christian work. Church people have always known the importance of the pastoral call at the hospital or home of the sick member. Somehow they have failed to realize, however, that every qualified lay person in the church should be involved in this type of visitation program as well as the pastor. Not only does this encourage the sick, but it will also bring about a deep spiritual experience to the person making the call.[8]

The following should be sufficient to challenge each one to minister to the sick:

1. Personal contact with the patient is vital and necessary to give him the spiritual help he needs.

2. The patient realizes his need at this crucial time more than at any other.

3. Many patients have no regular church home, so they know no pastor will call.

4. Many patients who are reluctant to ask for spiritual help will accept it when the skilled Christian worker takes the proper initiative.

5. Even where professional help may be rejected, a "neighborly call" by a "fellow layman" may not be in vain!

6. Many of the patients, unless reached under these circumstances, can never be reached at any other time.

7. It offers the decided advantage to the Christian worker of systematic follow-up, making possible greater success in a newly adopted Christian life.

8. It is essential to meet the spiritual needs if the physical needs are to be fully met.

Instructions for the Christian Worker

1. The worker must have a good knowledge of the Scriptures. It is essential that time be spent daily in prayer and Bible study to be spiritually fit to help others.

2. The worker must be led by the Holy Spirit.

3. He must speak in a soft voice, refuse to create or be any

---

[8] *How to Organize Your Own Local Unit of the Light Bearers Association.*

part of unpleasant scenes, or cause embarrassment by presence or attitude.

4.   He will not force himself or his literature on the sick. His service is voluntary and he must be received voluntarily. He will not go where he is unwelcome, nor will he linger longer than he is welcome.

5.   He will not promiscuously distribute religious literature. In some public institutions this is illegal. However, if permission is obtained, literature may be offered as a service to the patient.

6.   He will never speak disparagingly of another man's religion nor distribute any reading matter which mentions other religions by name.

7.   He will always seek to be helpful and systematic. He will seek definite guidance from God, have no motive other than a genuine burden for the lost and dying.

8.   He will be selective in his literature. Tracts with such titles as "You May Die at Midnight" are not in good taste.

9.   He will use tracts which point to the great theme of God's matchless love as revealed on the cross. The tracts must be plainly written, printed on fine quality paper in larger than usual type.

10.   He will refuse to argue or enter into a heated discussion with anyone. Instead, he will speak about Jesus Christ in a reverent tone and do what he can to encourage the patient.

11.   He will not promote any ism, cult or even his own denomination.

12.   He will never disturb either patient or guest.

13.   He will minister only after permission has been obtained to pray with the patient, read the Scriptures, or minister to him in some other way.

14. He will not interrupt nurses, doctors, or other Christian workers. He will not intentionally duplicate or overlap another Christian's work.

15.   He will never suggest to the patient a change of doctors, hospitals, treatment or medicine. He will never criticize the hospital management or policies.

16.   He will seek to maintain a sweetness of breath as well as a sweetness of personality.

Singing to the Sick

1. Some souls can be won to Christ through song who could never be reached any other way.
2. It is the easiest way.
3. It is welcomed by a large number of patients.
4. It is often welcomed by public officials.
5. It remains a vital means of presenting the gospel when all others fail.
6. It forms a link in furthering good relations with the hospital.
7. It lays the foundation for a later, more complete institutional ministry.

Suggestions for Organizing a Singing Ministry

A good idea is to make hymn singing so attractive that the hospital will not object.

Christmas is a good time to begin, when the caroling spirit prevails.

Discreetly avoid too close contact with patients and personnel, except through the leader.

Come back on Easter, then on other occasions. Keep coming back. Always be brief; always have the work well in hand; always remain cheerful and polite to all.

Once established, don't be tardy or absent; don't give up. Keep your assigned dates.

Observe the rules for good group singing. *Remember* — in all these cases, Christians must not antagonize or show lack of respect for those in public office. Officials are always cautious because of heavy responsibilities.

Christians should remember that there are ways to ingratiate themselves, and so they must learn patience and serve in ways that will be both legal and rewarding. When Christians have thus proved themselves in small services, bigger responsibilities often present themselves.

In the meantime, pray much. Be sensible; move slowly and depend utterly upon God.

Some Singing Rules to Observe

1. Come to the hospital only after rehearsing. Each one should

know what numbers are to be sung and the order in which they will be sung.

2.   The singing group must be well supervised by a leader whom all respect and obey.

3.   No more than fifteen members should be in a group.

4.   Do not sing too loudly, too slowly or too sadly. No one member of the group should be permitted to sing louder than the rest or sing "off-key."

5.   Neatness of dress cannot be overemphasized.

6.   Know the importance of good posture for both singing and good effect.

7.   Do not block passageways or doorways.

8.   Do not chat with each other while ministering to the sick.

9.   Do not chew gum.

10.   Encourage the leader by standing quietly while being introduced.

11.   Show politeness and consideration for nurses, doctors, attendants and guests, as well as the patients.

12.   Sing the more familiar church hymns.

13.   Limit the singing to two or three numbers.

14.   Never use more than one member of the group to offer Christian reading matter. The rest of the group will remain in their singing position and sing.

15.   Wave a friendly good-by as the group leaves the sick ward.

16.   While walking to the next singing station, walk in pairs, and quietly hum some Christian hymn or song.

Conclusion

The vision of this work for the Lord emerges. As the dawn of great challenge approaches, shafts of the new day will throw light upon that vision until it will be seen more clearly than ever before.

There can exist in our beloved America no more fertile field, no more challenging ministry, no greater home missionary opportunity than that afforded by the growing number of hospitals and convalescent institutions. We must reach these sick, sorrowing, suffering people with the Saviour!

This coming day brings with it a new spiritual hope for hospital ministry. The new vision emerges into the day — a vision to meet man with the one message he needs more than any other, at the one time in his life when he will be more responsive to it than any other!

"And Jesus went about in all Galilee, teaching in their synagogues, preaching the gospel of the kingdom, and healing all manner of sickness and all manner of disease among the people" (Matt. 4:23).

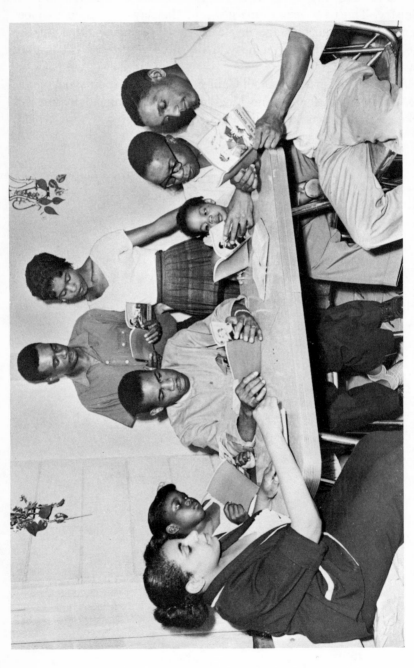

Bible study group in a public housing project apartment. (Courtesy of Chicago City Missionary Society.)

19

City Opportunities

J C WELLS*

THE GROWTH OF INDUSTRY and the mechanization of farming have brought many changes in the structure of American society. Foremost has been the vast rural to urban population shift. The growth of the cities is a phenomenon that demands close study.

City planners are also faced by tremendously complex problems as new suburbs spring up almost overnight. The problems of providing adequate transportation facilities for the rapidly increasing urban population are matched only by the problems of providing enough educational and social facilities. Yet city planners are not the only ones faced with problems, for the task of providing spiritual care for the new city residents is also a complex one. And only the church of Jesus Christ can meet the spiritual need so evident on every hand in today's cities.

The Christian worker in the modern city is confronted with masses of people who have been uprooted from a rural environment and transplanted into an entirely new social, economic, educational and religious environment. Many are confused. The adjustments to city life are great in a good many instances and create many pressures both within the individual and within the family. The church can be of real aid in such situations, helping to provide a warm social climate, new friends, an outlet for those needing activity, and the faith in a living Saviour that can help people over the rough spots in life. Various factors make city missions the only church-related agencies many of these new residents contact — and they thus are often in a real way the "arm" of the church.

*For biographical note, see chapter 8.

Classification of Cities

In order to understand the complexities of the problem, we need to look at the different types of cities.

Industrial cities. In an industrial type city manufacturing predominates. Transportation problems prevail, too. Residents adjust themselves to a regular routine. The workers represent a mixture of people from all sections of the country.

Seaport cities. Seaport cities usually have a foreign flavor. Social life becomes much more complicated. Many of these cities ship to ports around the world. Here live families whose husbands, brothers or fathers sail the seas. Foreign customs, habits, traditions and social life give such cities problems all their own.

The college town or city. Many large universities and colleges are located in industrial, seaport or farming centers. Usually, however, the cultural or educational element will overshadow the other.

A strictly college city is a difficult one for several reasons. There is a constant shift in population, which affects the business life of the city. The cultural emphasis will be felt not only in the social life, but also in business and even in church life. Many of the working class shy away from college churches.

The rural city. By this we mean one located in a farming community. There may be many industries in it, however, and it may also be classed as an educational center.

The small city. In the past the small city has been overlooked because it was thought its problems were not severe or there was no outstanding challenge. The last few years have proved how wrong this attitude was. All over the country many a small city has grown into a large city overnight. There is a constant shifting of population, usually because of industries, the building of a new airfield, or some other new development. The shifting population is like the sand bars of the river.

The Urban Problem

Urban growth poses many problems, particularly in the South and the West because of the rapid change of industry. Causes for this are varied.

The city is constantly moving out onto new lands. Industries are located where there is space. Soon new subdivisions are opened and new homes are built near the industry. There must be schools. There must be churches. These people must be taken care of.

The center of an older city begins to deteriorate. Business in the downtown area begins to fade. Churches begin to lose people. Many of the wealthier people build new homes on the edge of the city. New shopping centers open in new areas. The old city, where once business, churches and schools thrived, has decayed. People do not care to live there and business does not pay. Yet something must be done to take care of the people who remain.

Housing Projects

Governmental housing projects, owned and operated by the government for the benefit of low-salaried or retired people with low income, create other problems. In many cases these projects are the direct result of slum clearance in the downtown sections of the city. Schools and churches must be provided off the project. Because of the transient nature of the occupants, the churches nearby are reluctant to do very much for them.

Many of those who live in the projects hold membership in nearby churches, but socializing is generally difficult. To remedy this, some denominations are using workers to enlist the people in different kinds of activities. Meetings are held in the homes. Parties are held for the young people on the project playground. These workers enlist the people in Bible classes, study courses, prayer meetings and other activities.

Many churches send buses to the housing project on Sunday morning to take the people to Sunday school and church. Unless the churches reach the boys and girls of these projects in this generation, the projects may be the slums of tomorrow with a high percentage of juvenile delinquency. Even today, as young as the projects are, there is a fertile breeding ground for delinquency.

The city mission program has been found best in interesting the people and giving over-all supervision to the work. This, of course, must be through the local churches and with their help. The mission program can unite efforts of the neighborhood churches and give the project a spiritually uplifting effect.

There are numerous other kinds of housing projects, subdivisions, apartment buildings and hotels that must be considered. Each one calls for a specific program of its own. There is no over-all program that will fit all.

Hospital Ministry

A social, economic and religious problem has also been created by the sick, maimed and crippled of the different communities. Hospital insurance is now carried by many of the people, even those in the low-salary bracket. This means when people are sick they are frequently hospitalized. Doctors make few house calls.

Naturally the pastors will visit their members as often as they can, but a chaplain is needed and needed quickly in many instances. The sick need daily spiritual comfort and help. The hospital is aware of the need.

Again the city mission program steps in to help. The churches in the district, co-operating with the missions committee and the hospital, provide a chaplain or chaplains. The tie with the church is kept intact.

In some instances, one man looks after the sick in two or three smaller hospitals. In the large state or city charity hospitals many denominations have chaplains to take care of their sick members. In such cases, the hospitals provide quarters for the workers. Here again the city mission program is the tie that binds the forces together for the benefit of the people.

Approach to the Problems

First we need to discover the area in need. A glance at the situation may not be enough. A thorough study must be made from several angles. The following suggestions are offered.

1. Make a complete survey. Find out the number of people who are members of churches. Prepare a list of those making no profession of faith in Christ. Find out who is employed, who is unemployed or retired, and some idea of the salary range. Discover what percentage is on welfare or receiving aid from sources other than employment.

2. Get an evaluation of the future trend of the project. Does it

show stability, or are the people transient? The industries or what-ever is backing the project needs close study.

3. Make a survey of the churches nearby as to their attitude toward such work. Enlist as many as possible to help. Provide something for each church to do. Give them a definite responsibility. Perhaps each church can agree on someone to spearhead its phase of the work, with an understanding that it will help in the finances or whatever way it can.

4. Be sure that a definite plan is worked out in every case and that a church or churches agree to sponsor the work. In this case the city mission program can be of real value.

5. As intimated earlier, each mission or project must be church-centered to do its best work and to be of lasting benefit. There must be a sponsoring church. The program of the mission must be cor-related with that of the sponsoring church. This will give growth and stability to the mission.

Putting the Program into Effect

The churches as a group must have a well-organized, integrated promotional effort. They must be sold on the idea. It must be such that it can be adjusted to the different types of programs. Some suggestions follow:

1. A general committee should supervise all work. This com-mittee may be selected by the churches making up the group.

2. The general committee should have several other committees. One should be the expansion or new-work committee, whose duty will be to evaluate all new calls, look for a new site and buildings, and then report to the main committee.

3. The general committee will assist in working out the program with the sponsoring church. This church then underwrites the financial support or works jointly with the general committee to provide for it.

4. This mission or new project may progress in one of several directions. It may grow into a self-supporting church, or it may continue as a mission and Sunday school. In some cases the mission may grow into a weekday goodwill center. The entire program will be shifted if this is done. The first program will be preaching and teaching, the latter will be more of a teaching program.

The Mission Investors Program

The financing of new work is always a problem. Even though a mission is sponsored by a strong church, it must be remembered that the church has its own financial needs to carry on. It, too, must provide new educational space for its membership. Lots and building materials have doubled and trebled in the past few years. This poses a serious problem. A partial remedy has been found.

In several sections of the country a plan known as the mission investors program has been used very effectively in financing new projects. The plan is simple and easy.

A group of churches working together on a project agree to enlist their members to sign a pledge to give a certain amount over and above their church obligation when the committee calls on them by letter, provided the committee does not call more than twice each calendar year.

Suppose a new project has been organized. It is being sponsored by a church that cannot raise the funds for the new lots, etc. The expansion committee studies the case. A plot of the new ground is made. Full particulars are given, including the cost of land or new building. These facts, with a warm letter from the general committee, are mailed to those who have signed the cards. They are asked to send in a minimum of $5.00 through their own church, designated for this project. The church then has credit and the individual also has credit on his income taxes. A letter of thanks may be mailed in about four weeks. Those who have not paid will be reminded and will likely send in what they have pledged. This is "gleaning" the field.

Among those using this plan effectively are churches in New Orleans and Washington, D.C. It is a good sound plan.

Conclusion

The spiritual needs in our cities cannot be overemphasized. It is essential that an army of faithful prayer partners be enlisted in active prayer support. In addition, a definite plan of reaching every boy and girl as well as every adult with the gospel must be worked out. This project should involve every Christian in personal witnessing on a house-to-house visitation basis. Along with the visitation program should be suitable literature that can be left in the home for follow-up.

The Moody Correspondence School has a community evangelism program in which the church can enroll an individual or family in a Bible correspondence course. The course is sponsored by a local church, and when it is completed the certificate is presented to the individual by the church. This makes for continued follow-up opportunities and is an effective means of bringing a program down to the local level.

BIBLIOGRAPHY

Community Evangelism. Chicago: Moody Correspondence School. A pamphlet outlining the program.

EAVEY, C. B. *Starting Branch Sunday Schools*. Chicago: Moody Press, 1959.

LONGENECKER, HAROLD. *The Village Church*. Chicago: Moody Press, 1961.

STRACHAN, KENNETH. *Evangelism in Depth*. Chicago: Moody Press.

A representative of Moody Literature Mission presents books
to a captain of a ship docked in Chicago harbor.

20

Specialized Services
for the Church

by

STAFF MEMBERS OF THE RESPECTIVE ORGANIZATIONS

PIONEER GIRLS

PIONEER GIRLS is properly termed a home mission work because it is designed primarily to meet the need of the young girl at home. Its type of ministry, however, is to be distinguished from other forms of home mission work by the fact that it is a *service agency*. It provides a program which the local church may use as a tool to meet a specific need. It does not operate independently.

Briefly defined, Pioneer Girls is a weekday activity program for the local church, geared to meet the needs of girls aged eight to eighteen years old. Although it was originally founded to help reach the early adolescent girl who was leaving the church in such great numbers, its scope now embraces three separate age divisions: Pilgrims, for eight- through eleven-year-olds (third through sixth grades); Colonists, for twelve- through fourteen-year-olds (seventh through ninth grades); Explorers, for high school girls. Its program includes a weekly club meeting, an achievement program, and a camping and missions emphasis.

Pioneer Girls' distinctive goal is to present to the girl the reality of "Christ in every phase of her life." It recognizes the importance of counseling with girls individually and places great stress on this personal work in the structure of its program. It places equal emphasis on the initial step of conversion and the necessary follow-up in encouraging a girl's spiritual growth. It contends that "to the Christian, nothing is secular." Consequently its program is packed with interesting activities which every normal girl enjoys, but it presents them as a means of showing Christianity in action. The place of the leader of the club is pivotal in this, for it is by her example that a positive, vital Christianity is demonstrated rather than preached.

The total program of Pioneer Girls attempts to carry out these basic ideas, or its philosophy. The weekly club meeting, for example, includes informal activity as well as Bible "exploration." A pattern plan for the meeting has been set up as a guide for the leader. Based on experience with effective programing, this pattern meets the psychological needs of the age group for which it is designed in as skillful a manner as possible. The individual local leader works out her own program flexibly within this general framework. If she chooses, she may use the free program helps sent to her monthly from Pioneer Girls' headquarters office. Other program materials are available for purchase as well.

A System of Achievements

The system of achievements is the very heart of Pioneer Girls. Each girl progresses through the three ranks in each age division at her own rate. The requirements lead a girl into Bible study, a limited amount of *meaningful* memorization, and many activity projects. She may choose from a wide variety of badges as she goes along: handcraft, nature lore, sports, sewing, photography, citizenship and dozens of other fields of girl interest.

The genius of the achievement program lies in the opportunity it provides for natural personal counseling. As the girl comes to her leader to pass an achievement test, it becomes easy to lead the conversation into spiritual matters. Particularly is this true in the case of such requirements as that in the first rank for Colonists: "Learn these verses from the Gospel of John and use them to explain the way of salvation to your guide (leader)." Many girls have sensed their need of a Saviour as they have talked over their achievement tests with the leader.

Camping has always been an important emphasis of Pioneer Girls. It encourages group camping on the part of the individual clubs.

In addition, it operates several official area Pioneer Girls Camps Cherith, the name always given to their camps. In these camps, a full scale activity program is offered, majoring in outdoor skills indigenous to the natural setting. Spiritual emphasis permeates the entire day's program; it is not isolated to a special part of the day when formal instruction is given. Maximum personal attention is provided by a small ratio between counselor and her cabin group: one counselor to each six campers.

Training Emphasis, Too

Pioneer Girls does not stop at reaching the girl; it places great importance upon training the girl so that she may, in turn, reach others. Throughout the achievement program and in camp and club alike, there are frequent opportunities for girls to participate and to have leadership experience and training. Girls are also taught the importance of witnessing by life and by lip. Missionary preparation begins with this emphasis. Missions, as such, are stressed in the achievement program, where a badge is required in missionary activity. Every fourth week, the club offerings are set aside in a missionary fund. Many Pioneer Girls' groups combine their missionary "shares" in a national fund to go toward the support of several special Pioneer Girls missionaries — young women serving in various parts of the world under interdenominational boards who receive their financial support and prayer backing from the members of Pioneer Girls. The missionary program is optional, as is the official camping program at Cherith, but groups are encouraged to use the missionary and camp emphases in some way.

The steps in organizing a unit (or fortalice) of Pioneer Girls are simple:

1. The church, or pastor, sends for free introductory materials describing the program. If the church is located near a staff field worker, it may request a personal presentation from her, or she may send a descriptive film if she is unable to come herself.

2. The church, having decided upon adopting Pioneer Girls' program, sends for the organizing packet (for which there is a nominal charge). Simultaneously the pastor and/or church board appoints a Pioneer Girls sponsoring committee, who read the materials in the organizing packet and who subsequently appoint suitable leaders, approved by the pastor.

3. The church (or committee) sends for the instructional packet for guides. The prospective guides (leaders) read the materials, fill out the necessary forms (including an open book test) and mail them to Pioneer Girls' headquarters.

4. The headquarters office processes the forms from the leaders and mails them a packet of important materials very helpful in effective beginnings of the club program. The church is ready to start Pioneer Girls.

"Pal" Program Important

The place of the sponsoring committee is strategic to the integration of Pioneer Girls into the whole program of the local church. The committee acts as a liaison between the clubs and the rest of the church program, interpreting the needs of one to the other. The committee performs an important public relations job in the church and community as well. There are also many mechanical factors for which they are responsible: selection of leadership, securing of a meeting place, handling of any necessary finances, arranging for transportation.

Most important of all, the committee helps to integrate Pioneer Girls into the total church program by securing adult women called "Pals" to help in Pioneer Girls in a unique way. Each Pal "adopts" a specific Pioneer Girl as her own prayer partner. She prays for her girl daily and befriends her in any way possible. She makes a definite attempt to visit the home of the girl — possibly encouraging the girl's parents to attend church, if they do not already go. She makes it a point to see that the Pioneer Girl is invited to Sunday school and youth groups for her age, and in other ways draws her and her family into the entire life and fellowship of the church. It is by the means of an active Pals program that Pioneer Girls becomes an arm into the community reaching whole families for Christ and the church, and a permanent influence in lives rather than just a once-a-week club for the girl.

The potential of the Pal program is unlimited. It has been a means of great blessing in local churches. It is also vital to the national organization, because Pals are the means of financial support of the total work. By giving regularly what they can, either through individual pledges or through the church home missions budget, the total national ministry of Pioneer Girls is maintained.

Information may be obtained by writing Pioneer Girls, 111 N. Cross Street, Wheaton, Illinois.

※   ※   ※

The counterpart to Pioneer Girls is the Christian Service Brigade for boys. The two groups, while organized separately, work hand in hand as integral parts of the local church's program to reach into the community to win boys and girls for Christ.

Information pertaining to the boys' organization may be obtained by writing Christian Service Brigade, 109 N. Cross Street, Wheaton, Illinois.

THE EDITORS

CHILD EVANGELISM FELLOWSHIP INTERNATIONAL

TODAY'S CHILDREN have material and educational advantages never before available. Despite the criticisms now being leveled at education, and the poverty which grips much of the world's population, it must still be granted that more children have more advantages today than at any time in the past.

Having said that, we must recognize that the most important privilege of the child from the Christian standpoint — that of hearing about Christ's claim on him — is being denied more children than ever before. Secularism, materialism, and atheistic socialism conspire to deprive children of the opportunity to hear the gospel.

It is therefore evident that a special ministry is necessary, one that will carry out the instruction to bring children to place their trust in God that they might not be as their fathers (Ps. 78:7,8).

Leaders in both religious and educational work describe the years of childhood as those in which the basic attitudes and habits are formed. The Child Evangelism Fellowship challenges, organizes and instructs Christians to utilize these early years to win the children for Christ.

The history of the Fellowship is essentially the story of one man's response to a need.

J. Irvin Overholtzer became aware of this need among America's children and set about finding ways of reaching them for Christ. He discovered that practical methods for evangelizing boys and girls could be developed, and it soon became possible to enlist the active help of men of the caliber of Dr. Paul W. Rood and Dr.

H. A. Ironside. As a result, the Child Evangelism Fellowship was incorporated in the state of Illinois in May, 1937.

Since that time the ministry of the Fellowship has developed until there are active branches in all fifty of the United States, many parts of Canada, and in more than fifty other countries. Millions of children have been given the gospel, and many thousand have placed their trust in the Saviour.

In 1942 the magazine *Child Evangelism* was begun. It has served well those who evangelize children.

Realizing the need for trained leadership, the Fellowship founded the International Child Evangelism Institute in 1945. Since that time more than eight hundred students have received this specialized training. Many of them are serving overseas. Still others are serving in the United States and Canada.

Basic to the ministry of the Fellowship are three principles, all of them biblical:

1. There is an earnest belief in the possibility of child conversion (see Matt. 18:6, 14; Ps. 78:7).

2. There is a conviction that the gospel must be *taken to* the lost (Acts 1:8).

3. The Fellowship is committed to a ministry which is undertaken by volunteers as well as by clergy and other full-time personnel (I Thess. 1:8).

Upon these principles an effective program has been developed. In the United States, the national division charters state and local fellowships and commits to these the responsibility of reaching children in their areas.

This program is implemented by recruiting volunteer workers who conduct Good News Clubs, a name given by the Fellowship to its home Bible classes. In addition, the Fellowship urges Christians to engage in open-air, hospital, and other ministries, in order that children may hear the gospel and be won for Christ. The Fellowship provides training for these volunteer workers to make them more useful in the Lord's service.

On the foreign fields, the CEF workers establish a national headquarters, provide the Child Evangelism Fellowship's literature in the language of the country, challenge national Christians regarding the need to evangelize the children, and train and help them begin to win the children to Christ.

In many countries, the Fellowship already has excellent and responsible committees and has more full-time national workers than the number of representatives commissioned by the overseas branch. The indigenous principle is working out in practice in this effort.

Guiding the work is a board of trustees whose members come from all parts of the United States. These dedicated men determine over-all policy, develop budgets, examine candidates for foreign service, review appointments, and give guidance in the expansion of the ministry. The Fellowship charters state and other organizations which are guided on these levels by state and local committees.

The Fellowship has no membership among the children. It emphasizes the need for the child to associate himself with an evangelical church and Sunday school.

Many Christians are unaware of the vast numbers of children (under sixteen) who are receiving no Bible teaching (now estimated at 39 million in the United States alone). Most of these are lost — out of touch with Christ and the church — and a special effort is needed to win them. The ultimate goal is to give children everywhere the gospel and an opportunity to trust Christ as Saviour.

Opportunities abound — to teach, to assist in teaching, to open our homes for the neighborhood Bible class, to serve in organizing and using our influence to promote this ministry, to provide funds so others may be enabled to give full time to the work, to pray.

The dividends which accrue through the investment of lives, prayer and gifts in this work are large. A larger investment would, under God, result in yet greater yields.

The mission field at our doorstep requires active participation. For both men and women it is more than an opportunity and privilege; it is a spiritual responsibility — yours and mine.

The national headquarters for Child Evangelism is Grand Rapids, Michigan.

YOUNG LIFE CAMPAIGN

Two AMAZING PHENOMENA are easily observable among American high schoolers. First, a vast number of these boys and girls have never been vitally involved with any church, even though the church building and its program are easily available. Second, a staggering percentage of those who were active in younger days drop out from almost every church in the land during the teenage years. The numbers represented in these two groups plus the importance of the formative teenage years make the American high school crowd one of the most strategic mission fields in the world.

In 1938 a pastor in Gainesville, Texas, told his new assistant minister, a seminary student named Jim Rayburn, to leave the church program with the couples already running it and to find some way to interest the crowd of high shool students who wouldn't come to church. From that assignment slowly emerged the Young Life Campaign.

Young Life is characterized by its staff as a research project in earning the attention of disinterested teenagers. Several basic propositions form the underlying philosophy of the organization. One is the conviction that a most prized ability in a Christian witness is *flex* ability. In applying the New Testament principles of missionary endeavor to young moderns, the church cannot be glued to copying all its techniques and approaches from the past.

Another conviction is the primacy of the gospel. The young heart uncommitted to Christ can be helped by recreation programs; he will profit by training in leadership and citizenship; but above all, his basic need is Christ. Consequently, Young Life is a gospel propagating society. Any other activities are simply means to that end.

Great stress is placed on the role of the leader. As E. M. Bounds expressed it, "God's plan is to make much of the man, far more of him than of anything else. Men are God's method." This seems to be Paul's contention, too, in I Thessalonians 1:6: "And ye became followers of us, and of the Lord."

Building Bridges of Friendship

When a Young Life leader looks at a high school as a mission field, his initial step is to build a bridge of friendship and confidence with some representative members of the non-Christian element in this "tribe." Like any missionary, he will particularly seek out "chiefs and witch doctors," not because he is so impressed by the class offices and letter sweaters, but because other members of the tribe are so impressed by them. The leader may spend hundreds of hours at this phase of his job before he ever has the first "earned opportunity" actually to present Christ; but the result of an easy, lasting, wide-open door to that student body is worth it. In this phase he has two aims: really to know some boys and girls (not too difficult), and really to be known by these boys and girls (extremely difficult).

The best vehicle Young Life has found so far for the presentation of the facts of the gospel to teenagers is the Young Life Club. This is an hour-long weekly meeting open to anyone in school who wants to come, but begun initially by the leader with his young pagan friends. The same meeting begun with youngsters already known around school as religiously inclined would never have the same drawing power among the irreligious.

The group approach lets the disinterested boy and girl become familiar with the intellectual content of the gospel without feeling "on the spot" as he surely would in a private talk about religion with an adult. When antagonisms and suspicions have been stilled by the beauty of the gospel, the private counseling becomes effective and unstrained.

Geared to Youth

The content of a Young Life Club is deceptively simple. The location and length of the meeting, the exclusion of adults and children, the role of the leader, the singing, the language and content of the message, all this is the result of emphasis on another scriptural principle. In Colossians 4:5 Paul commands, "Walk in wisdom toward them that are without." The basis for evaluation of a program in Young Life is its effect on the teenagers, not its effect on the leader. Sadly, in many circles programs which appeal only to leaders are pursued year after year, and the youngsters must assume that either no one realizes he's bored stiff, or no one knows what to do about it. If every leader of teenagers could suddenly know what the teenagers themselves actually think of the program offered to them, we would have a revolution in youth evangelism.

Summer Camping Program

Supplementing the school-year club is a summer camping program centered in four Young-Life-owned camps. Star Ranch, Silver

Cliff Ranch and Frontier Ranch are in the Colorado Rockies. The Malibu Club is a hundred miles north of Vancouver, British Columbia. From across the nation teenagers come for a week or two of outdoor fun in exceptional surroundings and are again presented with the gospel story. The quality of facilities and program offered tend to erase many barriers and win an attentive audience from the very beginning of camp.

The camps, like the clubs, have a very permissive air. The gospel is presented clearly and in an interesting manner, counselors work hard at "being available," but great care is taken not to abuse the God-given freedom of choice. High pressure and emotionalism are avoided because Young Life has a clearly stated ultimate goal.

The goal of the Young Life program is *to build lives for Christ*. Its leaders know that the young person's commitment to Christ must be voluntary, must be intelligent, and must be understood as a first step in a long journey. The leader has to assume some responsibility for spiritual parenthood and provide assistance for baby steps into prayer and Bible study. He knows full well, though, that his touch with the boy or girl is temporary. God has provided the organized church as the lasting source of food and shelter for His flock, and the new lamb must find his place there.

Young Life personnel number 120 full-time staff workers and 400 volunteer club leaders, with approximately 600 adult committeemen who sponsor and promote local programs. Thirty-nine centers are active in twenty-two states, British Columbia and France. The school-year program directly touches about 40,000 boys and girls, and camp attendance is currently about 7,000. The national headquarters of Young Life is Colorado Springs, Colorado.

THE NAVIGATORS

THE NAVIGATORS is an international, interdenominational service agency specializing in the training of laymen for Christian leadership.

The various facets of The Navigators' work, as well as their particular approach in the training of disciples, are the outgrowth of a life—the life of Dawson Trotman. During his thirty years of service for Christ, Trotman was used to bring back into focus certain foundational truths. The influence of these truths had only begun to be felt before his death in 1956.

Converted to Christ at age twenty while meditating on two Scripture verses he had previously memorized, Trotman's hunger for the Word of God led him to continue the practice of hiding God's Word in his heart. For three years after coming to Christ he memorized a verse a day. Memorization of Scripture for the purpose of victory and growth had no greater champion in subsequent years than this man who had seen its remarkable power in his own life.

Although Trotman's life was full of fruitful evangelistic activity in the years following his conversion, he began to realize with disappointment that few of his converts were actually following on with the Lord. He met people he had personally led to Christ whose spiritual lives had not developed. Upon reflection he began to see a principle which, like Scripture memorization, was to become almost synonymous with The Navigators—follow-up, or the need for serious parental care of every new-born babe in Christ.

More and more Trotman realized that after conversion the new life must be nourished. This meant not only that he should challenge young Christians to study the Bible, to pray, to witness, but that he should actually show them *how*. Navigator Bible study methods now in use in the United States and around the world developed from those early days with a handful of sailors and their Bibles.

As this conviction deepened, Trotman began to spend hours with Lester Spencer, a young sailor aboard the *USS West Virginia*. Three months later, when Spencer brought another sailor for instruction, Trotman countered, "No, *you* teach him!" Thus a third principle emerged, that of spiritual reproduction. The Apostle Paul followed this method of spiritual reproduction. "And the things that *thou* hast heard of *me* among many witnesses, the same commit thou to *faithful men,* who shall be able to teach *others also*" (II Tim. 2:2). Reproduction, rather than mere addition, remains today a keynote of Navigator ministry. It is being practiced not only in the armed forces but on the college campus, in the church, among laborers, housewives, businessmen.

As his ministry expanded, Trotman and his wife, Lila, rented a larger home where servicemen could be invited to come when on liberty. From that time on The Navigator Home became a key center of operation in the ministry. Today Navigator Homes are located in major cities of the United States. In 1958, fifty young men were trained in the family atmosphere of various Navigator Homes for the work of winning and training others for Christ. Servicemen's work still continues side by side with the civilian growth.

Ex-servicemen whose lives were touched by The Navigators in the armed forces now work for Christ under more than twenty-five mission boards in every major field of the world. Many others are pastors. Still others joined The Navigators staff to give their full time to the vision expressed by Paul in Colossians 1:28: "Whom we preach, warning every man, and teaching every man in all wisdom; that we may present every man perfect in Christ Jesus."

Servicemen discharged into civilian life took these principles with them. Churches began to call for the Bible study materials and other helps. Consequently, the Topical Memory System was made into a correspondence course. Since 1947 more than 90,000 have enrolled in the TMS. In recent years more than 700 churches were using Navigator follow-up materials. In the same year twenty-nine conferences, training lay people in the "how" of victorious Christian living, personal evangelism, and follow-up, were sponsored by The Navigators in various parts of the United States.

In 1951 Evangelist Billy Graham urged The Navigators to help provide some sort of follow-up for those who made decisions for Christ in large, city-wide crusades. In the months following, Trotman and his assistants developed a system of follow-up for mass evangelism that has since been copied in evangelistic crusades around the world.

It should be noted in passing that The Navigators is not solely a home missions agency inasmuch as Navigator staff serve seventeen countries on every continent.

Headquarters in Colorado

Glen Eyrie, an estate near Colorado Springs, Colorado, serves The Navigators as their international headquarters, summer conference grounds and as a training center. Since 1954 some 500 young men and women from forty-one states and eleven countries have participated in the training program. In an average summer

450 Christians attend the conferences. The Navigators' Topical Memory System and Bible study courses are distributed from Glen Eyrie.

Thus The Navigators serve the Body of Christ not so much in terms of a geographical field as in demonstrating the validity of certain biblical principles, the adoption of which invariably tends to strengthen the church. Some of these principles, mentioned in this article, might be summarized as follows:

1. *Personal evangelism,* the great ministry of the layman.
2. *Follow-up,* parental care of the young in Christ.
3. *Reproduction,* each mature believer reaching and training men to reach and train others also.
4. *Scripture memorizing* as a means to victorious Christian living.
5. *The "how"* of the Christian life, the practical aspect of personal growth, including development of "tools" for training.
6. *Service,* training young men and women who serve with other Christian works, or with The Navigators, for the ministry of recruiting, building and sending laborers.

Information on The Navigators training program, summer conferences, or materials may be obtained by writing The Navigators, Colorado Springs, Colorado.

INTER-VARSITY CHRISTIAN FELLOWSHIP

INTER-VARSITY CHRISTIAN FELLOWSHIP is an interdenominational work among college and university students and nurses, with a program of evangelism, Bible study and prayer groups, missionary recruitment, literature, and camps and conferences.

More than 400 colleges and universities are reached by Inter-Varsity through affiliated but autonomous student chapters, non-affiliated groups, and active student contacts. Through the Nurses Christian Fellowship division, Inter-Varsity reaches more than 300 nursing schools and hospitals. The Student Foreign Missions Fellowship division of IVCF assists in a specialized program at 80 Bible institutes, Christian colleges and seminaries.

Inter-Varsity is a *student movement,* in contrast to other forms of Christian activity among students which could be described as *missions to students.* By this it is meant that the initiative and direct responsibility for a witness to the Lord Jesus Christ are in the hands of students themselves, rather than (as is the case in a mission *to* students) being the responsibility of a professional Christian worker or national organization. These students represent most denominations and Inter-Varsity serves as a channel of ministry to and for the young people of the churches of America. As an evangelistic arm of the church, Inter-Varsity extends the witness of the church into areas of college and university life where the student often has sole access.

Student Responsibility Emphasized

In Inter-Varsity the staff worker is a spiritual coach and counselor who aids and encourages students, gives them counsel and instruction, but never functions in such a way as to wrest from the students their personal responsibility and initiative for an individual and corporate witness to Jesus Christ in their own university.

Obviously, students themselves, with their limited time and relative immaturity, seldom possess all the requisite gifts for an effective, united witness, for evangelistic preaching, for biblical apologetics, for Bible exposition, and for the presentation of Jesus Christ to the entire university.

Despite this, students do retain the initiative and responsibility for the fulfillment of this task through the local Inter-Varsity chapter. They invite to the campus suitable ministers and professional people with the requisite gifts to lead a university-wide evangelistic mission or lecture series. Such a series of meetings provides a context in which the Christian faith may be defined and the Bible taught.

But the heart of Inter-Varsity's campus witness is the life and testimony of students themselves as they individually and collectively live in the power of the Holy Spirit, speak to their friends about the Lord Jesus, and bring them to meetings. Students conduct in their own residences small discussion-type evangelistic Bible study meetings. They meet daily for prayer to intercede for the campus and for their friends whom they are seeking to lead to Jesus Christ.

Inter-Varsity chapters have their own constitutions, develop their own programs in harmony with the tradition of their university, elect their own officers, initiate their own procedures and programs.

They are advised and counseled by traveling staff members. The staff member is a spiritual coach, but the captain of the team is the student president.

Aims of IVFC

What are the aims of an Inter-Varsity chapter? The objective for the individual Christian student is that he may mature in his Christian faith so that he will live a total Christian life in the university and endeavor to lead friends to personal faith in Christ as Lord and Saviour. The objective for the chapter is to maintain a united witness to Jesus Christ in such a way that, as one generation of students succeeds another every two or four years, each group of students will have the vision and ambition to evangelize the students of their generation.

By Bible study and prayer the members increase in their devotion to the Lord Jesus Christ, their understanding of and obedience to the Word of God, and the sincerity with which they unreservedly seek God's will for their lives.

Undergraduate years are that crucial time during which life decisions are made, character is crystallized, destiny is often determined. There is, therefore, an earnest endeavor to have each student face up to the command for world evangelism and his personal responsibility to seek God's will for his vocation, that each may be God's man or God's woman in the place of God's appointment.

Historically, the roots of Inter-Varsity go back to the Cambridge (England) Intercollegiate Christian Union, which grew out of the evangelical revival in Great Britain in the 1870's. Similar movements were established throughout the British Commonwealth after World War I. Work started in Canada prior to 1930 and in the United States in 1939.

Organization

The national organization seeks to assist the traveling staff and local chapters in achieving the objectives outlined above. The work is organized according to nine geographical regions, each with a regional secretary who supervises and works with his staff members, provides liaison between the national office and staff and students, ministers at various intercollegiate functions, represents the work locally to the Christian public, and maintains official relations with university authorities.

Directing the field work nationally are a general secretary and a national secretary, who in fellowship with the senior staff council (regional secretaries and department heads) are responsible to the board of directors. The board represents the larger corporation of business and professional men and women from many churches and from all parts of the country who serve voluntarily and who govern the organization in its policies and financial decisions.

In addition to staff assistance on the local level, Inter-Varsity initiates intercollegiate week-end conferences throughout the year and operates four summer camps for leadership training: Campus by the Sea, California; Bear Trap Ranch, Colorado; Cedar Campus, Michigan; and Campus in the Woods, Ontario, Canada.

As part of its foreign missions emphasis, Inter-Varsity conducts regional missionary conferences annually. Triennially a national missionary conference is held.

Publishing Effort

Through Inter-Varsity Press significant books and booklets are published for students and the Christian public. These include doctrinal and devotional works, biographies, hymnals, Bible study guides, and apologetic and historical books. *HIS* magazine is published nine times a year.

The financial support for the staff and for the various ministries of IVCF comes from Christian individuals and local churches. Staff salaries are not guaranteed. By means of a monthly newsletter and prayer bulletin the needs are made known. The national headquarters are at 1519 N. Astor Street, Chicago 10, Ill.

Through the years since 1939 God has brought thousands of students to Himself through the witness of IVCF students and staff. Other thousands have been strengthened and encouraged to stand true to the Lord in the midst of the intellectual and moral attacks of Satan while they were students.

Inter-Varsity graduates today are serving God around the world in Christian service and in every area of business and professional life. Many have continued to be used by God in reaching students on the campus as university faculty members.

Inter-Varsity serves the church's young people during four decisive years, while at the same time providing a continuing source of leadership and witness for the church when these same young people complete their studies.

OPEN AIR CAMPAIGNERS

Campaigning for Jesus Christ in the open air—that is exactly the work of the Open Air Campaigners. It all began in Australia over sixty years ago when an eminent lawyer was miraculously converted to Christ and began outdoor preaching out of gratitude for what God had done for him. An organization was later formed. With the blessing of God upon it, it became established in every major city of Australia and in 1954 crossed the Tasman Sea to New Zealand.

From time to time American and Canadian evangelists and Christian leaders who visited Australia have said, "We have nothing like this in North America, why don't you come over and help us?" In 1957, therefore, OAC began on this continent, with headquarters in Toronto and Chicago.

The Pattern

Undoubtedly open-air work is the New Testament way. The apostles were primarily open-air evangelists; they went everywhere preaching the gospel. But the Prince of all open-air preachers was the Lord Jesus. In the village strees, the marketplaces, the fields, on the mountainside, by the Sea of Galilee, He proclaimed the power of God!

The church today has reversed this divine order. We say "come" to the people. Christ says to us, "Go to the people!" The question for us all to consider is not "Why don't the people go to church?" but "Why doesn't the church go to the people?"

The Presentation

The gospel van is an integral part of the OAC approach. It is painted attractively in blue and white with texts on each side and on the rear. It has a platform that slides out from the side doors, capable of holding four or five men. A canopy, folded on the roof when not in use, pulls out above the platform and is fitted with good lights for night use.

Parked at a curb for a street meeting, the van is ready for operation within one minute. A crowd never fails to gather when accordion, guitar and trumpet ring out the gospel story; and rousing singing, straight preaching and a direct invitation seldom fail to bring decisions for Christ.

The same approach is used at factories where men gather in groups for their lunch-time breaks; at parks, beaches, housing projects, construction jobs and fairs. For children, a sketch board, a ventriloquist doll, magic and a well-told Bible story are great crowd gatherers and attention holders. The motto of the OAC is "witnessing for Christ by all means everywhere."

The Prospects

There are 39 million boys and girls under sixteen years of age who never go to Sunday school, in addition to millions of adults not attending church. How are they to be reached? There is only one answer. Go—with the gospel!

Large cities are vast mission fields. Hundreds of vans and evangelists are required to come to grips with the need. Cities, churches, Christians are pleading with OAC to help them reach the lost. Your help is needed that we may by all means save some. National headquarters are in Wheaton, Illinois.

MOODY LITERATURE MISSION

IN THE 1890's, when few Christian books were being published in the United States, D. L. Moody (the evangelist who founded Moody Bible Institute of Chicago) decided to do something about this lack by publishing inexpensive paperbacks in connection with his evangelistic campaigns. Thus Moody Press was born—then called the Bible Institute Colportage Association. The profits of the Association were used to give away books and tracts in army camps, jails and hospitals. This part of the ministry was later separated and is now called Moody Literature Mission. The Moody Press is the publishing arm.

Since those early days there have been many changes in method, but the essence of Moody's vision remains firmly rooted—to reach the lost through tracts and to build up Christians through inexpensive paperbacks filled with spiritual vitamins. The distribution in the United States lumber camps has waned as the lumberjack's shanty has been displaced by a modern house in a nearby town. But now Moody films are shown in isolated Canadian lumber camps bringing out large nightly audiences.

The work among homesteaders in the west is ended, but now the same effort continues among school children, supplying them with Christian books and gospels.

The activities of the mission are extremely varied as it reaches many classes and conditions. Always its purpose is to get gospel literature into the hands and hearts of those who will not otherwise receive it.

In addition to millions of tracts published and distributed overseas, several million tracts go out each year to distributors in the United States who cannot finance the quantities they need. In a recent representative twelve-month period, Moody Literature Mission supplied gospel storybook paperbacks to 12,000 United States schoolrooms; 500 shipments for jails and hospitals. Five hundred sets of thirty evangelical books each went to public libraries (4,500 libraries have received the books in recent years), and 300 shipments went to army camps and naval bases. Sixty-five libraries of children's books were sent to welfare homes and villages in Alaska. Moody Literature Mission sponsored 1,000 showings of Moody Institute of Science films in 110 penal institutions in thirty-one states.

Miscellaneous projects during this representative year included:

The book *Way to God* by D. L. Moody given to hundreds of individuals who were not sure of their salvation.

Fourteen thousand vacation Bible school handwork packets given to needy rural areas in the United States and Canada.

Thirty-five missionaries and missionary candidates attending Moody Bible Institute Summer School received three weeks of intensive training by the Literature Mission staff along with assistance from outside specialists.

Two thousand Moody Colportage books placed on ships coming into the United States ports.

Moody Literature Mission's budget is sponsored by Moody Bible Institute, which in turn is sponsored by thousands of donors in all parts of the United States.

Index

281